D1614914

UNRAVELLED

For Charles

UNRAVELLED

A FAMILY LOST & FOUND AGAIN

FANNY MILLS

UNICORN

First published by Unicorn
an imprint of the Unicorn Publishing Group, 2023
Charleston Studio
Meadow Business Centre
Lewes BN8 5RW

www.unicornpublishing.org

Every effort has been made to trace copyright holders and to obtain their
permission for the use of copyrighted material. The publisher apologises
for any errors or omissions and would be grateful to be notified of any
corrections that should be incorporated in future reprints or editions of
this book.

10 9 8 7 6 5 4 3 2 1

ISBN 978-1-911397-72-4

Cover design by Unicorn
Typeset by Vivian Head

Printed in Exeter, UK by Short Run Press

CONTENTS

PROLOGUE

2002 – a letter

On an ordinary day in 2002, over two years after I lost my beloved mother, and still desolate, I received a letter.

It was a cream-coloured envelope with a first-class stamp. Nothing special about that, but the reason that I picked it up and turned it over, examining it closely, was that it appeared to be written in her very own handwriting. There were no particular clues – 'Royal Mail Watford Mail Centre' it said. After hesitating a moment, I opened it.

Dear Mrs Mills,

I was deeply shocked and saddened to read of the death of your mother in 1999. This information came to me by chance when I was sent a proof copy of an entry in 'Debrett's' for correction. Subsequently I discovered that a notice was placed in the BD&M section of the *Times* after she died but we did not see it.

I understand that she was cremated in Exeter. I would be grateful if you could let me know if a plaque exists anywhere to commemorate her life or if her ashes were scattered in a particular place. This information could be helpful by way of closure, as she was my sister.

With best wishes to you and your family,

Yours sincerely
Robin Boyd

I re-read the letter. Her *brother*. That explained the handwriting. I did not really know of the existence of this person at all. My father used to wave a hand and say: 'There *was* a brother… absolutely hopeless.' I suppose I had the impression that he was either dead (as indicated by use of the past tense) or perhaps abroad. I knew that my mother had an older brother called Alastair, whom you couldn't mention, as my father would rant and my mother cry. But here was a letter from a different brother altogether. I took it through to the sitting room and showed it to my husband, Charles, who said, 'Why don't you ring him up?' I considered this idea, and that very evening, having plucked up the courage, I dialled the number at the top of the letter.

The man who answered the phone took away all my fears. He was chatty, easy and quick to laugh. It was just like talking to my mum; I can't remember much of it, but I do remember that he said: 'I expect you're breaking ranks by talking to me.' To which I had to reply that I was terribly sorry but I had to confess that I wasn't really aware of his existence at all. We both laughed, and when I put the phone down the world felt like a slightly different place.

I suppose I must then have written to him, for the next letter I have from him is dated from two months later:

14 April 2002

Dear Fanny,

I was delighted to get your letter. Thank you for writing and for taking the trouble to telephone me after I wrote to you about Laura. It was immensely helpful to talk to you about your mother. I felt we shared something of great importance and certainly your words helped me to grieve in a more realistic way.

Robin's letter continued:

Having heard from you that Laura's ashes were scattered somewhere on Dartmoor, my sister Juliet and I recently made a trip to the edge of the moor and planted some flowers (primroses and cowslips etc.) on a hill close to a stream. Juliet had written out a card with some words from *The Winter's Tale* and we placed it with them. (Perdita's words: 'Daffodils That come before the swallow dares and take the winds of March with beauty; violets dim, But sweeter than the lids of Juno's eye…') The connection between this play and your mother was a panel of shutters at the house we lived in while growing up, which was painted by various artists, including your mother, with scenes illustrating that part of the text.

My mum had a sister too? Juliet. And what magic was the Universe practicing? For at that moment I was working on a production of *The Winter's Tale*.

I knew I had a difficult task ahead. I had my dad and two brothers to think about, and I did not wish to do anything underhand. I steeled myself and went to see my father, about an hour's drive from where I was living in Devon. I climbed the steep lane up to his house, and soon we settled in the conservatory, as we always did. As we began talking in our usual slightly awkward way, I tried to spot an opportunity to introduce my startling discovery. My apprehension grew as I tried to find the right moment to throw my bombshell casually into the midst of our conversational norms. Eventually I spotted a silence and spoke up, my voice not quite steady:

'I got a letter… from… Mum's brother.'

My dad stared hard at me, held out his hand and said:

'GIVE ME THE LETTER.'

'No,' I said with all the firmness I could muster. 'He wrote it to me.'

'Oh… I see,' he said. 'What did he want?'

'He was sad to hear… about Mum,' I said.

'Oh. I see.'

'I wrote to explain.'

My heartbeat slowed down to something more like normal. Our grief for Mum was still pretty raw.

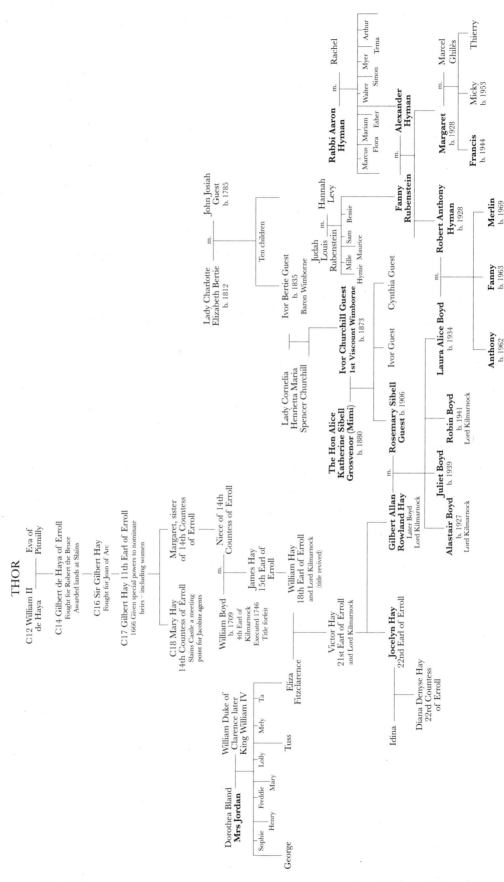

THOR

C12 William II de Haya — Eva of Pitmilly

C14 Gilbert de Haya of Erroll
Fought for Robert the Bruce
Awarded lands at Slains

C16 Sir Gilbert Hay
Fought for Joan of Arc

C17 Gilbert Hay 11th Earl of Erroll
1666 Given special powers to nominate
heirs – including women

C18 Mary Hay
14th Countess of Erroll
Slains Castle a meeting
point for Jacobite agents

Margaret, sister
of 14th Countess
of Erroll

Niece of 14th
Countess of Erroll

William Boyd
b. 1709
4th Earl of
Kilmarnock
Executed 1746
Title forfeit

m.

James Hay
15th Earl of
Erroll

William Hay
18th Earl of Erroll
and Lord Kilmarnock
(title revived)

Dorothea Bland
Mrs Jordan — William Duke of
Clarence later
King William IV

Sophie | Henry | Freddie | Mary | Lolly | Mely | Ta | Tuss | Eliza
Fitzclarence

George

Victor Hay
21st Earl of Erroll
and Lord Kilmarnock

Idina

Jocelyn Hay
22nd Earl of Erroll — Diana Denyse Hay
22rd Countess
of Erroll

Lady Charlotte
Elizabeth Bertie
b. 1812

m.

John Josiah
Guest
b. 1785

Ten children

Ivor Bertie Guest
b. 1835
Baron Wimborne

Judah
Louis
Rubenstein

m.

Hannah
Levy

Mille | Sam | Bessie

Hymie | Maurice

Lady Cornelia
Henrietta Maria
Spencer Churchill

Ivor Churchill Guest
1st Viscount Wimborne
b. 1873

Ivor Guest

Cynthia Guest

Fanny
Rubenstein

Rabbi Aaron
Hyman

m.

Rachel

Marcus | Mariam | Walter | Myer | Arthur
Flora | Esher | Simon | Tema

Alexander
Hyman

m.

Margaret
b. 1928

Marcel
Ghilès

Francis
b. 1944

Micky
b. 1953

Thierry

The Hon Alice
Katherine Sibell
Grosvenor (Mimi)
b. 1880

Rosemary Sibell
Guest b. 1906

m.

Gilbert Allan
Rowland Hay
Later Boyd
Lord Kilmarnock

Alastair Boyd
b. 1927
Lord Kilmarnock

Juliet Boyd
b. 1939

Robin Boyd
b. 1941
Lord Kilmarnock

Robert Anthony
Hyman
b. 1928

Laura Alice Boyd
b. 1934

m.

Anthony
b. 1962

Fanny
b. 1963

Merlin
b. 1969

Chapter 1

*H*ampstead is a very particular place. Broad leafy streets of beautiful Georgian or Victorian terraces climb up a steep hill on the edge of the Heath. A considerable area of near-countryside, and very much more than a London park, the Heath rolls out northward towards Highgate and Hampstead Garden Suburb, clothed in wide areas of grassland, coppices of oaks, beech, lime, silver birch and poplar trees, long straight avenues and little rough paths, red brick arched bridges and extensive ponds.

This exceptionally pretty little area of *rus in urbe* had long been colonised by a certain sort of person. During my childhood there in the 1970s, everyone seemed to be a writer, an artist, or a thinker of some sort. To grow up in Hampstead was to share this particularity. As life has unfolded, as I have met new people, adjusted, tried to find common ground, a glint of shared experience, or humour or preoccupation, I have always found that if I have a 'Hampstead encounter' with someone we understand each other immediately. Like the 'fame nod', the 'Hampstead nod' acknowledges a world of shared understanding.

My parents, Laura and Tony, seemed as bound up with Hampstead as it was possible to be, and we lived in a house that was a dream of Arcadia. Our street was called Downshire Hill, and of all the lovely streets in Hampstead it had a special elegance and beauty. Wide and straight, it ran from the High Street all the way down to the Heath; its houses were gracious Georgian residences with pretty front gardens and stone steps running up to arched front doors, brick façades and sash windows. Our house was in the lower part of the street on the right-hand side; set back, and mock-Tudor in style, it was rather different from its neighbours.

My parents lived for each other in a very complete way. They were always together on the streets of Hampstead – Laura in her duffle coat, her thick chestnut brown hair in a long ponytail, Tony, tall, striking and mercurial, in his greatcoat, striding along and lost in an interior monologue. They could be found walking down the hill, following South End Green as it skirted the Heath, to catch the number 24 bus. You might see them heading up to the High Street to buy fruit and vegetables, or a Sunday joint from Joe Steel, the butchers in Flask Walk, or strolling up to the Everyman Cinema to see *Les Enfants du Paradis* for the umpteenth time. '*There's* a happy union', an

American friend would say, looking at them in a puzzled way as she headed inexorably towards her divorce.

In 1957 when my mother, Laura Boyd, met my father she was studying textile design at the Central School of Art and living in digs somewhere in London. Laura rode a Vespa, hung out in coffee bars, and was talented and hardworking. One day she went to a party thrown by fellow student, Neal O'Casey (son of the famous Irish playwright Sean). When Neal invited his older brother Breon to the party, Breon showed up with his friend and flatmate Tony – a tall, brilliant, awkward young physicist. Laura thought Tony was 'smashing'. She was completely smitten after the first dance.

They danced only with each other that night. Laura's friends looked on with interest as they saw their shy friend being wooed so assiduously by a surprising type. Laura thought what a change this fellow was from her arty friends. He really seemed to know his own mind. Tony was six foot one, with thick black-framed glasses, intense, utterly brilliant and very, very certain about everything. Laura chattered away, artlessly; she was optimistic, happy-go-lucky, easy to get on with and shy, but with a deep down confidence. Tony responded to these qualities in her. For he, an ebullient talker, a towering intellect and very forceful, was also tortured, and a little unsure of himself socially. When the evening drew to a close, neither of them had any doubt in their mind that they would see each other again.

Over the next few weeks Laura discovered that Tony was on the Left of politics, and a former member of the British Communist Party. This only added to his appeal. He was young, radical, Jewish and wanted to be at the heart of a new egalitarian postwar era. Nervously, she tried to understand his interests – the brutal thoroughness of Marxism and modernism, writers James Joyce, Samuel Beckett, Sean O'Casey, artists Braque, Léger, Brancusi and Espstein; thinkers Marx and Engels; the British Labour Party; and singers Woody Guthrie, Pete Seeger and Leadbelly. I have on my shelves a copy of James Joyce's *Ulysses* with Laura's name written in her free-flowing artist's hand – a sweet testament to her desire to please Tony. She wasn't an intellectual, nor did she have an analytical mind, but this was 1957, so she accepted it as perfectly fine that the man took charge of these things. Things at home were complicated, and her overwhelming sense on meeting Tony was that she didn't have to *think* any more.

Soon Laura and Tony were going steady, and it was not long before she had moved into the flat he shared with Breon O'Casey in St John's Wood, and taken up her place behind the ironing board, exactly like Alison in *Look Back in Anger*, with Tony as her Jimmy Porter.

Laura had made her choice – with Tony she felt so much more confident. She gradually shed her art school friends. Together they began to form a world view: a little bit Parisian, existentialist, black polo-necked, jazz obsessed; and a lot 'Folkie'. They hated world-weariness, irony, brittle socialising; they despised self-deprecation as fake. Laura's *bête noire* was '*fausse bonhomie*'. They aspired to total candour, simplicity, emotional honesty; they considered their partnership to be based on such real, earthy truths that they despised those around them who struggled with more human, flaky problems with their relationships and their understanding of the world. Their position was absolutist, and they had no time for relativism.

The ménage of Laura, Tony and Breon in Abbey Gardens continued for some years until Laura left the Central School of Art and tried to set up as a textile designer, and Tony got a job in Harlow. Laura and Tony moved there for a year, truly in the heart of suburbia, and kept their sense of the avant-garde by painting one wall orange.

Their marriage was hastily arranged and attended only by their two fathers. It took place one Thursday morning in January 1962 in a Marylebone registry office; Laura wore a blue silk suit with a skirt and pretty short jacket. Soon afterwards they left for Israel, and another new posting for Tony – at the technical institute in Haifa. They had a sun-drenched and happy year. Their first child, a boy they called Anthony Arie, arrived safe and well in May. Laura filled up sketchbooks – charcoal drawings of Tony, usually deep in thought, of her new baby – she loved motherhood – and bright, light yellow and blue pencil sketches of flowers and balconies. Eilat was a paradise on the Red Sea, undiscovered, un-built-upon, idyllic.

Tony's posting came to an end, and, poring over a map, they put their finger on the wilds of the West Coast of Scotland. This is where they would go. To the Mull of Kintyre. They would forsake the sunshine of Israel for a gruelling winter in Scotland. They took the stables of Carradale House, which was lived in by the intellectual and writer Naomi Mitchison. Here their daughter came into the world – that's me – in the midst of a freezing cold, snowy, Scottish winter. I was nearly born by the side of the road, but we just made it to Campbelltown. Laura was offered porridge by the nurses, which she politely declined.

The Scottish dream lasted six months. After that Laura and Tony confronted the financial reality that they were not going to be able to earn a living doing a few bits of writing, painting and lecturing, packed their things, and returned to London.

Where else would they go but Hampstead? It was the obvious place, and here they settled, buying a brand new small modernist terrace house in Belsize Park.

Chapter 2

My earliest memories are of family life in Ornan Road, Belsize Park, in the late 1960s. These memories are fragmentary – of climbing up onto a high stool to reach the fashionable 'island' in the middle of the kitchen; of crouching in the gallery looking down on an adult dinner party, with all its disquieting mystery and sophistication.

I am lying on the bottom bunk with my feet above my head, pushing with the soles of my feet at the lump of my brother on the top bunk through a metal network of springs, strung between blue metal poles. His annoyingly familiar curly-haired head appears, hanging over the edge. On Sundays, I climb into my parents' bed as they read the *Observer*; I dip an unusually shaped spoon full of caster sugar into their little cups of coffee, and watch the liquid creep up the sugar until all the white granules have turned brown. Then I put the mixture in my mouth and suck it like a sweet. I now know that the unusually shaped spoon is a modernist masterpiece designed by Arne Jacobsen, but then it was just a strange spoon. When I am not fighting my brother I am taking my bike up to the garage to practise my moves, or climbing up to the garage roof to eat forbidden sweets.

I am in the garden in summer, playing in a long, cotton, blue and white stripy tunnel that keeps its shape with metal hoops. Tony's face, looking relaxed with jet-black hair and Michael Caine glasses, is framed in the circle, as if at the wrong end of a telescope; I crawl inside – the tunnel traps the warm air and feels hot.

Expeditions from Ornan Road included trips to piano lessons, which I dreaded, and much more appealing expeditions to the bakery. Here were delicious smells, tempting macaroons, Viennese fingers, all sorts of different loaves and rolls, little cakes and almost always we would buy iced buns. They were meltingly soft, with a generous layer of icing on top. One day, although I had no idea of it, there was a man standing behind us in the queue. He was an impressive, highly intelligent looking youngish

In the garden at Ornan Road

man, well built, like a rugby player, with thick bushy eyebrows. He kept shooting furtive looks at us and at one point made as though to come over, an expression of greeting stealing over his face. But he changed his mind and looked at the floor. Laura hurried out of the shop with me at her side, with our paper bag full of buns, and didn't look at him.

I remember an unusual tea party somewhere in West End Lane with Auntie Marion – a formidable presence – and lots of 'Other Children' whom I did not know. Who was Auntie Marion? She was aged and imbued with a sort of mystical wisdom, and was not my actual aunt.

Somewhere, in the streets of Belsize Park, Swiss Cottage and Hampstead, we did not know it, but a woman was searching for my mother. Sure that she had found her, she would follow someone, only for them to turn round and present a stranger's face.

One day Tony put on a dark suit and went off to what we understood was his own father's funeral. I had never met this grandfather in the flesh, and only had the vaguest sense of a mean-looking man in a wheelchair, and that he made Tony unhappy. Then some time later my mother disappeared for a few days and our father was left in charge. I thought that he wouldn't know how to do the warm milk properly. I needn't have worried. He did it fine. Mum returned with my little brother, Merlin, and the family was now complete.

ᗡᘉᗡ

In 1970 Laura and Tony moved with their family of three children the short distance from Ornan Road to 38A Downshire Hill, its name, 'Moel Lys', written in wrought iron above the front door. This house was to be the centre of our existence for the next twenty-three years.

I can't remember the exact day of moving in, or indeed anything much about the move. I just remember having my own bedroom. No more brothers, no more bunk beds. Apparently I wrote a letter in rounded seven-year-old hand to Tony saying, 'Dear Daddy, Thank you for earning enough money so that we can live in our lovely new house.' Tony always thought this revealed a kind of underlying suspicion that this money might not always be so forthcoming, which turned out to be rather prescient. My room was a fairytale, situated upstairs at the back of the house and nestled in amongst trees and gardens. It had three large windows and was flooded with light.

My big brother and I raced around our new domain, pushing open the light wrought-iron gate, running down the red brick path to lift the brass knocker on our new front door. At the front of the house was a small garden, threaded with little stone paths, planted with hydrangeas and shaded by a spreading lime tree. Inside you came straight to a hallway, dark and still, with Arts and Crafts style wooden panelling up to about three feet high. The other side of the hallway brought you out onto a small wooden 'gallery' from which you could survey the loveliest room in the house – a large, light, square sitting room, which our parents immediately transformed by laying a bright yellow carpet. They then added a black leather Liberty sofa, a whole wall of Habitat modular bookshelving, an enormous hi-fi cabinet, and a large, bold, modernist Léger print of the face of a lady with a schematic tree. It hangs in my own sitting room now, and many people think it looks like me. Perhaps when my parents bought it in the 1960s they were unconsciously attracted to a picture that looked a bit like themselves. I can see myself sleepily stretched out in front of the gas fire while a Beethoven piano sonata plays.

We had one or two visitors and I can call to mind the frantically squealing two dogs rolling up and down the orange-carpeted stairs, lost in the crazy joy of the moment – our new golden retriever puppy and a friend's grown-up terrier, of the same size as our puppy, called Jinkie. My mother's laugh rings out.

Sketch of Ant by Laura

While my brother, Ant, and I were involved in taking possession of our magical new kingdom, Laura rolled up her sleeves and set about applying coat after coat of emulsion to the kitchen until the last trace of Germolene pink finally disappeared. Then she got to work in the garden, planting cerea, little yellow puffs of flower, orange blossom with its dark green glossy leaves and creamy flowers, geraniums, wild strawberries and many other flowers. Her colour palette was white, cream, mauve, green, pink and yellow. When Tony tried to plant a bright red camellia she vetoed it immediately.

Ant and I loved the garden too. You had to give the metal frame of the French windows in the sitting room a good kick to open them. You came out onto a stone terrace adorned with a pergola, next to which Laura planted a jasmine, encouraging it to grow up the wooden struts and spread itself over the terrace. Rough stone steps descended to the lawn, planted on either side with geraniums and wild strawberries.

We drove our wooden trolley round and round on the grass until it scored a deep muddy track. A huge oak tree dominated the lawn, and one of its long, horizontal branches ran along the intersection of a shed roof with a high garden wall, providing a perfect place to hang out. We played up there for hours, surveying the adult life below, and it didn't take us long before we discovered the neighbours: two boys with staggeringly posh little voices called Nicholas and Henry who pronounced 'I ain't' as if they were the queen. Henry would walk up and down on the low wall dividing our two gardens saying 'Now… now, now, now… now… (pause) now, now… (pause) now… now… now (pause) now…now… now… now (pause), as if about to reveal the most brilliant game in the world, but nothing ever came of it.

On the other side, a trellis separated us from the other set of neighbours, who were all grown ups. We could hear Gill Greenwood, the wife of Tony Greenwood, Harold Wilson's Minister of Housing, moving about and talking. We fell rather silent then and a slight tension entered the air as Gill had lots of cats and our golden retriever, who was slightly out of control, had found a place to get through the fence. The very far end of the garden was shady and dark, planted with trees and shrubs; a low wall divided it from the back garden of a house in Keats Grove lived in by a lady called Jess Weeks, who seemed ancient.

The final place to explore was upstairs. The orange-carpeted staircase took you up to a half landing, where the first thing on your left was a door leading to the upstairs bathroom. It was a pretty room with a window onto the side passage, with an old-fashioned, free-standing, lion-footed bath, a lino floor, a black-and-white cloth bathmat with three elephants of increasing size, each holding the other's tail with its trunk, and a wooden slatted door to the airing cupboard, which was just the right size for my seven-year-old self to curl up and hide in. Straight ahead was my bedroom. The next room to mine was much narrower, also looking out onto the back garden. This was the residence of my little brother, Merlin, who started digging a hole from his side through to mine, perhaps for spying purposes.

A little flight of two or three steps brought you to a generous landing, big enough to be a room in its own right, with a window that looked out onto the street, where my mother established her ironing board. Everywhere was No. 38A's characteristic dark wood panelling. The curtains were bright blue, geometric, 1960's flowers. We put Laura's leather saddle, worn and shiny with years of use and love, on the banister to stand in for a horse. On the other side of the landing, looking out over the street, was the largest bedroom with the same generous bow window as the room below. This was our parents' bedroom. Finally, more or less above the kitchen, was Ant's lair. It had black-and-white checked curtains, and you could hear his foot drumming on the floor when he worked.

There were a few things in the house that did not fit the modernist aesthetic of Laura and Tony. On one of the top shelves in the kitchen cupboard lived a set of fancy cut glasses, which we were never allowed to touch – I found them rather intimidating. Upstairs, in my big brother's bedroom, was a framed collection of large and exotic butterflies pinned to a black backing and covered with a glass front. These things were remnants from the life of my father's family, which seemed to us to be steeped in mystery and gloom.

Chapter 3

$\mathcal{W}$alks on Hampstead Heath made a framework for our life in Downshire Hill in the early '70s. For all my parents' avant-garde credentials, Sundays were absolutely conventional and predictable, consisting of a traditional lunch of roast lamb, roast potatoes and vegetables, or a beef stew with dumplings, after which we would sally forth onto the Heath. My brother, Ant and I, both of us fashionably clad in tank tops with asymmetrical pockets and orange flares, or shirts with long collars, would run ahead and climb trees. We had a particular favourite which was twisted into a sort of seat, worn shiny with years of use; you could climb up this tree and lie along a horizontal branch watching for the parents, and drop down at the precise moment they finally caught us up.

Sometimes our walk would take us to the very far end of the Heath, and we would invariably visit Kenwood House. It was impossible not to be struck by the alteration in the character of the Heath here. The landscape became a manicured parkland under which you could feel an artist's controlling intelligence at work; several Henry Moore sculptures lay about the grounds and were looked down upon by the house itself, a generous, elegant, white Georgian villa, remodelled by Robert Adam, with a collection of paintings and gardens full of azaleas and an orangery. We visited Kenwood House so often that the paintings became my close friends. I felt I knew the Gainsborough lady in a sharp, flat-topped hat and pink, gauzy dress, or the little girl in a bonnet with a blue ribbon holding a kitten. I also became familiar with every inch of Rembrandt's face after hours of contemplating his self-portrait, painted in every conceivable shade of umber, which hung in one of the airy high-ceilinged rooms. Life in art; art in life – the two were closely interwoven in my childhood, and those enticing portraits hanging on the walls of Kenwood House inhabited my mental landscape as vividly as any childhood friends.

Kenwood House

My favourite painting, however, and the one which I spent the greatest number of hours standing in front of, was a small oil painting of an actress. She was painted in costume, playing Viola in *Twelfth Night*; the portrait shows her in profile. On her head is a tall hussar's hat, draped in a red scarf and sporting a gilded tassel. She wears a military coat with gold braiding on the shoulder, a white waistcoat and a red scarf at her throat. With a leather-gloved hand held to her breast she looks beseechingly at someone just out of the picture, her mouth slightly parted, just about to utter her next line, little curls escaping from her hat, framing her face. I was utterly entranced by her. Part of the reason for this special feeling was that my mother told me that she was my ancestor, Mrs Jordan, brilliant comic actress and mistress of William IV, so not only could I sense her overwhelming vitality, but I had the pleasing sensation that she was part of me.

Behind this painting, which I communed with on such a regular basis on my walks on Hampstead Heath, lay an extraordinary woman, and one who assumed an important place in my imagination. It is worth taking a short detour to look at her life, as she seemed to echo down the centuries – a sort of Foundation Myth on my mother's side of the family. In 1994, Claire Tomalin published her brilliant biography, *Mrs Jordan's Profession*, which brought my heroine to vivid life. Dora Bland was the daughter of gentlefolk who were already theatrical. She went on stage when her father deserted the family for an heiress. She reinvented herself as Mrs Jordan, and in classic theatreland style became pregnant by her wicked, sexually-harassing manager, Richard Daly, a determined pursuer of women, very handsome and with a marked squint.

That quality she had, which made me want to reach into the Kenwood painting and throw my arms around her, was shared by everyone alive at the time from the moment she arrived in London. She dominated the stage, a comic genius who specialised in 'breeches parts', so hilarious that riots threatened when she cancelled a performance. 'Her face, her tone, her manner', wrote William Hazlitt, 'were irresistible, her smile had the effect of sunshine and her laugh did one good to hear it.' Charles Lamb strived to put into words his captivation, describing her delivering her lines as Viola 'as if by some growing (and not mechanical) process, thought springing up after thought… She used no rhetoric in her passion; or it was nature's own rhetoric.' John Boaden wrote: 'Of her beautiful, compact figure she had the most captivating use, its spring, its wild activity, its quickness of turn.'

There are so many images of her in mid-theatrical gesture, with her great mass of curly, brown hair and eyes full of pathos, her whole being overflowing with movement, with comic vitality and attack. Original paintings were turned into prints for her growing fan base. She was endlessly painted, sometimes in idealised form, sometimes in conventional style, sometimes in mid performance, like a photograph in a modern theatre programme. It is nearly impossible to come away with an exact idea of her features since they seem so different from one painting to the next, almost as if she was too full of movement to capture. She was not considered conventionally beautiful, as she had too much nose and chin for that, but through every picture shines her wit and energy.

A sensitive and serious young man called Richard Ford wooed Dora, and together they had two children, but Ford refused to marry her. Dora and Richard Sheridan, who was manager of Drury Lane, both moved in the orbit of the royal family, who were keen theatregoers, and before long Dora caught the eye of the King's second son, William, Duke of Clarence, who lived nearby in Richmond and of course saw her at the theatre. He set about wooing her with great ardour, and although she held out for some time, when Ford refused to marry her she eventually accepted William's suit.

An absolute storm of abuse broke out when the newspapers got hold of the story. The royal princes were not popular, and the fact that 'Jordan' was a contemporary word for a 'chamber pot', was a gift for the vicious pens of caricaturists. 'Public Jordan open to all Parties' was a nasty jibe in a Gillray cartoon; another shows the Duke's red-stripy trousered lower half as he thrusts himself inside a huge cracked chamber pot with dainty female feet – the 'cracked vessel' of biblical morality.

However, the partnership was a real one. William was a lonely figure who felt his royal parents' disapproval, failed in the Navy and was 'already half sickened by his years of debauchery'. He was exuberant, warm and outgoing, passionately in love with Dora and looking for domestic happiness. For her part, Dora 'was not the first commoner to have her head turned by the power, magic and special quality of royal blood'.

The virulent attacks subsided as Dora and William settled down to a very domesticated life at Bushy House, a rural paradise where they lived in real and deeply felt happiness for fifteen years. Dora raised ten children, at the same time continuing her brilliant career. The same quality that made people love her on stage suffused her home life. The nursery filled up with George, Sophy, Henry, Freddles, Mary, Eliza, Lolly, Tuss, Mely, Ta... There were dogs and ponies and an excellent education for all the children. Often she would take the babies with her during the theatre season. When she was away from them she worried about them, dreamt about them, wrote to them and took intense pride in every single one.

But after all this the Duke finally allowed himself to be worked on by those who thought his domestic arrangements were unsuitable for a future king. Claire Tomalin tells the story of Dora's final rejection by the Duke so movingly: 'was there no one to tell the Duke', Tomalin demands, 'that his behaviour was that of a monster?' Mrs Jordan, aged nearly fifty, had to endure a sudden withdrawal of the affection of her life partner; the Duke began scattering marriage proposals in a most undignified way; and there are heartbreaking letters where she tries to give him advice on how not to make a fool of himself. An inexorable progress towards rejection and separation began, with the Duke keeping all the younger children. The story goes that Dora received news of the Duke's insistence on a separation in mid performance of *The Devil to Pay*. She was supposed to laugh immoderately at a certain point in the script, but instead burst into tears. Her leading man rose to the occasion and changed the line 'Why Nell, the conjurer has not only made thee drunk, but has made thee laughing drunk' to 'has made thee crying drunk'. Real life, in its cruellest guise, entered into her art, and Tomalin points out that comedy turned to tragedy in that moment.

Dora's son Henry, away at sea, read about the separation in the papers. His letter, unseen for two hundred years, made Dora's biographer weep, with its clear, true tone of outraged grief: 'My God!! To think a father, such a father, should have done such a thing I can assure you I have been literally very ill ... If this be true I will never more go home except once to see my dear Mother whom I consider as a Most Injur'd woman.' To her friend, Boaden, Dora wrote she was 'heart sick and almost worn out with this cruel business'. She was up against the power of the royal family. The fight was on unequal terms and she was bound to lose.

Dora's worries piled up; the Duke distanced himself from her and would only contact her through advisers; extremely oddly, he started collecting pictures of her when she was still alive and desperately in need of his help, preferring Dora in art to the real living breathing woman. She had to leave Bushy and scarcely saw her children. Her son-in-law swindled her, building up a terrifying tangle of debts in her name, and she decided to flee to France to try and sort out the mess.

She took a house near Boulogne with a companion, where the landlady reported that the unhappy lady played her guitar to herself and appeared anxious. Madame James, as she called herself, paid her rent regularly and appeared to live for the arrival of letters. The days became weeks. No one summoned her home. Sophy, her eldest daughter with the Duke, was on holiday in Paris enjoying balls and parties and made no reference to her mother in her letters. Her son, Frederick, was stationed in Paris too, and it was probably to be near him that she moved to lodgings in Saint-Cloud, where the barracks were. The rooms were comfortless and shabby. She spent her days reclining on a sofa, unheard of for a woman of such energy and spirit.

Dora was still trying to sort out the money business with her son-in-law, who was now living in her house in London, safe from arrest for debt, since everything was in Dora's name. When she wrote to the Duke's adviser, Barton, she received no reply. Barton did nothing, did not attempt to clear the debts, or pin down her son-in-law, or inform the Duke. Dora, although sinking into illness and despair, still wrote cheerfully to her children. Frederick was posted to a distant part of France, and Dora was left with not one of her dearest around her, just a few visits from curious people who had divined who she was. Here she died, alone and broken-hearted. The Duke defended himself, saying he had always paid her allowance. 'So it was', writes Tomalin:

but how little that signifies. It is the failure of love, friendship, imagination and simple decency that appalls. A woman who should have been honoured and supported, surrounded by her family, comforted in her illness, was instead first driven from her home, then separated from the sons who were her natural protectors, and divided from her young daughters, who were encouraged to forget about her while she lived. No one took up the case against her swindling son-in-law; no one lifted a finger to help her in practical matters; no one spoke for her in her isolation and illness.

'No one dies of a broken heart, perhaps', Tomalin concludes, but Dora was broken-hearted when she died in 1816.

Dora's reputation died with her. She dropped out of public favour brutally quickly. When *The Life and Times of William IV* was published in 1884, her twenty happy years with William were summed up like this: the Duke of Clarence had 'formed a connection with a well-known actress … There is no need to do more than to chronicle the fact, as the subject is a distasteful one.'

Yet William was in some ways regretful. Some years after her death, William, now King, commissioned a lifesize statue of his former love from Francis Chantrey, the leading sculptor of the day, with two of her children and two emblems of her profession, the comic mask and pipes, at her feet. It was intended for Westminster Abbey, to be placed 'beside the monuments of the Queens'. But objections were raised in various quarters, including from Dora's own son, George, and after the King's death the statue was still in Chantrey's studio. The Rev. Lord Augustus Fitzclarence (Tuss) had his mother's statue crated and carried to his parish of Mapledurham and placed in his church. Perhaps his parishioners thought it was a representation of Mary with St John and the infant Jesus on her lap. Eventually it was left to the Queen and was finally installed in Buckingham Palace in May 1980. William also developed a habit of giving his children portraits of their mother as wedding gifts, as if he had not behaved so terribly towards her, a habit that seems redolent of his guilt and regret.

My favourite portrait of Mrs Jordan these days hangs in the National Portrait Gallery. *Mrs Jordan as Hippolita in 'She Would and She Would Not'* by John Hoppner. In this painting her brown eyes are full of humour, her mouth turned up at the corners, as if barely able to contain laughter; she wears a trademark dashing military outfit of blue and cream and a marvellous blue military hat bursting with feathers. Her curly hair sticks out wildly from underneath it, and she holds a lorgnette in her hand (she really did need glasses). Her unquenchable vitality is concentrated in this painting; it is quite impossible to look at it and not feel lighter in spirit.

The painting was inherited by Mrs Jordan's daughter, Eliza, who entered the aristocracy when she married the Earl of Erroll at St George's, Hanover Square, in December 1820. Thomas Creevey, the politician and commentator, wrote: 'What a handsome, spanking creature Lady Erroll is, and how like her mother. She looks as if she was uncomfortable in her fine cloaths and wanted to have them off.'

It was from Eliza that my mother, Laura, was directly descended. Her name, her choices, her imagination, her artistic genius, her attempt at building an idyll far removed from the stresses of the world occur over and over again, like ripples, in the later history of Mrs Jordan's descendants. She was always present for me in that entrancing portrait in Kenwood House, which seems as if it can barely contain her.

Chapter 4

*O*ur little magical world of Downshire Hill was very closely bound up with my mother, who instinctively created a relaxed, warm and happy atmosphere wherever she went. The idyll she set out to create was her own faint echo of Mrs Jordan's Bushy. Like her ancestor, Dora, she was wonderful with her children, and to have her as a mother was a blessing of infinite value. When I think about her now, we are in the kitchen at Downshire Hill; I can feel my arms around her waist, my feet on her shoes, while we walk around the kitchen. Many years after she died, I feel the physical ache of her absence and find myself in the middle of something quite ordinary, missing her.

Laura was five foot seven, quite large-boned, with an oval face and straight but characterful nose. She had hazel eyes and thick, chestnut brown hair usually drawn into a high ponytail which ran right down her back. Everything around her was always comfortable and happy. She was kind and polite, never lost her temper or got angry – the occasional 'ruddy hell' was about as cross as she got. Laura's perspective on life tended to be rather different from other people's, as she couldn't be bothered with the chitchat and game playing of 'society'; Sartre's remark that 'Hell is other people' was one of her favourite sayings. She never once wore make-up, only a dab of 'Je Reviens' by Worth. Although shy, and incapable of public speaking, she was extremely chatty at home. Stoical and completely level-headed with her children, she hid her own emotions, concerned to put others at their ease. Laura barely reacted to our childish ailments; I see Ant on the terrace in the back garden, his hands clasped to his head after an encounter with a nail, blood pouring out between his fingers, wailing 'IT'S REALLY SERIOUS THIS TIME!'

Like Dora, the thing that really interested her, apart from her children, was her art. In Downshire Hill, sitting in the kitchen, or in the garden, or on Hampstead Heath, Laura filled up sketchbooks, working with charcoal, soft pencils, metal boxes of Winsor & Newton, or tubes of gouache. I picture her sucking the end of a sable brush to get it to come to a point, and frowning deeply as she regarded her subject, usually one of us, or a tree or some flowers. We were scarcely aware of quite how talented she was, as she was incapable of showing off. An art school contemporary wrote: 'I tell you on my honour, Laura had a very rare and important gift that we were all privileged to receive on viewing and re-viewing her work.'

Perhaps it was a part of her nature as an artist, but Laura really only felt absolutely comfortable in the moment, brush on paper, wooden spoon in saucepan, mop in hand. But more than this, she had a strange relationship with her past: she almost never talked about it, and seemed uncomfortable if you tried to persuade her to discuss it. She was not the sort of person who would say, 'Do you remember the time when?' If it was in the past, it wasn't interesting. She developed pleasant relationships all around her with neighbours, people Tony was involved with, or the parents of

RIGHT: *Pencil sketch of the author in a tutu by Laura*

our friends, but she didn't really seem to have any old friends of her own or any family. Every now and then, walking up Hampstead High Street feeling relaxed and happy, chatting to my mother, I would suddenly feel panic in the air as she swerved to avoid someone who had clearly recognised her.

Although we knew very little about her past, we did know that Laura was posh. This was brought home to us because we were not allowed to say the words 'toilet', 'pardon', 'settee', 'pleased-to-meet-you' or 'perfume'. Other hints of aristocratic antecedents were the Coutts chequebook (Coutts was Dora's banker), the fact that her father was a Lord, and that she was 'The Hon'. We also knew that we had Royal Blood. This was a great nugget and could be exploited to maximum effect in the school playground.

My brother was sent to quite a rough school called Marylebone Grammar, where his friends called him Tony; one day one of his new friends rang up and Laura picked up the phone. 'Can I speak to Tony?', the boy asked in a strong London accent. My mother replied, 'There is no Tanya here.'

We children gradually came to realise that the past, in our family, was not just vague; there was in fact an absolute block – a sort of invisible wall. You only knew it was there because it stopped you when you tried to put your hand through it. My brother was asked to do a family tree at school and found that unlike everyone else's, there seemed to be no branches, only Laura, Tony, the three of us, and the dog. Did our parents have mothers, fathers, brothers and sisters like other people? They didn't appear to.

If you looked closely, however, there were some faint smudges of family which hadn't quite been wiped away. I was stealthily aware that Laura *did* have a brother, the mysterious 'Uncle Al'. A well-worn, heavy-duty, Navy-issue, fawn duffle coat with enormous toggles hung in the hallway amongst our mini dark blue or green duffle coats from Colts, which we knew was in some way connected with him. He was just a strange figment, a shy ghost who appeared occasionally at the dinner table only to fade away when confronted by Laura's pressed together lips and downcast eyes, or Tony's angry ranting, and withdrew back into the safety of the fawn duffle coat, his usual residence.

A framed drawing of Tony's mother hung on the sitting room wall. It was an unforgettable portrait. From black and sepia chalks or very soft pencils and a slight wash on rough cream paper, an arrestingly beautiful and sad face looked out of the picture as if at someone just behind and to one side of the viewer. Her eyes are enormous and liquid, her face a lovely shape with strongly drawn, dark eyebrows and a well delineated jawline, her dark hair is cut short with her ear just showing and parted at the side. I knew little about her, but always knew that she was of Russian origin, which sounded wonderfully exotic.

A memory so hazy that I can barely recall it reveals a few fleeting visits from a tall man in a greatcoat. I knew that this was my grandfather – Laura's father – he brought me a mistletoe brooch, inlaid with seed pearls, which I treasured, and a little solid gold horse which was part of a charm bracelet. I cannot remember his features at all and I am sure he never stayed the night with us. I have no sense of that precious thing, a grandparent-grandchild relationship. His visits seemed to cease after a couple of years.

The final trace of family was an occasional reference by my father to a sister. He definitely had a sister. We knew that for certain, as he used to say 'My *sister!*' looking anguished and struck with horror. 'She ran away to North Africa.' We had the strong impression that she might be dead? Or at any rate doomed. From this moment North Africa lodged in my imagination as the *mother* of all degeneracy; it had claimed my dad's sister who was lost to all decent society. Like a sort of Victorian fallen woman, I supposed. I did not know her name, or what she looked like. She was beyond the pale.

We three all understood that our parents' relations shouldn't be talked about. I cannot recall a single occasion when my mother talked about her own mother. She never mentioned her once. I had no idea who she was, what her name was; it was just as if she hadn't existed at all. She was completely airbrushed. Certain stories were fed to us, but everything was carefully curated. There was a mystery that we mustn't probe.

Chapter 5

$\mathcal{B}$ack in the twenty-first century, in that strange year 2002, my grief for my mother still raw, I continued my correspondence with this unexpected uncle, this much younger brother of my mother's, of whose existence I had been entirely ignorant. The envelopes continued to arrive on the doorstep, addressed to me in handwriting that was just like hers. His letters were extremely light and funny and we seemed to have developed an instant rapport. We exchanged photographs of our families and eventually he wrote in one of his letters 'Perhaps I could suggest myself for a cup of tea. Do you think we could stand the shock?' Our growing friendship through correspondence, his generosity and humour in writing, our mutual quest for understanding had become imperceptibly rather precious to me, and I did not want to jeopardise it. Would an actual meeting do that?

The wheels had been set in motion, and before long the day of our meeting came upon us. I fussed endlessly over tea service, cake and sandwiches and paced up and down, trying to shake off my nerves. Suddenly a red car drew up. Our house is set high above a little crossroads in rural North Devon, and I watched as the car drew up by the village green. A man in his sixties of square frame and average height got out and looked about him with frank interest, before walking purposefully towards our house.

There is a sudden transition from 'man approaching' to 'here he is'. We are talking, and I am taking him indoors to have a look around the house; his voice is clear, lively and full of laughter. In fact his laugh rings into the air, so natural, so full of charm that it takes over his whole body. Easy chat, spreading a happy atmosphere, these were things Laura did as naturally as breathing, and he is just the same. Now we are sitting in the front garden and having tea, he is questioning me closely about my mother's death; he wants to know every detail. I can see how pleased he is to learn that his sister was brave. He is a doctor, so these matters interest him very much. As we talk I am shooting glances across at him. Is he like Mum? He talks just like her, he doesn't look exactly like her, but his mannerisms are just the same. He is ordinary and extraordinary at the same time. The moment is crystalline. And now my children and husband have returned, having been instructed to leave us an hour or so alone together, and everyone starts chatting.

And then, when I've only just got used to the idea of his presence – my real, living, breathing uncle – he is gone. Walking away from the house, climbing into his little red car and driving off. In the silence that follows, I cannot hold back the tears. I think about this lovely man I have just met. Why was I not allowed to know him? He would have been twenty-two when I was born – a young, fun uncle – everyone wants one of those, don't they?

Not long after his visit, Robin sent me a most overwhelming, heartfelt letter.

1 September 2002

Dear Fanny,

Please forgive the typing but my medical hand is becoming increasingly illegible. I'm sorry it has taken me so long to write and thank you for your warm welcome and the tea party, but life has been a bit of a whirl for the last week.

I was utterly overwhelmed by meeting you and Charles and your delightful children – every one of you so charming and not at all middle class – in fact very aristocratic! [this in response to something I had said about Laura wanting to create an ordinary, middle-class family]. But I suffer from a surfeit of emotion and the consequence, I felt, was that I made little sense and must have appeared muddled and discursive. [He didn't.] Nevertheless I am very glad I came and I thank you for having invited me. Perhaps some day, you will permit me to come again.

Haydn. I'm glad you approve. His understanding of the human

condition always seems to me to exceed that of all other composers; there is the warmth, the humour, the compassion, the containment, the nobility of spirit and the calming effect on the nerves. I often think I would not have come through the dark patches in my life without him by my side.

Alice. This time in Spain, in a half-light and in oblique profile, her resemblance to your mother as a youngster was quite shocking. I almost felt it was Laura beside me.

I send you all my love, *un fuerte abrazo* and again many thanks for your kindness and hospitality.

Xox

Robin

Chapter 6

After my parents moved from Ornan Road to Downshire Hill in 1970, the new reality was that Tony, instead of being a slightly distant figure who went out to work, became 'Dad at home'.

Tony's lair was the downstairs room at the front of the house, flooded with light from the huge and magnificent Tudor-style bay window, which took up almost the entirety of one side of the room. You didn't go anywhere near his study unless invited, and he could be a fearsome figure. The room contained a large cupboard and a roll-top desk full of tiny little drawers and cubbyholes which housed propelling pencils, Allen keys, miniscule screwdrivers, padlocks, Sheaffer fountain pens and Tippex – always lots and lots of Tippex. There was scarcely a spare inch of wall space, as the room was covered in the same Habitat modular bookshelving as the sitting room. Several shelves bore his sculptures: bronzes and wooden Cycladic forms, fish and strange trunks of women with holes all the way through where you might expect the navel to be. His days were spent bent over his electric typewriter, clad in an oiled wool, fisherman's sweater, ferociously concentrated. His glasses were so much part of him that they were almost moulded into his face. If he took them off, perhaps to peer closely at something that needed fixing, his face looked unclothed. The bridge of his nose was

RIGHT: *Tony in absolutely characteristic pose, resting his chin on his hand*

deeply rutted and his eyelids seemed very pronounced and studded with fascinating little balls of skin.

Tony's day began later than ours, as he wasn't good in the mornings, and he would allow our mother to preside cheerfully and chattily over breakfast. He would always be there to help with homework at the end of the day. At weekends, though, we would coincide at breakfast, and I would observe him as he shaved in the kitchen with his state-of-the-art electric razor. I watched its hypnotic circular movements around his chin and listened to the burr of stubble disappearing under its blades.

Whatever time or day of the week it was, Tony's habit of muttering to himself was liable to burst out at any moment, so that my brothers and I were in a condition of constant alert when we were out of the house, evolving elaborate systems for signalling to him that he was doing it. He talked to himself at quite a volume – disjointed but clearly articulated sentences, spoken as if the person he was addressing was actually in the room. He might be standing in the kitchen, gently or with more anguish, biting the side of his hand: 'Christ in tights… we've been through this several times already… mutter mutter… once again let me explain… mutter mutter… this really *will not do*…'

'Dad…'

'One more time… mutter mutter.'

'Dad!'

'Sorry darling. What did you say?'

'You were talking to yourself.'

'Sorry.'

Tony had a strange obsession with his feet. At the slightest sign of athlete's foot a battery of powders and unguents would be produced and dire predictions of the consequences of foot neglect. You might find him downstairs with the hairdryer plugged in and set to top setting, one foot on the table, bent over and carefully drying between his long toes, talking to himself as usual, completely immersed in the world of his mind. He would look up as I came in. 'You've got to be so *careful*,' he would say dramatically 'with athlete's foot.'

If there was any sign of the mildest of illnesses in himself or any member of his family he went into a panic. The family would be thrown into a State of Emergency. He seemed to want to protect us even from the inevitable weaknesses of the body. Illness and death were distasteful matters (nobody ever said the word cancer in those days) which were not allowed to enter into our pastoral bower. Years later, my brothers and I really had a strong sense that he would live forever, or at any rate would outlive us. Surely when the Reaper pitched up Tony would just sit him down, like he did with Jehovah's Witnesses and canvassers for political parties, and talk at him (I've never met anyone who could talk as much as Tony) until he gave up and went off to find someone else. Later Ant and I shared the thought that if our father were still alive when we were on our deathbed we would feel very cross.

But for all his neuroses Tony was very good with small children. He got right down to your level and said things that really mattered. There was something reassuring about him at that time. He seemed to have the answers to everything and life was very *definite*. I like to think about those early days with him. He and Laura were so comfortable with each other; they seemed to me to be very wise and knowing.

Tony was an *enfant terrible* – a fully paid-up member of the awkward squad. He set about raising us as little atheists and Communists. He saw everything in terms of dialectics, like Karl Marx, who was really a sort of alter ego, and while other people were raised learning the Lord's Prayer, for me it was some words from a little pamphlet that always seemed to be lying about: 'WORKERS OF THE WORLD UNITE – YOU HAVE NOTHING TO LOSE BUT YOUR CHAINS!' Not that he knew much about workers, or work, come to that.

Sitting side by side with his Communism was an absolute obsession with the British Establishment. He had read maths and physics at Trinity College Cambridge, had a very Cambridge voice, and in a way, in spite of his firebrand of the Left persona, he longed to be a part of the Establishment. He saw spies everywhere and delighted in trying to outwit them.

In the hallway at Moel Lys was a black Bakelite 1950's telephone with a silver dial. I can still feel the texture of that heavy dial, my small finger in the number pulling it round as far as it went and watching it purr its way back to its starting place. It was quite hard work getting through all the digits in a phone number, and this lent a great sense of anticipation and occasion to any call – a sense that was amplified by Tony's closely held belief that because of his left-wing activities our phone was being tapped. Just in case, he used to sign off his phone calls with the words, declaimed, rather than spoken: 'And here's asking for HIGHER PENSIONS FOR MI5 STAFF!! – if you're listening.'

Tony was an arguer, a provoker, a polariser and our dinner tables were places of debate. You had to be ready to defend your position absolutely or you would be subject to the crushing remark, 'What do you *mean?*', said in a quiet but lethally clear and articulated voice, and your argument would be dismantled. He loved James Joyce, a modernist writer who embraced the science of the unconscious mind, just as Tony always sought to prove that science had all the answers. 'Riverrun, past Eve and Adam's, from swerve of shore to bend of bay...' I don't need to look that up to reproduce it. Joyce's extreme intellectualism, wearing his cleverness on his sleeve, really appealed to Tony, and a circular novel was tailor-made for his very theoretical and abstract mind.

When Tony was in a room, any room, everyone reacted to him – his height, his colossal brain, his talking, his personality. We're all trimming our sails, swapping glances, giggling or arguing. But we're all reacting to him. 'You idiot!!!!!' I can hear him shouting in panic, if one had done some everyday thing, like screw the lid on the coffee pot slightly wrong, although he would immediately apologise and realise he had gone right over the top. Here's a thing he used to say, with drama, 'I said to myself now Whoa boy! Let's just stop and think here, Whoa boy.' Whoa boy? Where on earth did he get that – from watching too many Westerns?

The impression we had of Tony's early life was pieced together in a series of stories, and conjured up an image of a boy who was precocious and conceited to a high degree, and utterly infuriating. He told about the dinner lady offering him cabbage, at the age of six, and his reply being, 'I would like an infinitesimally small amount of cabbage please'. His favourite story was one about the time when he and some school friends made a snowball on the roof of a garage. It got larger and larger and larger, until finally they rolled it experimentally over the edge of the roof. I can see him – he is at the head of the table, his face consumed with uncontrollable laughter. 'We were so pleased with the size of our snowball' – pause to check we are all listening – 'and we went to the edge to look over…' – pause for more hilarious mirth – 'there was this sleek, expensive car with a soft roof…' – pause again as he was overcome – 'it fell right through the soft roof *and then through the floor.*' Helpless now with laughter at the memory, I can see him holding his stomach, his face convulsed with almost painful mirth. It is hard not to join in such all-consuming hilarity, so, at least in the early days, we laughed too.

Then there was the one about finding himself seated on the lap of his grandfather, who spoke English with a strong Eastern European accent, and saying, 'I am sorry, Sir, I only speak English'.

∿

Slutsk, the ancient Jewish city in the Russian Empire, bears little trace of what it once was. It is now an ordinary city in Belarus, close to the Polish border, of about 60,000 souls.

It was attacked by gangs of Polish soldiers soon after the First World War, and then Jewish life was suppressed by the Bolsheviks. A remnant survived until the utter calamity of the Nazi occupation.

In October 1941, in what became known as the Slutsk Affair, between 3,000 and 8,000 Jewish residents were herded towards pits in the Gorovakha Ravine and shot. Over several days during the spring of 1942 between 3,000 and 4,000 inhabitants were taken to the forest near the village of Bezverkhovichi, six miles west of the city, and were shot or murdered in gas vans. In 1943, the 'town ghetto' of Slutsk was liquidated. Its residents were driven to a place called Mokharty, three miles east, where they were shot from behind in mass graves by the Minsk security police office. When some of the residents of the ghetto tried to defend themselves, shooting at the German and Latvian soldiers, the ghetto was burnt to the ground.

There is virtually nothing left of the extraordinary place where my great-grandfather, Aaron Hyman, later rabbi, was born in 1862 – the man with the strong accent whom Tony offended as a small boy. A square, black plaque affixed to a rock in a down-at-heel playground and park surrounded by parked cars and flats, is a barely noticeable reminder that this was the site of the Slutsk ghetto.

But as I start to explore, I realise that a place possessed of such a spirit does not die with its physical removal. JewishGen and the Yizkor Books project have gathered together the memories of the Jewish diaspora from Slutsk, 'the nest of our good and warm childhood'. It emerges 'out of the fog of the past as a homeland that no longer exists on the earth, but hovering in the heavens, rising sometimes, in moments of solitude, in our thoughts, in our minds, in our longing for what was and what is not'. With this beautiful image of my great-grandfather's birthplace hovering in the heavens I plunge further into the ancient city.

Slutsk was a centre of faith. The *Slutsk and Vicinity Memorial Book* contains a number of studies. Y. D. Abramsky in *The City and its Fullness*, describes it as an open city, surrounded by satellite towns, 'each like a limb of the city itself, from it, and in it. Slutsk was the hearth, the fire of the Torah blazed there, and each House of Sparks, from near and far, was lit by its fire.' The city was a centre of learning, crammed with synagogues, arranged in the pattern of a Star of David, which were always heaving. Nachum Chinitz in his essay 'Professions and Vocations' gives a vivid picture of the glorious vibrancy of the place. It was a lively centre of plenty and of industry, set in an area of pleasant forests and overflowing with vegetable gardens and orchards, all benefitting from a fertile soil. 'Slutsk cucumbers' were famous through the region.

The city was at its liveliest on market day. Stalls were packed in tight, making it hard to move, and 'it was possible only with difficulty to squeeze between the wagons, whose shafts were very high'. Stalls were laden with fowl, eggs, strands of flax, pig hair and flax seed, also flasks of butter and cheeses, and there was livestock – cows, calves, pigs and horses. The noise and

Studying the Talmud in Slutsk

Slutsk synagogue

the tumult were deafening. Business was transacted in high-octane style – furious haggling finishing up with pats on the back, handshakes, signing of the deal and finally the 'magaritz'; a liquor bottle was whipped out and downed with a piece of pastry until both sides were content with the deal.

To read on is to be drawn in further to the bustling life of the place – makers of Slutsk cakes (fried portions of tasty pastry cut into pieces with a saw), tanners, shoemakers, scribes producing Torah scrolls for export to America, and makers of combs and *shofar* (ritual horns). There were hatmakers, who:

> … produced hats and caps in various sizes, both for the summer and winter seasons. The members of their families worked on this endeavour in their homes, and their stores were in the marketplace, on the Street of the Road and on Zaretze Street. They even had their own synagogue, known as Kirznershe Shul. For the most part they supported themselves by the sale of hats to the farmers of the area, who loved to outfit themselves by wearing these various glittering hats on their heads.

There were water-drawers, latrine cleaners, smiths, butchers, shoemakers, carpenters, Slutsk rickshaws, wagon drivers, doctors, firefighters and my favourite – an eye licker. If you had some grains of soil in your eye, you needed the services of the *oygen lekere*, she would put the tip of her tongue into your eye and remove the granules with a single deft movement.

It does not take much to imagine Aaron striding along (he looks tall in the photographs I have now seen of him) between the high axles of the wagons, absorbing the clamour of the marketplace; he is a serious young man, good looking and intent, with small round glasses. Perhaps he stops to buy one of Slutsk's famous cakes, taking a break from the depth of his thoughts as he watches the saw cutting through a fresh batch of pastry steeped in honey. From quite an early age he had his sights set on the rabbinate, so at some point he needed to leave Slutsk to find a bigger stage. He went to Lviv, in Ukraine.

Lviv was, and is, an intensely cosmopolitan place, one of the great Hapsburg cities, and it must have been a place of possibility for the young scholar from pastoral Slutsk. Lviv was a centre of Jewish culture and learning; Jews are first recorded living there in the tenth century, and about a third of its population was Jewish.

The location of the two significant places in Aaron's life – Slutsk and Lviv – reflects the fact that since the Middle Ages Eastern Europe had been home to the largest Jewish community in the world. Jews had migrated from France and Germany to the Polish Lithuanian kingdom, where they prospered. But at the end of the eighteenth century the kingdom fell under Russian rule. Unlike the Polish/Lithuanians, the Russians did not welcome Jewish competition and Jews were confined to the Pale of Settlement. Simon Schama in his *Story of the Jews* tells us that in the *shtetls* the most extraordinary Yiddish-speaking life developed – a self-sufficient mini state where Jews could survive the repressive policies of the Tsars. A deep culture of self help emerged. There was nothing Jews didn't do in the way of trading and manufacturing, even felling wood. Never mind that Jewish tradition held that demons lurked in woodland: they still mastered the lumber business. Driven in on themselves, they looked to their own history and culture and established schools where children were taught every word of the Torah and Talmud. My great-grandfather was an unsurprising product of such a world.

Then in 1881, Aaron's bustling, lively and stimulating life was thrown into darkness. On the 13 March 1881, Tsar Alexander II was assassinated in St Petersburg by a left-wing terrorist organisation. One Jewish girl was among the plotters, and a wave of anti-Semitic violence was unleashed. It began with incidents in Elizavetgrad, in what is now Ukraine, and spread rapidly through the Pale of Settlement. Bands of Cossacks and disorganised peasant mobs tore through the peaceful life of the *shtetls*. In the middle of an industrious, ordinary day you might hear the pounding hooves of approaching horses, and minutes later find your store smashed to pieces. Your life would be turned upside down. Shouts and tramping feet might presage an invasion of your home; if you were a woman you might be dragged out and raped. If you were a man, the approaching mob might start kicking and beating you until you had no fight left, or send you hurtling through your own window. It was all random, terrifying, inhuman, to satisfy a bloodlust. You were a scapegoat once again. You might be in and out of your friends' houses, trying to work out ways of defending yourself, but in the end what could you do?

Aaron has left no trace of his thoughts or experiences during this time, and the first written record of him is an English naturalisation certificate of 1885. He joined the almost three million Jews who fled Eastern Europe between 1870 and the 1920s. With a wife, Rachel, and a young son, Marcus, he made his way to England and settled in the East End, in Whitechapel, at 3a Tenter Street. As usual in the Jewish story, uprooted Jews gathered together with fellow immigrants in particular areas. In New York it would have been the Lower East Side, but in London, where Aaron and Rachel began a new life, it was Whitechapel.

The same strands of Jewish life that were to be found in the *shtetls* developed here. Russian Jews who were drawn to Russian revolutionary politics encountered plenty in London. Revolution was in the air and, for a while, prosperous and respectable citizens lived in genuine fear of an army from the East End, preparing to attack under the cover of fog. William Morris often came to the East End on speaking engagements and research trips, and he was shocked by what he saw. Commenting on the living conditions of a Socialist League friend, he wrote: 'It fairly gave me the horrors to see how wretchedly off he was; so it isn't much wonder that he takes the line he does.'

For my great-grandfather, Aaron, Whitechapel was certainly better than the terrifying daily existence he had fled, but it was not free of anti-Semitism. Only three years after his arrival in the East End things took a darker turn when Jack the Ripper struck. Journalists and police speculated that the killer could have come from the world of Russian Jewish immigrants. The body of one of the victims was found near to the back entrance of the International Working Men's Club on Berner Street, and on the door jamb close to another was a message dashed off in white chalk: 'The Juwes are (not) the men that will (not) be blamed for nothing.' The message was cryptic, and not necessarily written by the murderer, but the Chief of Police hastily had it removed to avoid an anti-Semitic backlash. Even *The Illustrated Police News* depicted Jack the Ripper as a vicious caricature of an Eastern European Jew.

Rabbi Aaron Hyman　　　　*Rachel Hyman*

Against this backdrop, Aaron Hyman settled down to raise a very large family. As I sift through the threadbare details of his life, I am disappointed to find that Aaron (grandfather to my Communist father) was about as far from joining the revolutionaries as it was possible to be. In the midst of this bubbling cauldron of Socialism, he tacked firmly towards respectability.

His focus was on education – education as a life-or-death necessity, to make sure his children could succeed, be manoeuvrable, and get out of trouble quickly. In their house with seven rooms, I am sure that the stern and ascetic rabbinical tradition and hard-as-nails mother meant that the world was disciplined and driven, focused on learning.

I catch up with my great-grandfather in the 1891 Census of Great Britain and Wales, still living at 3a Tenter Street N, and listed as having five children: Marcus (eight), Flora (six), Mariam (four), Elick (two) and Moses, the baby. Aaron is listed as 'Slaughterer of Cattle and Poultry Butcher for the Jewish Community'. Elick, the second son, I realise was my grandfather, Alexander, the mysterious, gloomy and dark figure of Tony's brooding remarks. I suppose 'Elick' is just 'Alec' with a Russian accent.

By the 1901 Census, Rachel has had four more children, and some of their names have been changed, which gives the impression of many more children than there actually were. We still have Marcus (now seventeen), Flora (now fifteen), but Mariam has changed to Maud (now thirteen), Elick is eleven, Moses is nine. And we now have Esther (seven), Myer (five), Symall (three) and Tema (six months).

In the 1911 Census, Aaron and Rachel are still at their Tenter Street address. Marcus and Flora have flown the nest. The eldest is now Mariam (not Maud this time), the next is now listed as Alexander (no longer Elick), then we have Walter. Who is this Walter then? Ah, he used to be Moses. Then we have Esther (seventeen), Myer (fifteen) and Simon (formerly Symall); Tema, the baby, has grown up and is ten years old, and there is now Arthur, aged five. Ten children in all.

Aaron was an important figure in London's Jewish community. He was a rabbinical supervisor and head *shohet* (official slaughterer of acceptable meats) as well as unsalaried rabbi of a congregation. He was an activist, founding the Zionist Mizrachi organisation in Great Britain. I start to get a measure of the man when I see the work that he published. 'Commentaries on commentaries on the Talmud' is how Tony expressed it wearily. His first work was a large collection of sayings from Talmudic and Rabbinic literature alphabetically arranged according to the catchword. Then came his *magnum opus*, which took him ten years to complete in three volumes: a biographical dictionary of the Sages of the Talmud. According to everything I read, these works – a careful, scholarly, detailed, determined task that stretched over years – have all been indispensable to scholars. I understand that his writings have been a great inspiration to the Israeli right wing.

A few years after that, in 1905, Aaron would have read in his daily paper of the most vicious Russian pogrom yet in his former home:

Men and women were barbarously felled and decapitated with axes. Children were torn limb from limb, the streets were littered with corpses, hurled out of windows, and the houses of murdered Jews were systematically destroyed. In this way the Jewish population of the district was wiped out.

An optimistic belief circulating at the time, that non-Jewish Leftists in Russia would come to their aid, proved to be an illusion.

Aaron arranged for the immediate evacuation of his sister, Annie, her husband, David Bernstein, and their children, who were still living in the Pale, in Rostov on Don, finding a home for them close to his own in Whitechapel. Although Annie's husband was already fifty-nine, Aaron managed to find work for him as a Hebrew teacher in the East End. The Hymans and the Bernsteins were in and out of each other's houses. I get the impression that a lighter atmosphere prevailed among the Bernsteins than their disciplined and driven Hyman cousins. They used to frequent Anarchist clubs full of handsome Mensheviks and dashing Bolsheviks, and one of the Bernstein girls, Rae, danced with Maxim Litvinov, a charismatic figure in the Russian Revolution. The oldest Bernstein boy, Mikhail, was a talented artist, returning to Russia where he helped found the Leningrad school of painting. Another of the girls, Maroussa, married fellow Russian émigré, Jules Goldstein, and moved to Paris. Her musician daughter, Fania, would later write an extraordinary account of how she survived the Nazi concentration camps.

Chapter 7

$\mathcal{A}$s life unfolded in our Hampstead Arcadia I knew almost nothing of this immigrant past. Life was happy and stable for my two brothers and me, and almost everything of importance took place within the walls of No. 38A, as always with Laura at its heart. The house did have an especially comfortable quality, perhaps reflecting the fact that its architect, Norman Hunter, had designed it for his own use.

In the summers we had supper on the terrace under the pergola. The air, scented with jasmine, was soft and warm, and the days seemed to stretch to eternity, safe, happy and unchanging. In the winters I would lie in front of the gas fire in the yellow-carpeted sitting room, listening to my parents' records (strictly Bach, Beethoven or Mozart). I would read or look up at the Mark Gertler painting of sunflowers above the mantelpiece, losing myself in the thick yellow, orange and green brushstrokes, or staring at the Emilio Greco pencil sketch of a female nude, which was endlessly absorbing. Sometimes to me the head looked as if it was just an oval, drawn in profile, looking straight ahead. At other times I could see it as if the head was turned towards me. That is the correct way of perceiving it; but I would flip from one perception to another.

The winters culminated in the most glorious Christmases. From the moment when I would see Tony manhandling large bags into his office and stuffing then hastily into his special cupboard, excitement would start to build; it continued through my birthday on the 19 December, an expedition to Camden Lock Market to buy a huge tree for the sitting room, and on to the ceremony of decorating it with exquisite Liberty baubles and real candles. It didn't let up until Christmas Day. Our full and lumpy stockings were from Harrods and adorned with our names in beautiful glittery script; carefully chosen and lovingly filled, they never disappointed. There were no packets of Hula Hoops or Curly Wurlies for us.

Laura's practicality and focus were at the heart of the day. Behind it lay her determination – all the extra shopping, buying and preparing the turkey, making the stuffing and the Christmas pud, and cheerfully stage-managing the day. Tony, always on the brink of being overpowered by his emotions, found the day difficult, and the muttering and hand-chewing would increase. Laura would say privately to me, 'He's thinking about his mother'. She would give him a single task, which was always making the brandy butter. This used to take him about three hours. As he added the brandy drop by drop he would drink a lot of Château Lafitte and start singing Georges Brassens' songs in a loud and tuneless bass.

There was nothing suburban about our enormous Christmas trees, always the biggest that could be found and more suited to a stately home, or about the real candles, which, given Tony's nervy paranoia and our rumbustious out-of-control behaviour about the house, seemed to be a strange choice. As Laura clipped the little silver candleholders to the branches, searching out those that grew horizontally, and fitted the little white candles, I used to sense that she was expressing some experience of a different world. She never described her childhood Christmases, or mentioned a mother, or brothers and sisters, but she possessed an absolutely natural knowledge of how to do it graciously and beautifully. Every now and then she would breathe the name 'Mimi'. Mimi would always have real candles. Around this name gathered my sense of something grander. I knew that she was Laura's maternal grandmother, and Mimi's ghost would invariably slip into the house and move about gently on Christmas day.

∿

In the twenty-first century, I drop in on my new Uncle Robin. Our relationship has continued since his visit, mainly through letters and emails, and the occasional cup of coffee in London. It is fraught with emotion, lurching forwards with confessions, outpourings of tentative feelings of family affection, and then pulled back by the unavoidable truth of so many lost decades. Our meetings are full of nervous laughter, self-deprecation, half disclosures and hints; tears (on my part) and exhaustion afterwards.

We are always edging around a deep pool of loss and sadness, for there is no doubt that he adored my mother. 'I send you this (Casals playing Haydn) – especially track 12 – in memory of your dear mother, my big sister whose private mind I never knew but who, as a teenager growing up in the Forest of Dean, I always loved – and never stopped loving even though we seldom met thereafter.' On this occasion I want to ask him about Mimi. Who was she? He has a photographic portrait of her by Cecil Beaton on the wall. He waves his hand towards it, laughing his ringing, infectious laugh, and declares, 'What a bitch!'

The most commonly reproduced portrait painting of Mimi, by Sir John Lavery, shows her in a white backless dress, a long string of pearls and a slash of red lipstick. Christie's catalogue, when the picture was to be sold, described it: 'Lady Wimborne's portrait perfectly reflects both its sitter's personality and the moment in which it was created. Her confidence, independence and Hollywood-inspired glamour are the perfect encapsulation of the modern attitudes and quickly changing pace of life in inter-war Britain.'

Mimi was born the Hon. Alice Grosvenor, one of five children of Robert Grosvenor, 2nd Baron Ebury, and great-granddaughter of the Duke of Westminster. The Grosvenors were the richest family in Britain. An early portrait of her reveals a young woman with the perfection of a porcelain shepherdess, her dark hair surmounted by a wavy hat bedecked with flowers. Her skin is flawless, dark eyebrows are slightly raised, and her liquid eyes are cast upwards. She started off conventionally enough by marrying Ivor Guest, grandson of John Josiah Guest, the successful founder of the steelworks at Merthyr Tydfil, the largest in Europe, and cousin of Winston Churchill through his mother, Lady Cornelia Spencer Churchill. Ivor was elected Conservative MP for Plymouth in 1900; six years later he crossed the floor and joined the Liberals, then went to the House of Lords. With Churchill's help he was appointed Lord Lieutenant and Viceroy of Ireland in 1915.

Uncle Robin gets out some more photographs of Alice, in her role as Vicereine of Ireland. Here she sits in an open-topped carriage for a state occasion, driving through the streets of Dublin. She is smiling graciously from beneath a period hat – really just a headband topped off with enormous Hermès-like feathers. Ivor sits beside her in military uniform and is also smiling in genial fashion. The couple exude entitled charm. Mimi's ghost is beginning to take more solid form.

A little more flesh is added to her bones in the biography *The Red Earl*, Selina Hastings' account of the life of her father, Jack, Earl of Huntingdon. The families were acquainted in Ireland, and Jack's sisters were placed as ladies-in-waiting to Alice. The Guests were, on the whole, not approved of in society: Ivor's father was a snob and a social climber, widely known as 'the paying Guest', and Ivor himself was regarded as a bore, pompous, far from intelligent and a shameless importuner: 'We must assume that God knew best when he created Ivor Guest', ran a rude little saying in circulation. Asquith thought him 'very unpopular', and Margot Asquith thought him 'just a fairly frank bounder'. Ivor's brother, Freddie, was considered even worse – a snob, a playboy and a lightweight, he suggested that the best solution for working-class unrest was to drug their tea. He was regarded by Viscount Gladstone as Lloyd George's 'evil genius', and even his obituary hinted that Freddie was not a nice man to know.

Alice was regarded as a cut above her husband, and Selina Hastings makes it clear that her father was completely besotted with her. Sexy and flirtatious, golden-eyed, with beautifully cut lips and charming dimples, Mimi inspired animal passion in the opposite sex: she required it, contemplating her own reflection in their eyes. In Ireland, she played a part, the part of vicereine, queen of her own little kingdom, decked in a fabulously expensive wardrobe, exuding beauty and charm. Her part carried utter conviction. Behind her back, people called her 'Queen Alice'.

In 1916, Ivor and Mimi's grand existence in Dublin was violently rocked when the Easter Rising erupted. 'A terrible beauty was born', wrote Yeats. The highly decorative Alice found herself in the eye of a great storm. A group of rebels emerged through the front door of the captured GPO building; Patrick Pearce stepped forward and read from a sheet of paper, his voice charged with emotion: 'We declare the right of the people in Ireland to the ownership of Ireland, and to the unfettered control of Irish destinies.' A republic had been declared; James Connolly clasped the hand of Tom Clarke and said, 'Thanks be to God, Tom, that we have lived to see this day'. After that events began to unfold fast and with violence.

Ivor, although his role was often ceremonial, now found himself at the centre of an explosive situation in which he was called upon to act. Alice wrote a vivid letter home to her mother: 'My darling Mummie, it has all calmed down now but it has been a terrible time. One more awful tragedy in this beloved land. It makes my heart ache.' Trapped in the Viceregal Lodge, she gives her mother a blow by blow account of that terrifying Bank Holiday Monday. 'I was washing my hands for luncheon when I was rung up and told to stay in my bedroom', she wrote, 'Sein Faners [*sic*] have attacked the castle and might come down here. I went down and found Ivor very calm, but very white.' She dashes on in characterful, flowing, hard to decipher handwriting, describing how Ivor urged her to evacuate, but she 'would rather die'. He tried to telephone, only to find all communication wires cut. A report came up from the police that the rebels were marching towards the Viceregal Lodge. Alice reports that they readied the children and ladies-in-waiting before sending them off to Luttrelstown in a brougham. 'We found ourselves with two footmen, two A.D.C.s and the clothes we stood up in.' Defenceless, they were 'at the mercy of the enemy… it being Bank Holiday, everyone was away', and awaited their fate.

Alice writes loyally that since Under Secretary Nathan was locked up in the besieged castle, and General Frend commanding the forces was in England, 'Upon Ivor and Ivor alone Ireland and all of us relied to pull us through and magnificently he did it'. Ivor moved to ensure the electric light plant was guarded. Then by a stroke of luck he discovered that the only wire that had not been cut was the one to the Curragh, where British troops were stationed. 'Had this been cut, I think we were done. Before long the troops were on their way. From 12.20 to 10 o/c that night when the curragh troops began to arrive and till 3 o/c that night I never left Ivor for a moment.' Alice it seems didn't lack courage. Ivor got a detachment sent to Kingstown (which he said must be guarded as the only link with England), and tried every means of getting in touch with England. He at last got a wire through to London asking for more troops and a wire to the Admiralty warning them that there might be an attack by Germany on the south coast. Finally, he decided to declare martial law on his own authority. The days of that terrible, extraordinary week, so hugely significant in the history of Ireland, rolled on, with Alice reporting 'We were in agony lest the provinces should rise… the suspense was terrible'.

Most accounts I have read of the Easter Rising say that the British authorities were totally unprepared for what happened, but Alice in her letter home tells her mother that Ivor had been urging action for some while. He was prepared to stake his political reputation on arresting all leaders of the military council, but no one else supported him. Ivor sensed something in the air and changed his plans for Bank Holiday Monday: he had been planning a trip to Belfast but cancelled it; he advised Alice not to draw too much attention to the change of plan, and that if she drove out, she must go on the North Circular Road to avoid the town.

The events of the week are well rehearsed, and with British reinforcements arriving in large numbers the Rising was eventually quelled. Over 3,000 arrests were made, and 187 people were tried at secret courts martial, without a defence. Fourteen men were executed by firing squad at Kilmainham Gaol. Some of those executed were not leaders and did not kill anyone; as the executions continued, public opinion began to shift: thousands of people who had opposed the whole Sinn Fein movement began to change their minds. Over 1,800 men were interned in camps and prisons in England and Wales, many of whom had nothing to do with the Rising. Many of the camps became 'Universities of Revolution'. A bloody phase of Irish history had begun.

Ivor Churchill Guest 1st Viscount Wimborne with the troops in Dublin in the aftermath of the Easter Rising

After the Easter Rising was over Ivor tendered his resignation, but was exonerated of all blame and reinstated. He finally resigned after he had opposed Lloyd George's policy of conscription in Ireland in 1918. Ivor and Alice moved back to England. Stripped of their positions, they began to descend into decadence. Despite being married to the most irresistible woman in society, Ivor turned into a predatory and serial womaniser. A contemporary described him as 'a disappointed man at a loose end'. The stages for their careers of adultery were both extremely grand.

In London they moved into Wimborne House, just behind the Ritz – one of the grandest houses in the capital. Their country residence was a Tudor manor house in Northamptonshire, Ashby St Ledgers, famous as the gathering place of the Gunpowder Plotters. Mimi employed Lutyens to renovate and improve it. It was perhaps to this romantic house, with its pretty warm-coloured stone, Tudor-style windows, steep roofs, tall chimneystacks, beautiful manicured lawns, perfectly trimmed hedges and stone balustrades, that my mother's mind was returning when she lit the candles on our Christmas tree in Downshire Hill.

Ashby St Ledgers (above)

Royal visit on the occasion of 'Polo week' at Ashby St Ledgers 1921. The Rolls Royces belong to Ivor Churchill Guest, 1st Viscount Wimborne and HRH Prince of Wales (left)

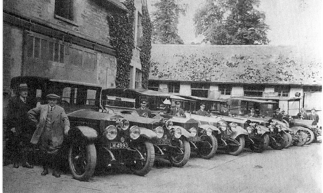

Queen Alice, ignoring her husband's affairs, took up her position as irresistible Liberal society hostess with graciousness. Her greatest success was her bid to end the General Strike by bringing together a group of leading politicians and trade unionists to lunch at Wimborne House. Lords Londonderry and Gainford, for the major coal owners, met the chairman of the Trades Union Congress, the 'endearing' Mr J. H. Thomas, as well as Lord Reading, Philip Snowden, J. A. Spender of the *Westminster Gazette*

and, of course, Lord and Lady Wimborne themselves. It seems to have been a most placatory affair, with everyone convinced of the importance of a return to the status quo as soon as possible. Four days later the General Strike quietly and gratefully collapsed.

Wimborne House was not just the scene of political lunches but was known for Mimi's parties which were laid on with her special talent for perfect loveliness in everything. A contemporary, Dora Foss, leaves us a description of one:

> It was a never to be forgotten experience. We passed through a series of anterooms till we came to a large salon where we were received by Lady Wimborne. Huge pyramids and columns of white lilacs and lilies rose from the floor; champagne cocktails; and I got entangled with mine and my handbag, trying to shake hands with Lord Wimborne in the middle of this spacious room, with no flat space near on which to park my drink.
>
> We then moved into the supper room where we sat at a number of round tables. I counted thirty-five guests and seventeen footmen. The tables were massed with yellow roses in silver tankards; we drank soup out of silver plates and ate the most exquisite food. After supper, we moved into the vast music room, with its fantastically lovely crystal chandeliers lit by hundreds of candles. It was a scene of great splendour and beauty – yet as a *party*, it was ineffably dull. Siegfried Sassoon joined Hubert and me and we sat together on a brocaded seat and contemplated the magnificent room, and the distinguished company. 'This is Rome before the Fall', Siegfried Sassoon said.

But as the 1920s developed it became clear that Mimi wanted to shape her own, rather different, life. She began to move into more avant-garde circles, becoming a close friend of Osbert Sitwell. She was thirty-eight on her return from Ireland, at the height of her powers, and used to having her own way.

The Sitwells epitomised a myth of romanticised, artistic aristocracy. A group of Oxford-educated, middle-class young men like Harold Acton and

Mimi in full fig

Evelyn Waugh, on a mission to rebel, aped the Sitwells' upper-class habits of speech, dress and attitude. Effortlessly upper-class herself, vastly wealthy, with considerable musical talent, Mimi felt she too could become a patron of young geniuses. She wanted to be a free spirit and patron of the arts, just like the Sitwells.

Cecil Beaton was an early beneficiary of the Sitwell patronage, so it is not at all surprising that one of his early photographic subjects was Osbert's friend, Alice Wimborne. Beaton first caught sight of Alice at a ball in 1926, during a stay at the Venetian family palazzo of Baba, Princesse de Faucigny-Lucinge. Alice appeared in a gold crinoline dress, 'wagged her hips and pranced about', and Beaton found her to be dazzlingly glamorous and mystifying.

The young photographer took her picture in 1928, and included the 'Shingled Vicereine' in his exhibition at the Delphic Studios in New York in 1931. The photograph is simple compared to some of his more extravagant society portraits; she wears a tiara set with rubies and an understated, but perfectly tasteful, dress; she rests her hands on a surface and gazes serenely to one side. Exquisite, lovely, unforced perfection. Many society women refused to be photographed by Beaton, because he saw too deeply into them, exposing all their exotic tricks and affectations. (Stephen Tennant observed: 'You may think Cecil is listening intently to what you say. He isn't. He's counting the hairs in your nostrils as you speak.') Perhaps in Mimi he met his match, for she was as confident of her own beauty as he was of his talent.

Looking over the many photographs of Mimi, I find myself baffled by how very different she looks in different pictures. Her expressions are never anything other than a gentle smile, her photographs always heavily staged.

Robin tells me that she was actually quite a large-boned woman, expert at concealing her size. And then suddenly I come across a photographic print called 'Lady Wimborne in a Silk Wrap Dress' by Edward Steichen. It is as if the veil has fallen away and she suddenly looks like my mother. She looks softer, she looks nicer, her face oval, like Laura's. The photographer has caught something.

In 1934, Osbert introduced Mimi to the composer William Walton, the Sitwells' brilliant protégé, whom they had taken into their home, almost as a member of the family. 'He has a very clever shaped head', the youngest Sitwell, Sachie, had remarked when he met him at Oxford. Mimi, at fifty-four, in Catherine the Great style, very much enjoyed making younger men fall in love with her, and this is what she did with Walton.

After a painful period of creative bloc, Walton was staying at Sacheverell Sitwell's house in Weston, close to the Wimbornes' grand home, Ashby St Ledgers, working on his First Symphony. The Sitwells apparently left him working alone, but when Sachie returned from holiday the taxi driver who picked him up from the railway station told him he had driven Mr Walton to Ashby every day. A guest at Ashby reports coming down from Mimi's room at about 11.45 in the morning and seeing the footman apparently waiting for her with half a bottle of champagne on a silver salver with a glass and a dish of sandwiches. She went up to him and said, 'How very nice. Just what I fancied', only to be told, 'No milady, this is for Mr Walton'.

I plug my Iphone to my large speakers and listen to the fourth movement, imagining Walton getting into his taxi at the end of a day's work to relax into the luxury of Ashby St Ledgers, and the arms of sexy, youngish grandmother Mimi. 'I even got on very well with her husband', Walton reported. 'The family seemed to like me, I don't know why.' I am probably being fanciful, but from the beginning drum rolls, rich orchestral sound, bringing in of the main tune, and the little echoey bits of flute to the huge and triumphant final chords, it seems to me an optimistic and even triumphal piece of music.

It would be tempting to see Mimi as part of a world of superficiality, of *façades*, to borrow the title the Sitwells used ironically for their famous work of performance art, but that would be to miss something of her. For her sexy, glamorous, dressy persona masked a keen intelligence and more serious interest. Her affair with Walton turned out differently from all her other affairs with younger men. She seemed to be reaching for something a little more real, more disciplined, and more meaningful than her 'set' had to offer. Walton was a Northern, working-class boy and *enfant terrible*, happy to enjoy the patronage of aristocrats, but ultimately not sharing their values. Gradually Mimi began to shed her old circles, to adopt a more Bohemian lifestyle, to devote herself to her lover's genius, and to become his muse.

Osbert Sitwell reacted with spite to news of this new relationship between his protégé and his friend. Perhaps he was jealous of both parties. He asked William to leave the house and wrote to a friend, 'I saw Willie and Alice walking down the King's Road yesterday. She looked old, and footsore and slummy.' Walton loyally responded that it would have been almost impossible for Alice to look slummy.

Alice Guest and William Walton's affair lasted for fourteen years. Ivor looked upon it with perfect equanimity, being fully engaged in his own career of seduction. Alice supported and looked after William, providing stability, money and patronage, using her contacts to bring people together. For example, she introduced him to the poet Christopher Hassall through a mutual friend, Eddie Marsh, former secretary to Winston Churchill. Their partnership coincided with a most fruitful period of Walton's creative life: he started composing for film, writing the music for *As You Like It* in 1936, then *Dreaming Lips*, *A Stolen Life*, and later *Henry V*, which he scored for Laurence Olivier. He also composed for the ballet, working for Frederick Ashton, and wrote 'Crown Imperial' for the coronation of George VI. In this success Alice was an active help and collaborator.

After Walton was operated for a double hernia, Alice rented the whole of the Villa Cimbrone in Ravello to help him recover. Walton wrote that she was very good at making him work and would get very cross if he messed about. The violin concerto that he wrote there expresses the depth of his feelings for Alice. Caught up in their romantic dream, they conceived a plan to build a house on the cliff below the villa in Ravello, on a point known as 'I Quattro Venti.' Willliam spent hours planning and building a little model of it out of matchboxes. But for Alice and Willie, as for so many, the war intervened, and the dream house was never built.

Roy Douglas, a collaborator of Walton's, described a visit to Ashby St Ledgers in November 1940. Ivor had died in 1939, so William was a bit more of a permanent fixture. The house was cold; the three of them ate their meals in the long, draughty dining room, and each of them had an oil stove beside their chair. 'We can have butter with our muffins today, William,' Alice said, 'because Mr Douglas has brought his ration.' After dinner Walton would depart to compose, while Douglas and Lady Wimborne sat on the club fender with their feet in the fireplace trying to keep warm and talking of music, literature and people. Douglas reports that she was always friendly and relaxed, and had a low, husky, attractive voice. On another occasion in 1941, Alice is described as reclining on a sofa in a silk gown, smoking one of the cigars occasionally sent to her by Winston Churchill.

As the war progressed, its effects began to show at Ashby. The gardens were neglected, sheep grazed the lawns. By 1943, one of the retired gardeners became butler, very short-sighted, with thick spectacles. Quite often when he left the room a loud crash of crockery was heard. In 1942, Douglas joined them again at Ashby and wrote warmly of Alice: she was far more than a society hostess – in fact a charming and very cultured person of 'much artistic and literary discernment'. Walton would go away and write some film music after dinner and bring it to play to 'Lady W', who had been known to say 'that's not really good enough, William, you can write a much better tune than that'. He would meekly go back to his music room and re-write. Douglas also thought she had a very beneficial effect on Walton's character: when she was with him he was inclined to be a kinder, more thoughtful man, less bitchy. At the very end of the war Walton and Alice were spotted by Alan Frank of Oxford University Press acting 'like a couple of kids enjoying themselves'.

A fictionalised portrait of Alice, as 'Mrs Wentworth', captures and exaggerates something darkly extraordinary about her:

Polo week at Ashby St Ledgers in 1921. Edward, Prince of Wales is seated front right. Mimi is second from the right

A Slutsk family from about the same period

Crossing the new mown lawn with an unhurried step, sauntering with enjoyment, strolling with a leonine suppleness of movement, smiling a little under the shade of her green-lined parasol, she achieved a charmingly period appearance in clothes and accessories of the richest and latest simplicity. ... Lightly and gently Mrs Wentworth twirled her parasol, tilting it so that not so much as a stray sunbeam should touch her dazzling neck. She put up a white gloved hand and felt the splendid column of it. Mrs Wentworth sat and thought about herself. She thought about her beauty, her brain, her attainments, the impression she made on others. Looking at her life, there seemed no reason why it should ever end. For herself, and indeed for others too, she had no age. She had abolished age, and with it, the abstraction of death. Her belief in herself was in turn translated to others. In watching her it was possible to react to one aspect of her only, the completeness, the totality, the apparent immortality of her beauty. She had other assets, but they were neglected … for her loveliness was of an obliterating strength, and nothing else could live beside it. Long ago Mrs Wentworth had decided that this quality and the preservation of it was worth the sacrifice of all else she might acquire or be possessed of.[1]

Mimi was still with William Walton when she died in 1948. Her death was painful, and Walton wrote of being utterly traumatised, seeing her go quite black through lack of oxygen. Thirty-three years later when he spoke about it in a documentary the pain was visible in his eyes. Walton's 'Sonata for Violin and Piano' that he wrote the year after her death, one of his greatest works, contains a strong dramatic conflict between melancholy romanticism and rhythmical power which reflects the tension he was feeling after the trauma of her death.

---

[1] Evelyn Jordan, unpublished fragment.

Chapter 8

$\mathcal{M}$y mother, Laura, whose middle name was Alice, would have been fourteen years old when her grandmother died, and yet she never really described her to me. She would murmur the name Mimi most obliquely, hinting that her grandmother was very particular about being addressed as Mimi, and never Granny. Laura did not mention Ashby St Ledgers either, although she must have spent many holidays there and certainly experienced fairytale Christmases. Throughout those fourteen early formative years of Laura's life she would have seen her grandmother in action and must have been profoundly influenced by such a figure.

Laura seems to have inherited far more from her grandmother than a penchant for real candles on her Christmas tree. From Mimi, Laura gained a sense that it was a reasonable role for a woman to support a man of genius, and confidence that it was of no consequence to move outside your class in order to do so. When she found Tony, her very own William Walton-style *enfant terrible*, with his very own 'clever-shaped head', she must have felt a deep sense of recognition. As I read about the charming and cultivated Mimi, as she managed the practical and emotional side of life while Walton composed, it all seems very familiar to me. I can see Mimi managing everything most charmingly so that you did not even notice that she was really in command, just as Laura did. A contemporary noted that Walton's character was much improved by Alice, and I think you could say the same of Tony under the influence of my mother. Laura perhaps inherited all of this from Alice, but there was no trace in her of her grandmother's narcissism or casual acceptance of infidelity.

Tony's genius was real. He had a very powerful brain, so overpowering in fact that he was often trapped within it and lacked the skills to relate himself to the world of his peers, or to find a suitable route with some institutional backing. Far too much of his time was spent in conflict with a world that was far beneath him intellectually. Laura could see how distracting and tiring these brushes with the world were for him, and sought to protect him, surrounding him with peace, calm and beauty. 'He has a rich inner life', she used to say to me. And so the philosopher sat in his ivory tower and simply thought and wrote.

I can hear the clackety clack of his blue manual typewriter and clearly remember the excitement of his first book coming out, not long after we had moved to Downshire Hill. It was called *The Computer in Design*, a square hardback full of glossy pictures, including one of my very own hat, a pointy, woollen Peruvian one with earflaps. But it was a side issue connected with the new reality of 'Dad at home' that really affected me. One day two men came to the house, picked up the television and took it away, in order, we were told, that Tony could concentrate on his work. I sat on one of the lowest orange-carpeted stairs and watched as the beloved magic box disappeared out of my life. Ten years later, Merlin used to set out on a twenty-minute walk to a grimy electronics shop on the Finchley Road in order to press his face against the glass to watch television. Only then did Tony relent and allow the window into other worlds back into our house in Downshire Hill.

With the television gone, all routes to an understanding of popular culture or the fast changing world of the 1970s disappeared, and Downshire Hill became a temple to highbrow culture. Education was God; there was no subject that our brilliant father could not explain to us, giving us the tools to analyse things for ourselves. We were encouraged to be intellectual snobs on a grand scale.

Our school was called New End, and was a ten-minute walk up Willow Road. It was an eight-storey, red brick, Victorian building with seemingly endless lino staircases, an infants' playground with outdoor loos, a girls' playground with a covered area where we played Elastic, and a boys' playground, shaped like a long thin wedge of cheese, which was really just a football pitch. It was no ordinary primary school, crammed as it was with the children of artists, writers, actors, philosophers and scientists. Apparently one of the teachers handed in their notice in quite a fit of pique, crying 'I'M TIRED OF TEACHING LITTLE GENIUSES!!' Whatever the truth of that remark, my memory of this time is a myriad of small fragments – milk in little half bottles, skipping in the girls' playground, scraping my Clarke's shoes on the playground to wear them out so that I could have new ones, my red trouser suit, a girl of quasi-mystical womanly powers who wore halter-necked Biba dresses, and Miss Klotz, the reputedly sado-masochistic teacher whose hefty body swayed atop four-inch stilettos, and who doted on a few favourites called 'the jewels in the coalheap'. My brother, Ant, was left in no doubt about his status as a very sooty and ordinary piece of coal.

At home, although Tony was an intellectual and scientist there was a special reverence for the artist and the craftsman. We three children were all allowed, with the encouragement of the fashionable manual of childcare by Dr Spock, to draw all over the kitchen wall, and Laura sketched whenever she could find the time. Tony used to have a special voice, in a deeper register, all worshipful and portentous, which he assumed when mentioning artists he admired. I think he perhaps didn't quite understand how talented his own wife was.

Breon O'Casey came to visit every now and then. I can picture him seated comfortably in an armchair in our yellow-carpeted sitting room, the exact image in my mind of what an artist should look like, that is to say large and bearded. He would talk in his deep voice as slowly and deliberately as Tony spoke didactically and continuously, full of rhetorical flourishes, but perhaps because they were so very different they got on really well. I can recall Breon's shoulders shaking with laughter. His daughters Oona and Diobhna seemed impossibly ethereal, Celtic and godlike to me, but they hardly ever came with him.

Tony and Breon's unlikely friendship had been formed at Dartington Hall progressive school, where the arts were treated with great sophistication. This approach had printed itself firmly on Tony, and somewhere in his soul he felt that art was the highest form of human endeavour. There was always a tension in him between the intellect and the expressive, and some part of him wished that he too could be an artist, even though this was not where his talents lay. This conflict was playing out when he attended sculpture classes at the Working Men's College; Tony worshipped

Brancusi, and his weird sculptures showed this influence. He also produced simplistic Cubist-inspired oil paintings in black and white, or two colours, somewhat Sitwellian, a sort of crude artistic response to his preoccupation with Marxist dialectics.

Our life in Hampstead was itself an extension of this reverence for art – as if Laura and Tony were living *within* an artwork. There was a kind of artificiality about the place. Hampstead felt less like a neighbourhood than a stage. Everyone living in and around the Heath was acting out their self-appointed role as part of a company of thinkers, and trying to efface his or her roots in some way. Hampstead was full of all sorts of people dislodged from their backgrounds – Jewish immigrants, Irish literary types, musicians, artists, radical aristocrats and left-wing politicians. Michael Foot was a familiar figure, stalking eccentrically along in his donkey jacket, white hair untidy about his head. They had all come together to shape their own world of free thought.

We used to have very stagey encounters on Hampstead High Street – with Freddie Uhlman, a tiny figure with a stick and a heavy German accent who would conduct bellowed conversations with Tony while I lurked in the background trying to make myself invisible, or with Eric Hobsbawm, the historian. After a long boring conversation about history Tony would stride several paces ahead of me and re-live the conversation all the way home. None of these people ever seemed to appear inside 38A Downshire Hill – as if this was our dressing room and very private.

Like most members of the left-wing intelligentsia, my parents firmly distanced themselves from any religious roots they might have had. There were too many replacement gods for actual God to find any sort of place in their world. Our family culture in Downshire Hill was free-thinking, rational, scientific, artistic, intellectual. That was all you needed, Tony said. Religion was obviously bogus; when the body dies, it all dies. This was a central truth you had to confront and bravely live with.

However Laura wasn't really an atheist. She had been baptised and confirmed, and her confirmation present, a beautiful set of ivory hairbrushes adorned with a curly L, lay on her dressing table. I felt a religious sensibility in her. She used to say she was a pantheist, believing that God was in everything. To be lost in the primeval shape of a tree or the patchwork patterns of the Heath landscape, the blue intensifying towards the horizon, absorbing what she saw through every pore and expressing it through her brush, was for her a kind of religious experience. Tony mocked Christianity, calling it 'gibbet worship', so Laura could hardly develop any latent faith she might have had. Besides, it just wouldn't have been *à la mode*. Tony's atheism was so militant I think it concealed something, but as small children my brothers and I absorbed the atheism and despised religion. To me at that time the idea of God was inconceivable, and I had some early successes in conversion (or de-conversion perhaps): during the course of a walk up Willow Road to New End School I convinced my friend that there was no possibility of God existing, only to find her in tears the next morning at the loss of one of the important structural planks of her life.

And so for a long time I had only the haziest idea that Tony was from a Jewish family; I sort of knew it, but it didn't seem to have anything to do with me. I had to wait until a girl called Sophie Reddish at school asked me if I ate pork, before this vague sense firmed up. 'Yeah,' I answered, confused and defensive, 'why wouldn't I?' We were citizens of the world – what did religion have to do with us?

Chapter 9

Tony's study contained some relics and further hints of his family's Jewish past. The rabbi, Aaron Hyman, was the father of his father, Alec. But all of his treasures were from his mother's side. A small black-and-white photograph of my great-grandmother showed her to be possessed of a most calm and good face, full of depth and peace.

A second photograph shows this same lady, the mother in a group photograph with her family. I discovered that her name was Hannah Rubenstein. Hannah and her husband, Louis, sit in the centre with their knees together, three-quarters to the camera, rather serious and stern, anchoring the little group, surrounded by their seven children. Hannah wears a long skirt with large buttons running all the way down and an elegantly gathered silk blouse, also with pretty buttons running down the middle. Her fair hair is swept up into a bun. She exudes calm, while her husband, bearded and sharper of face, glances sideways. He is more difficult to read. Five of the children are quite grown up. Two daughters have a homely air, seated on either side of their mother. There are two older boys in the back row in smart jackets, white shirts and ties; and one younger boy at the back looks fairly extraordinary – his hair is cropped short and he sports an outsized Eton collar. In the front is little Sam in shorts, a jumper with diamond patterns at the neck and sleeves and ankle boots. And out to the far left, beautiful, independent and haughty, in a stylish outfit of long skirt and top with two rows of buttons, is my grandmother, Fanny. They present a very respectable, thoughtful and well-dressed group. A tailor's family, they seem imbued with much style and charm.

I had always been proud of the 'Russian' grandmother I never knew. And my father did actually *talk* about her. He spoke of her sharp tongue, as well as of her great beauty and formidable intellect. He spoke of her married life as 'one long round of dinner parties with tedious people'. She used to make remarks that were so barbed, but cleverly disguised, that

Fanny Hyme Sam Daddy Reaane Maurice MILLIE

The Rubenstein family. Fanny is on the far left

the poor old recipients didn't even notice until they got home, at which point the penny would drop and they would rage impotently in the privacy of their own bedrooms.

Fanny was a woman of style. We possessed a raspberry pink, velvet, long jacket of hers whose sleeves were so slender that I could not push my arms through them. I was quite skinny, but my bones were certainly bigger than her bones – she must have been really tiny. There was also an intriguing silk shirt with three-quarter-length sleeves, printed with panels of yellow, black and olive green, and a design of a long-stemmed flower with leaves printed in white or black all the way over each panel. I particularly liked its style, with a collar that was green on one side and black on the other, and I could just about fit into it, although it was a little tight around the shoulders.

Her interest in clothes became mine; casting back to my teen years I have vivid memories of a pair of flat, leather boots which rose high above the ankle with many, many lace holes; of jeans which I took in all the way down the inner seams until they were skintight and of lying on the floor of a shop to do up the zip of another impossibly tight pair of jeans. Every trip up Hampstead High Street brought with it the lure of the few clothes shops, strewn with temptations.

Fanny Rubenstein felt part of me, somehow, because she slipped through the invisible wall of silence. She was my namesake of course; I can't count the number of times I said, through gritted teeth: 'It was my grandmother's name.'

Fanny Rubenstein

It was not only for herself but as part of a partnership that my grandmother took up a place in my imagination. Fanny and Alexander – it has a glamorous, cinematic, opulent, early twentieth-century feel, conjuring up images from Bergman's film. My mind fills with beautifully dressed people, pinched-in waists and bodices, lavish meals served in expensive silver dishes, servants, candelabras, repressed and tortured family relationships.

Fanny and Alexander had much in common, both coming from large Ashkenazy families who had fled from Eastern Europe at the end of the nineteenth century to seek sanctuary in England. Fanny's father, Louis, set up business as a tailor in Manchester and remained committed to his faith. A keen Zionist, he served as warden at his local synagogue. Her maternal grandmother, a tiny lady of astonishing determination, had crossed Eastern Europe almost on foot, from Russia to Romania, in search of the husband who had deserted her, in order to obtain a divorce and start a new life.[2]

Both families had faced persecution; they had had to pack up their belongings and uproot themselves, settle in a distant country, learn a new language, find that they stood out with a strong accent, different religion and unusual way of dressing, cope with people staring at them and judging them, never losing their sense that life could be arbitrarily destroyed at any moment. Simply to arrive at the point of safe and purposeful lives in England had already taken huge courage. Out of this battle to survive came two young people who started at the bottom, but were fired with a great determination.

A glimpse of the Census of 1911 shows Fanny already asserting her ambition with great confidence. Louis Rubenstein, of 164 Cheetham Road, Manchester, is listed as Head of the Family. Occupation: 'Gents' Tailoring'. Birthplace: 'Russian Poland'. Nationality: 'Jew' – crossed out and replaced with 'Russian'. Then we have Bessie: aged twenty, 'Assistant Tailoress'. Fanny: aged eighteen, 'Student'. Milly: sixteen, 'Assistant Tailoress'.

At eighteen Fanny was clearly not prepared to settle for 'assistant tailoress' like her sisters. She won a place at Manchester University and stayed on to do an MA, the subject of her thesis being 'Trading Posts in Africa'. For a girl from a tailor's family this drive to explore the world, to investigate a subject so far removed from her own experience, breathes curiosity and ambition. At university she made new friends, developed independent habits of thought,

---

[2] Bessie Levy, who was deserted by her husband, and then lost all her three children in an epidemic, walked from Russia to Warsaw in order to find a learned rabbi. The rabbi told her she must seek out her husband and obtain a divorce. He would be overjoyed to see her, and not want to grant her a divorce, but she must stand firm. She finally tracked him down in Turkey where he begged her to come back to him. But true to the rabbi's advice, she stuck to her guns and ritually renounced him. She had to call the police in to obtain her divorce. Only then did she tell him that their three little children were all dead. She went on to remarry, and then, hearing of the wonders of England, she moved with her husband and daughter to Manchester.

and came to a left-wing, secular and Fabian position, quite different from her parents. On graduating, however, just about at the start of the First World War, she found that opportunities were somewhat limited, and she spent some time teaching history in Birmingham, where she made friends with a fellow radical teacher called Marion Weinreb (the Auntie Marion of my hazy childhood memory) and worked as a rep selling medicines.

Fanny Rubenstein

Meanwhile, in London, we can imagine the disciplined world of Aaron's family of ten, at No. 3a Tenter Street, Whitechapel. The patriarchal figure of the rabbi with his 'hard-as-nails' wife made sure that the family worked extremely hard. Obviously not all of the sons could become rabbis, so Aaron had to choose one. At first it was to be his eldest son, Marcus. But Marcus took himself off to India, where he became a tutor to a Maharaja. The expectation then fell on his second son, Alexander, who was sent to a Jewish seminary where his entire education was conducted in Hebrew and focused on the Talmud and the Torah. However, Aaron's carefully laid plans were to be overturned when Alec gradually began to realise that that life did not interest him and that he lacked faith. He was in a new country, a safe place, full of opportunity, and the war was over at last. Alec wanted to embrace all it had to offer.

Aaron showed realism, behaving in a way that was open-minded and forgiving. He could see that Alec had other ideas, so he began to ask around for opportunities for him. The Jewish community mobilised and the chief rabbi found the young man an opening at Shell Oil, a company with strong Jewish roots that had been created by a Marcus Samuel to import seashells from the Far East, originally run from a small room in Whitechapel. His sons then developed the company as an exporting business, revolutionising the bulk transport of oil. Alexander was found a place as an office boy, his job being to carry messages from office to office, but soon, and very impressively given the limits of his education, he began to rise in the firm.

Then Alec met Fanny Rubenstein, and the two young people, both extremely gifted intellectually and very ambitious, were married in 1918, on the threshold of a new era. They truly did feel that the world was at their feet. Alec knew that his wife had extraordinary charisma and a brilliant mind. She was described as 'just regal'. If she stepped into a room everything changed. With this star at his side he would surely sweep all before him. And for Fanny, her husband was the pillar of strength and stability she needed.

Fanny and Alexander's rise was spectacular. They set up home in Finchley and soon acquired a cook and a gardener. Before long they were embracing the cultural life of London, attending plays, concerts and the ballet. Their first child came along in 1921, a bright and outgoing girl. Although Fanny had given up her career, normal for a young mother at the time, she was an able member of committees, including the board of Governors of St Pancras Hospital. Their lives were entirely secular. If you had visited their house in Finchley you would have found no candelabras with eight branches; they celebrated Christmas, not Hanukah. They had left the world of their parents far behind.

There was a hiccup in their perfectly smooth rise. In 1924, Fanny became pregnant again but gave birth to a stillborn child. This event caused her terrible distress and she suffered a depression that became serious enough for Alec to search for help. He found her a German Jewish psychiatrist and she staged a good recovery.

Fanny and Alexander

Alec continued to be promoted in the company, eventually appointed to Head of the Division of Wax and Candles (when I learned this I couldn't help thinking about Tony's special ability to blow out a candle with a tiny and perfectly aimed breath from many feet away). At that time Shell, after a merger with Royal Dutch, was becoming the business of the moment. Prince Borghese won the Peking to Paris motor rally using Shell Spirit motor oil, Ernest Shackleton and Captain Scott used Shell fuel in their expedition to the Antarctic, and Bleriot's inaugural cross-Channel flight was made using Shell Spirit. To be successful at Shell was to participate in this world of glamour.

The lives of Fanny and Alexander progressed from comfortable to luxurious. They drove a Rolls Royce, and Fanny, true to her girlhood as a tailor's daughter, dressed immaculately and with enormous style, shopping in Harrods and Harvey Nichols in a characteristic colour palette of light blue and beige. They started travelling the world. On Shell business they took cruises to South America, New York, Rio de Janeiro and Buenos Aires, leaving a staff of four or five people to run the house. Fanny was always the centre of attention on these trips, during which she would change from one *haute couture* dress to another every day, choosing her footwear from a collection of eighteen pairs of Ferragamo shoes, and revealing a subtle glimpse of diamonds and emeralds. Fanny and Alexander were living lives of Hollywood style glamour and affluence, light years away from the Pale, the pogroms and the terrifying precariousness of the lives of their parents and grandparents.

Fanny had been swept into the fast lane and there is no doubt that she adored the glamour of it all, but at the same time there was something missing. She became famous for her extremely sharp tongue. Her considerable intellect was directed, in a gentle-voiced way, towards undermining the mediocrity of the society she found herself a part of. 'Talk of acid to clean the paint off!', Tony used to say. She found the Englishwomen she moved among to be overbearing, with shrieking voices and a tendency to laugh mirthlessly at unfunny things. These qualities were amplified in the presence of this diminutive, soft-voiced, exceptionally beautiful and alarmingly clever Jewish lady. Fanny used her sharp intellect to demolish it all. 'Did you see so and so?' she would exclaim afterwards – 'I mean she looked like a horse who had come in through the window and wrapped itself in a curtain.'

Fanny had been, after all, a serious student of history, and where did all her interests go in the midst of this life of luxury? She tried to keep it all going through reading and through membership of the Fabian Society, and with her perceptive understanding of the sweep of history she saw the way the wind was blowing in the 1930s. She foresaw the rise of Hitler, but felt passionately that Communism was not the answer. She became very interested in the ideas of Simone Weil ('the red virgin'), a philosopher known to a limited circle in the late 1930s, later described by Albert Camus as 'the only great spirit of our times'. Fanny saw her as a kindred spirit of intensity and sensibility.

Weil's philosophy and theology must have appealed to my grandmother, as she grappled with her own bipolar nature and with the increasing political extremities of the '30s. Weil's concept of affliction (*malheur*) encompassed the idea that only some souls are capable of experiencing the full depth of affliction, and the same souls are also most able to experience spiritual joy. Affliction is a total suffering which transcends both body and mind – a physical and mental anguish that scourges the soul. Here was a philosophy to encompass depression, which also promised the greatest ability to experience the fullness of spiritual wonder.

Weil was an extraordinary woman, who packed a rich and chaotic life into her thirty-four years. As well as writing many of the most lucent works of philosophy of her times, she worked in a factory in order to know what that was like. She volunteered to join the Rebels during the Spanish Civil War, despite her short sight and poor health. Everyone tried to leave her behind on missions as she was a terribly bad shot, and for God's sake don't let her use the heavy machine gun! Later during the Second World War as part of the French Resistance, Weil dropped her briefcase and secret papers spilled out all over the pavement. Fanny's contribution to the war effort was less dangerous. She bought shoes and posed for the cameras, and she smuggled a pastry chef, an Austrian Jew called Mitzi, out of Vienna in the 1930s, reputedly in the boot of her car, and brought her home to join the household staff.[3] Mitzi became a warm and central part of the

Mitzi

---

[3] Tony used to be overcome with a wistful expression when he remembered as a child the mouthwatering delicacies which used to parade out of Mitzi's kitchen. Years later, as I pushed Dad around in his wheelchair, he kept insisting that we visit an exquisite cake shop. 'Come on darling – choose something, whatever you like.' He was thinking about Mitzi.

household – an easy-going and lovely friend for the highly strung Fanny, and favourite of the two children who hovered around her as the most fantastic apple strudel emerged from her rolling pin.

Throughout the 1920s and '30s Alexander remained as devoted to his charismatic wife as ever. Knowing her nature and talents, he tried unsuccessfully to persuade her to continue working (she had had a good job selling pharmaceuticals). When he travelled widely in Europe on his own for work, he would send her a postcard every single day, sometimes starting a message on a card that arrived on one day and finishing it on the next.

In 1928, Fanny attempted another pregnancy, and this time all went well. She gave birth to a healthy boy, my father, whom they named Robert Anthony, known by his middle name. Here at last was the answer to her frustrated sense of needing an achievement of her own. Anthony was to be her work of art. The relaxed and happy mother she had been to her daughter disappeared, and her attachment to the new child verged on the neurotic. First, she commissioned her friend Marion to create a nursery school especially for him. Then, when he was seven years old, she chose to send him to Dartington Hall, a very unusual and progressive educational experiment in the heart of the Devon countryside. The teaching was highly unconventional, and pupils were taught by great artists from the Bauhaus as well as literary figures and scientists of renown. This was to be the place that would enable Fanny's work of art to take shape, and where her little prodigy would develop into the great figure that he should become. The family paediatrician warned that Fanny was developing a relationship with her son that was unhealthily close.

Rabbi Aaron Hyman

As Alexander and Fanny swept all before them in England, Alec's father, Rabbi Aaron, satisfied with the success of all his children, finally left London in the 1930s, and after nearly fifty years in England moved to Israel. He wished to die there and be buried on the Mount of Olives, overlooking the Dome of the Rock, to be sure of a front row seat for the coming of the Messiah.

Chapter 10

The walls of No. 38A Downshire Hill contained a lively swirl of family life – argumentative, sometimes explosive, accompanied by much laughter. We children found our way around Tony, we learnt how to argue, how to tease him, and we told him off when he behaved badly. We defended him to the hilt if anyone criticised him. Laura, although so self-effacing, had a much surer instinct for managing a family and knew how to make us all feel happy, bringing the best out of everyone. Our idyll continued to centre on her. If I close my eyes and think myself back to those days I am always transported to the kitchen, where she was generally to be found.

I am sitting at the kitchen table; a slant of sunlight comes through the window, alive with dancing particles of dust. Laura is making gingerbread with her back to me, chatting away. She is wearing pale blue Laura Ashley trousers and a cheesecloth shirt, her hair is up in a ponytail. Ant comes in, curly black hair, flares and National Health glasses, and struts over to the bread bin, one of those tin ones with 'Bread Bin' in very fancy writing, and pulls out a malt loaf. He rips off the packaging, doesn't cut a slice but eats it by pushing the whole thing slowly into his mouth and chomping until it is finished. Like a cartoon. He sits down for a bit, closes one eye and focuses the other on the window, tilting his head back and forth as if trying to isolate a small spot on the window frame. This is how he thinks.

Although Laura was calm, resilient and charming, if there was something she didn't want to do, a person she didn't want to see, she would dig her heels in with greater stubbornness than anyone else I ever saw. As a result she and Tony saw very few people. She was much at her happiest in the kitchen. She wasn't an adventurous cook at all, and she liked producing things that she knew well, so that she could muse on colour, line or form as she cooked. We had *petit Suisse* for breakfast, a yoghurty package wrapped in a piece of paper; ham, tongue and brown bread for lunch; gingerbread and Earl Grey tea with lemon at 4.30; and usually spaghetti with tomato sauce or chicken for supper. It tasted delicious and we didn't yearn for more exotic culinary experiences. The important thing was that she was there and we told her everything. She didn't judge, but brought her kindness and experience to make us feel better about any difficulty we might have. Sometimes, unnecessarily, she was given to pieces of homespun wisdom which in retrospect I think she must have picked up from her nanny, such as 'a woman needs a home like a snail needs a shell'.

Mum and I talked endlessly about every subject under the sun, as close and happy as it was possible for a mother and daughter to be. But she wouldn't speak of her past or her family, and I very rarely asked her, for it seemed to cause her unhappiness. I once tried to ask her about her brother, the mysterious Uncle Al of the fawn duffle coat. We were sitting in Cranks restaurant in Goodge Street eyeing up a depressing-looking wedge of homity pie. I can't remember exactly what I asked, but I do remember her reaction: she closed up, pressed her lips together and looked down at the table. She looked so upset that I dropped the subject and we went back to our contented chat.

Every now and then I would open the little jewellery case I kept in my bedside table and take out the soft velvet box which housed my mistletoe brooch. This was a really charming little twig with leaves, set with seed pearls, and it was infused with the presence of Laura's father – my grandfather, who was no more than a faint memory. From time to time this man, never named, never fully described, found a way through the wall of silence. Tony would tell us that he was the key to Laura's happiness. Laura herself didn't say much about him but smiled shyly. Just as darkness gathered around the person of Alexander, everyone's countenance lightened when they mentioned Gilbert. So, when in the twentieth century my new Uncle Robin sent me a little cache of letters from my mother to her father, I opened them with keen interest.

∿

I pick up one envelope after another, the address written in capital letters between carefully ruled lines:

CAPT. THE. HON. G. HAY. SPRINGHILL HOUSE. MORPETH

I unfold the little letters carefully, to see my mother's childish, joined-up handwriting running along lined paper, discoloured with age:

DEAR DADDY. I AM SO SORRY YOU CANT COME HOME. I HAD A LOVELY TIME AT FALCONHURST. LOVE FROM LAULY.

DEAR DADDY, I HOPE YOU WILL SOON COME HOME AGAIN. I MISS YOU VERY MUCH. I PLAY WITH ANN EVERY MORNING AND DO EXERCISES WITH HER. LOVE FROM LAULUMS

DEAR DADDY, I HOPE YOU ARE WELL. THANK YOU VERY MUCH FOR THAT LOVELY BIG COT. ALL MY DOLLS THNK IT IS LOVELY. ANGELINE WAS SO ANXIOUS TO REST IN IT THIS MORNING. ISN'T IT AWFUL I HAD MUMPS FOR MY BIRTHDAY BUT I AM GOING TO HAVE A BIG PARTY WHEN I AM BETTER, I DO SO HOPE YOU WILL BE HERE TOO. MUMMY IS GOING TO BUY ME A BIRTHDAY CAKE WHEN SHE COMES BACK. I AM VERY EXCITED ABOUT HAVING A BABY BROTHER AND I AM LONGING FOR MUMMY TO BRING

HIM HERE. HASN'T HE GOT A NICE NAME ROBIN. DOCTOR WOOD SAID I CAN GET UP ON SATRUDAY. WITH LOTS OF LOVE FROM YOUR DARLING LAULUMS XXXXXXX OOOOOOO XXXXXX OOOOOO

How could I not be touched by these early creations of my mother's? The patient but persistent longing for her Daddy runs through them all. But

Laura does her bit for the war effort

they are also full of references to Mummy and her siblings – the ordinary everyday fabric of a child's life.

You would never suspect, reading these childish letters, that she would one day blank out and deny them all.

Like Laura, Gilbert didn't make much of a fuss. He hasn't left a trail of writing, or a blaze of publicity. He didn't achieve anything very spectacular, apart from his mildly distinguished service during the war. He was tall, with a longish, handsome face, very like my mother's, and had a streak of grey in his hair which appeared while he was still in his twenties. Words that attach to him are 'steady', 'even-tempered', 'noble', 'conventional'. His nieces described him as 'The dream uncle, with enormous warmth and charm'. He was the second son of a highly distinguished diplomat, Victor Hay, Earl of Erroll, Chargé d'Affaires in Berlin, and then High Commissioner to the Rhineland after the First World War. His father was an important influence, but it was the actions of Gilbert's older brother, Josslyn, that were to have the most profound effect upon him.

Josslyn and Gilbert, the two sons of an Earl, both good-looking, upper-class and capable, should have been born to rule. From early on Gilbert was in the shadow of Joss – a golden boy with 'transcendental good looks'. While Gilbert went to Cheltenham, Joss was sent to Eton, where he became a bit of a bad boy, the object of numerous crushes. Arrogance took root in his character, as he barely seemed to have to lift a finger for the world to fall at his feet. Gilbert, by contrast, had to work harder and developed a more honourable and steady character. Joss was extremely able, brilliant even, and it was assumed he would follow his father into the diplomatic service. He passed the Foreign Office exams, but then abandoned his bright prospects when he fell in love with Lady Idina Sackville, twice divorced, unconventional, and eight years older than him. They went ahead with a scandalous marriage in 1923. His elders began to realise that he was spoilt, but also that he was vulnerable.

I have a photograph of Joss in front of me. He is devastatingly handsome, smooth and blond, clad in his wing collar and bow tie, with an exaggerated side parting. His wife, Idina, stands next to him in a strange shapeless coat

The TATLER

Vol. LXXXIX. No. 1159
London, September 12, 1923

POSTAGE
Inland, ½d.: Canada and Newfoundland, ½d.: Foreign, 1½d.

Price
One Shilling

LADY IDINA GORDON AND THE HON. JOSSLYN HAY

A snapshot recently taken at a well-known Italian resort. Lady Idina Gordon is the Earl of De la Warr's sister, and the Hon. Josslyn Hay is a son of Lord Kilmarnock and a grandson of the Earl of Erroll. The engagement of Lady Idina Gordon and Mr. Josslyn Hay was announced a short time ago

that looks as if it was made out of curtain material, a large string of pearls peering out from under her feathered cloche hat which casts a shadow over her eyes.

Joss and Idina emigrated to Kenya and became part of the Happy Valley Set. James Fox in his book *White Mischief* paints a vivid portrait of the scene, and my great uncle's place in it. Idleness and dissipation on a heroic scale characterised the life of these English expatriates in the 1920s and '30s, whose sole aim was the pursuit of pleasure. Everyone gathered at the Muthaiga Club, a pinkish, pebbledashed building with cream and green walls, polished parquet floors and deep armchairs with loose chintz covers which 'gave out the atmosphere of Thames Valley gentility and Betjemania'. It was a country club, open to women, but closed to Jews. During race weeks the drinking started with pink gins soon after midday, gin fizzes in the shade at teatime, cocktails for sundowners, and whisky and champagne until the lights went out. At the nightly balls the guests might have been dressing for royalty, and the dances didn't usually end until around 6 a.m. The club was famous for sexual escapades, and 'terrible grievances took root in the libidinous, drunken atmosphere'.

After their arrival in Kenya in 1924, Josslyn and Idina very quickly took their place at the heart of Happy Valley. Their residence was called Slains, and there they threw parties that were famed for their excess, during which Idina was like a high priestess presiding over a sacred ritual, deciding who was going to sleep with whom. Joss became immediately very popular in the colonial community, a striking figure in a white tussore suit, a polka dot bow tie and panama hat, clever, immensely charming, witty and tough, a natural born leader, and very attractive indeed. There was a cynical and bullying side to him too. He was unpleasant to his African servants, exploitative of the women who found him irresistible, and contemptuous of their husbands.

One possible serpent in Josslyn's Eden was his need for money. The Earls of Erroll, despite the immense antiquity and grandeur of their birth, had very little money. Joss did have a farm in Kenya, but he took very little notice of it and soon began to run up debts. His attempts to plunder Idina's money led eventually to divorce and Joss fell in love again with 'another married heiress and beauty, also older than himself, a petite, slender, animated woman with auburn hair', whose name was Molly Ramsay-Hill. After Joss was horsewhipped by her husband, Molly obtained a divorce and they settled into her house, known as the 'Djin Palace'. The descriptions of this place are like a drug-induced vision.

The Scottish lord must have felt at home here, beside this beautiful lake, that had the look of a wild highland loch, encircled as it was by mountains and plains, its wide grassy shore bordering the water which, seen from the veranda of the Djin Palace on a fine day, was a clear, cool blue pool. For decoration there were flamingos, herons, black duck, chalk white egrets, and hippos rose and sank in the water among the floating islands of papyrus. The bedroom doors of the house faced an inner courtyard with a tiled pool and a fountain in the centre. There was a sunken marble bath lined with black and gold tiles – to facilitate, so the story goes, the vomiting of over-indulgent guests. The rooms and terraces were furnished with deep sofas and armchairs loose-covered in flowered chintz. And Erroll's full-length portrait, in unpaid-for Coronation robes, hung at the top of the stairs.

Marlon Brando-like, Joss revelled in his own torrid kingdom.

But after a while he stopped being a pure waster, as 'boredom and an acute sense of his own abilities' began to have an effect, and he started to move towards politics. He joined the British Union of Fascists, but quickly dropped it when Mussolini invaded Abyssinia, was elected to the 'settlers' Parliament and was described by an observer as 'much improved'. He became secretary to Sir Ferdinand Cavendish Bentinck at the Production and Settlement Board and began to turn into an able and conscientious worker. His political views turned from Fascist to outright opposition to the appeasement policies of Chamberlain. By 1940 he had become military secretary to the Colony, was a Captain in the Kenya African Rifles and was head of the Manpower Board. He was responsible for marshalling an East African fighting force for the Abyssinian campaign, and his administrative skill was widely prized. Sir William Havelock, who worked for him, said, 'He was a demanding man, brilliant at his job.'

The war was starting to transform him, as it transformed so many others. But as usual, it was with women that the less attractive side of his character came to the fore. He began to lose interest in Molly, who took to drinking heavily and shooting morphine. One of Joss's servants recalls him saying, 'Give the woman as much as she wants to drink. If she wants to die, let her have it. If she wants a drink, let her have one.'

And finally, he went a step too far in his contempt for husbands. When he met and fell in love with the cool ash blonde Lady Diana Broughton, newly married and in Kenya with her husband, Sir Jock Delves Broughton, they conducted their affair with brazen disregard for Jock's feelings. On 24 January 1941 my great uncle was found shot dead in his Buick at the crossroads on the Nairobi-Ngong road. Sir Jock was accused of the murder and stood trial, but was acquitted, and committed suicide a year later.

Unlike Joss, my grandfather Gilbert was not brilliant, but nor was he a cad. When Gilbert was sent to a lesser school, Cheltenham, it was as if he was being designated a more pedestrian role than his charismatic brother, right from the very start. When the golden boy started veering from the path of honour and distinction that could so easily have been his, Gilbert more than ever assumed the role of the steady brother with the good sense. I quiz Uncle Robin about him, and Robin simply says, 'he was trying to be the good guy'. While Joss was indulging himself in Kenya, Gilbert married, became a loving and present father, worked steadily at a job he wasn't terribly good at in the City, and developed a respectable social life of somewhat dull engagements.

Then in 1941, after he had joined the Army, he received the news about Joss. The shadow cast by his brother became even longer in death than it had been in life. Gilbert carried on, as he always had, displaying a humdrum determination to keep things going, maintaining a kind of shadowy dignity through everything – through all the excesses.

A little mystery reveals itself in my mother's letters to her father, Gilbert; for by the end of the war her letters are no longer addressed to the Hon. G. Hay but to Major Lord Kilmarnock. In 1941, Laura suddenly found that she had a new surname; she was no longer Laura Hay, but Laura Boyd. The story of my mother's change of name from Hay to Boyd springs from this same desire of Gilbert's to patch things up, to tidy up, selflessly to keep things as steady as he was able to. It was closely connected to Joss's murder in 1941.

Gilbert and Joss were born with the name Hay – an ancient and powerful Scottish clan, who claim descent from the God Thor, ennobled as earls of Erroll, and further dignified with the powers to nominate their own heirs, including through the female line. As well as the complicated armorial achievement, it had its own symbol, the falcon, its own castle, Slains, which clung to the bleak Aberdeenshire east coast, its own war cry, *A Hay! A Hay!*, and even a legend. Its emblematic plant was the mistletoe, which explains my precious brooch.

In the eighteenth century the Erroll title passed to a woman. This Countess of Erroll married a William Boyd, Earl of Kilmarnock, head of another ancient Scottish clan. William Boyd fought for Charles Edward Stuart at the Battle of Culloden; he was captured, imprisoned in the Tower of London and beheaded by an axeman (a mark of his status) on Tower Hill in August 1746 in front of several thousand spectators. At this point the Kilmarnock title was forfeit; William's son James inherited the Erroll title from his mother, and decided to change his name to Hay to match the title.

The Kilmarnock title disappeared for nearly a century after all this, only to be revived again in 1831. It was recreated for James's descendant William Hay, who became not only the 18th Earl of Erroll but now also the Earl of Kilmarnock.

In the twentieth century, when Josslyn, Earl of Erroll and Lord

Kilmarnock, was murdered, he had one child – a daughter called Diana, also known as Puffin. She inherited the Erroll part of the title and became the 23rd Countess of Erroll and Lord High Constable of Scotland. The Kilmarnock title could only be passed on through the male line, so that went to Joss's brother, my grandfather Gilbert, who became Lord Kilmarnock. In a reversal of the events of the eighteenth century, Gilbert decided to change his name to Boyd, to match the Kilmarnock title, so my mother was Laura Hay until she was seven, and then found herself Laura Boyd. Gilbert had tidied up his side of the family; by assuming a different surname, he put some distance between himself and his disgraceful brother.

Gilbert Boyd, Lord Kilmarnock dressed in his robes for the Coronation, 1953

Gilbert, it seems to me, had many of the same qualities as my mother. Laura never, ever thrust herself into the limelight. While everyone around her was demanding to be heard, proving how entertaining or clever they were, throwing tantrums, dramatising everything, Laura hid her own feelings, strove to put others at their ease, put on a brave face, brought all her capability to bear on everyday life. Gilbert was clearly devoted to her, and she to him: 'I hope you will soon come home again. I hope you are well. I miss you.' I cannot understand how, years later, she allowed him to die without visiting him.

Chapter 11

*I*f you click the little wrought-iron gate of 38A Downshire Hill shut and turn left, your feet take you away from Hampstead Heath and up towards the High Street. Just a few paces, past a row of beautiful black, iron streetlamps, bring you to St John's, a gracious eighteenth-century cream-coloured church on the corner of Keats Grove. We used only to go inside the church, strictly speaking a chapel-of-ease, once a year, just before Christmas, to the carol service. For me, a church service was a novelty, a

St John's, Downshire Hill

rich experience – candles cast their soft light in pools around the elegant Georgian interior; we sat in the high wooden pews and let our voices join the others, an exhilarating but unfamiliar feeling.

Turn left at St John's and you find yourself on Keats Grove, a smaller and exceptionally pretty street, each house a jewel set in a pretty and leafy garden. To live in this street is to be very blessed; we experienced this when we visited Jess Weeks, whose garden backed onto ours. In typical Hampstead style, she wasn't just any old lady – her daughter was close friends with the drummer of Pink Floyd and, much to our envy, was given tickets to The Wall gig.

A short way down Keats Grove and on the right are Keats Grove Library and Keats House. It didn't take me long, after we had moved into Downshire Hill, and the TV had gone, to discover the library.

Keats House

The library had a very particular atmosphere, a weird hush, a booky smell, silent librarians with stamping devices – a riveting transaction which involved pulling a white tongue of card from its brown pocket with a little triangular section cut out of one corner; with an emphatic click, a new future date was added to the list of purple or blue past date stamps. The swing doors led to the grown-up bit that I only entered occasionally, intrigued by the outsize print shelf.

Then came the moment, full of anticipation, of stepping towards the shelves of treasures. I worked my way through all of E. Nesbit, hardbacks with orange covers and a see-through plastic extra layer – *Five Children and It*, *The Phoenix and the Carpet* (I remember being very entertained by the little brother who is suddenly transformed into a pompous grown up), enticing spines along the bottom shelf of the main children's room in the library. Then Geoffrey Trease, Henry Treece and Rosemary Sutcliffe. There was a freestanding case in the middle of the room which contained Enid Blyton. I wasn't allowed to touch those, as they were completely forbidden, I wasn't sure why, but I always felt shocked when I met people who *had actually read Enid Blyton*. I read and read, *David Copperfield* at ten years old – I was through with Dickens by the age of about twelve and never really attracted especially after that.

At home too our lives were built on books. A wall of the sitting room was entirely covered in bookshelves, crammed full without an inch to spare. There were encyclopaedias, books on science, art, economics, politics, Marxism and philosophy and a few sets of books that seemed to belong to a different kind of house altogether. There was a complete and very tiny set of Dickens with minuscule writing, bound in red leather with gilded titles, and with gossamer thin pages; there was a handsome set of Jane Austen hardbacks and row upon row of small, blue, hardback copies of Trollope. They would have looked more at home in a house of heavy mahogany furniture, silver cutlery, engraved glasses and starched white napkins, but there they were, and I devoured them all.

I would get so involved in whatever I was reading that I sometimes read all night and felt bereft when I finished. Then I would go and find one of my parents and say forlornly, 'I've finished my book'. They would then immediately rush off to the shelves and say, 'Have you tried this?'

There was one book, a blue hardback that took its place in the sitting room amongst Tony's books on thought, which I was vaguely aware of as an important work of art history, but which did not hold especial interest for me. It was, I suppose, rather a fashionable book of the time and would have been seen on any self-respecting Hampstead dweller's shelves. This was called *Ways of Seeing*, by John Berger. As far as I was concerned, it was just another of Tony's heavy tomes.

I suppose I would have thought that Berger's book appealed to Tony because of the fact that its author was a Marxist thinker, whose approach to its subject of art history was disruptive and challenging. I have a copy before me now and I find a typical section: 'Seeing comes before words. It is seeing which establishes our place in the surrounding world; we explain that world with words, but words can never undo the fact that we are surrounded by it. The relation between what we see and what we know is never settled.'

I have a clear memory of taking down that blue hardback many times. It was probably all quite embarrassing to my teenage self, because now that I return to it I see that there is a lot about nakedness and sex. 'What is the sexual function of nakedness in reality? What does this sight of the other mean to us, how does it, at that instant of total disclosure, affect our desire?'

In Berger's Booker Prize-winning novel *G*, you can see the writer going still further in his elusive quest to capture the sexual act in print, his search for exploring the reality of sex. The writer uses every analytical and artistic tool he can find in his quest, and gives us a combination of explicit description: 'Warm mucus encloses his fingers as if it were a ninth skin', and intellectual speculation, 'The focus of sexual desire is concentrated and sharp. The breast may be seen as a model of such focus, gathering from an indefinable soft variable form to the demarcation of the aureola, and within that to the precise tip of the nipple.' He even expresses it as an equation. 'The experience [sex] = I + life.' He goes on to wrestle with the limitations of language in trying to describe his subject:

All nouns reject the meaning of the experience to which they are meant to apply. Words like cunt, quim, motte, trou, bilderbuch, vagina, prick, cock, rod, pego, spatz, penis, bique – and so on, for all the other parts and places of sexual pleasure remain intractably foreign in all languages, when applied directly to sexual action.

This combination of bold honesty and intellectual rigour, joined with a cringe-making tendency to embarrass the reader, was very reminiscent of how sex education was treated at home in Downshire Hill, perhaps reflecting something of the zeitgeist of the times. Tony repudiated what he saw as the coy hypocrisy with which most English people discussed the subject of sex – a kind of giggling silliness on the surface, disguising unpleasant, loveless actions in reality. I can hear him declaiming the word 'prick', delighting in his own provocativeness. At the same time he would use art, just as Berger did, telling us about an exhibition where all of the pictures on one side of the gallery depicted straight lines, and all of the others were made up of circles. He thought it was utterly hilarious that so many people didn't notice. But somewhere amidst all this frankness and iconoclasm there seemed to be a weird detachment around the subject, as if something had got lost in all this intellectualisation of sex. This, combined with our mother's embarrassment and nimble jumping away from difficult topics, left us quite at sea. Tony was horribly embarrassing. Laura was silent. In classic Downshire Hill style, my sex education centred on a book called *Where do Babies Come From?* I picked it up and studied the weirdly shaped foetus in the womb.

But to return to *Ways of Seeing*, the only one of Berger's books we owned. If I had thought about it, it was in fact a slightly unusual book for my parents to have on their shelves. The book was an accompaniment to a television programme of the same name, presented by the charismatic author, and extremely fashionable at the time. Since my parents had no television and no interest in popular culture, there is every chance they would not have rushed out to buy the book of the moment. Tony was a scientist and did not really approve of literary or art criticism. He might well have considered Berger to be a bit of a pseud. Laura was an instinctive artist who would also have had no interest in such over-analysis of her art.

As it turns out, however, there was an overwhelming reason for them to have this particular book, by this specific author, on their shelves. During one of my early meetings with Robin he casually dropped in the following remark –

'Your gm was married to John Berger.'

'My grandmother was married to John Berger? What? You mean *Ways of Seeing* John Berger?'

Neither Laura nor Tony batted an eyelid when the Berger volume came off the shelf. Not a flicker of emotion appeared on their faces. Not a word of any special connection. Just another book amongst the many.

Chapter 12

I am in the kitchen with Laura. We are sitting at the kitchen table, clasping our cups of coffee, chatting away. She is waiting by the white fence near my primary school to greet me, wearing a duffle coat, with her hair back in her characteristic ponytail. She is just so physically *present*, so endlessly just uplifting. I smile in greeting and hug her.

As I think back to those times, I ask myself if I am exaggerating, but then, no, I realise that I cannot bring to mind a single instance of her saying the word 'mum' or 'mummy'. Did she even have a mother? My grandmother was missing. At least my other grandparents were allowed an occasional mention. But this one, the mother of my own wonderful mother, had been written out completely. And this is why – when Uncle Robin in 2006, four years after we had first corresponded, sent me a present of a slim paperback, I found its contents so astounding. For, of course, Laura did have a mother and this mother was mortal. Her mother was Queen Alice's eldest daughter, Rosemary, and for the very first time I was about to meet her.

The book was *Rosemary, a Memoir*, compiled by Alastair Boyd. Inside the front cover Robin had written *Only Connect*. This little book was nothing less than a complete assessment of the life of the grandmother I knew nothing about, written by her eldest son, Alastair, containing views of her children and friends, her own novels and poems and extracts from her diary.

This was a lot to take in. After a lifetime of knowing NOT ONE THING about her, suddenly to know so much is causing me some indigestion. I sit in my office with the book in front of me, studying the cover. Under the title is a black-and-white photograph of a girl with a side parting and short hair, wearing a white party dress, looking thoughtfully at the viewer. This is my very first glimpse of my Unknown Grandmother. I realise, by page 20, that she had been alive and well *and living in Swiss Cottage* until I was seven years old. I have to put the book down and go and tell someone this extraordinary fact. That's mad, I mutter to myself. *Swiss Cottage* – walking distance from where we lived. You could get there by crossing Hampstead High Street at the top of Downshire Hill and threading your way through quiet leafy streets – Thurlow Road, Lyndhurst Gardens, Wedderburn Road – or you could go straight down Ornan Road and Belsize Lane, past the Sigmund Freud statue and join Fitzjohn's Avenue that way. Swiss Cottage meant the modern grown-up library with several floors, not my cosy and beloved Keats Grove Library, but rather closer to distant things like University and Research. How did we avoid seeing her? Why was Tony's mother, Fanny, spoken of, but not Laura's mother, Rosemary?

I flip over to the photographs and draw in a sharp breath. A black-and-white photograph entitled 'The Firm' shows Rosemary with Cynthia, her younger sister. The face that smiles out at me is my mother's. I put the book down. When I resume, my grandmother, unmentioned, unseen, unknown, springs into vivid life before me.

It is a life of privilege, *immense* privilege. I turn to a picture of the family, standing in front of the Viceregal Lodge in Dublin, immaculately dressed, and very staged. Ivor, dressed in a top hat, long coat and a cane, holds his younger daughter's hand with his own white-gloved hand. Next to him,

Rosemary à la Velasquez

Mimi is dressed in eccentric *haute couture* – a dark trouser suit teamed with a white, lacy skirt with asymmetric hem, an enormously wide sash across her middle, long white gloves and a flat straw hat. One hand, as perfectly white-gloved as that of her husband, holds the hand of her older daughter. The girls themselves look like two little wedding cakes. They are wearing pure white little dresses, short white socks, white shoes, their faces almost covered with broad white hats piled up with swirls and adornments.

I sit in my office, absolutely riveted by this little book, and feel as if I am not really breathing properly. I *knew* somehow, I always

Ivor, Mimi and the girls in front of the viceregal lodge in Dublin

knew that Laura, if she had not been divinely created, must have had a mother who loved her. She *must* have, or how could she have learnt to be all that she was?

I turn back to study the photographs. Here is one – Cynthia has a hand on Rosemary's shoulder and is about to whisper something in her ear. Rosemary, with two enormous bows in her hair and a white silky dress with a square neckline, looks with a forthright gaze right out of the page as if straight into the future – as if she has no time for whatever trivialities her sister is whispering in her ear.

I am very cross with Ant. I have sent copies of *Rosemary* to both brothers (Robin had sent me extra copies), and he has left his out in a conspicuous place where Tony can find it. Tony duly finds it and has a terrible outburst. They have a great row and my brother defends me. 'He is her Uncle,' Ant says, 'she is entitled to develop a relationship with him if she wants to.' In truth the memoir says very little about Laura and Tony.

As I turn the pages, for the very first time I am allowed to meet my grandmother. I find out that she was about five foot seven, the same height as Laura, that she was of medium build with high cheekbones and a firm jawline (unlike Laura), and that her hair was mid-brown, very fine and difficult to shape (also unlike Laura, whose hair was always thick and plentiful). Her character is well defined: she had a deep voice, often mistaken on the phone for a man, and her hands were large and workmanlike; she liked to wear rings with big stones like onyx, topaz and opal. She always wore trousers, as well as two or three strings of cultured pearls, a Victorian rectangular gold watch and a gold bracelet. The compelling power of detail has me captivated, and little flashes of this banished grandmother flit around my brain – large hands, a deep voice, an elegant pair of evening trousers. Apparently she hated having her photograph taken. That's funny, so do I. Laura didn't mind at all, she was contented with her looks.

All of the entries in the little memoir show what an effect Rosemary had on people and the affection she inspired. Her cousin writes that she is his definition of a star, with her 'gaiety, lightness of spirit and slightly wicked sense of humour', and that he felt 'enriched by knowing her'. I read on, completely unable to put the book down and, as well as being fascinated, my emotions are being worked on to such a pitch that when I stand up I realise I am overwrought and upset. But I make my way through the little book. In old age she is described as having a deep, husky, seductive voice (like Mimi), constantly smoking filthy, black, tobacco cigarettes held in her large, practical-looking hands, dressed in gold lamé trousers, rather bent and limping a little. She had a whiff of Edith Sitwell, with hair longer on one side than the other.

'I will not forget her first words to me', writes one contributor: 'Pour me a gin dear boy.' I put down the slim paperback and a sense of loss spreads slowly through me…

∿

One of the first and most notable things I discover about my grandmother is that she loved to write. She was almost inseparable from her typewriter, and wrote page after page of diary. Her favourite subject in her diaries is her children. As I read I am riveted by a description of the teenage Laura, seen through the eyes of her own mother. This does not feel entirely comfortable to me; it is bound to transform my mother into a selfish creature, as all teenagers are selfish.

In her diaries Rosemary gives my mum a fanciful name: she calls her Lydia. Here she is as a teenager:

> As the summer wore on, Lydia became sloppier and sloppier, ruder and ruder, less and less civil and civilised with people. She obliterated her beauty. She moved as if chained and manacled. In repose she put her body into distorted and ungainly attitudes. Stooping over books she bit at her fingers. When addressed, her mouth fell open and she squirmed a little. She refused to look strangers in the face and shook hands with her head turned away. Her clothes were generally dirty and always the wrong colours. Was it an instinctive recoil from that horrible thing, love?

But more often Rosemary strikes a less critical note:

> Lydia came in, tramping noisily like a man. Her movements were always awkward and graceless. She wore someone's old duffle coat with the hood up. Her face was indescribably like some glorious Reubens portrait. I tried to see her as a lovely girl, my daughter. I could see nothing except the dimple and the Reubens colouring. Her youth reached at me, I felt the point of it at my heart, and I smiled at her. She had no idea why, but she was pleased because I smiled at her.

A ghost moment – my grandmother smiling at my teenage mother, and she is pleased.

> Lydia smiled over her palette. 'It's great fun painting hair,' she said.

'You just mix all the colours you can together and it becomes hair.' Carvali says, '*Pour les cheveux, il faut faire un peu la cuisine.*' Idly she drew a faint half-moon line through the green portrait. 'La divine proportion,' she said. 'That's what Carvali calls it.' In her overalls she looks demure and divinely young, gently absorbed. Her hair gave her the appearance of a sixteenth-century Italian youth.

I think about my mother. She is pulling a shopping basket on wheels down Keats Grove, a silk headscarf tied under her chin. We are on our way to the Co-op in South End Green, green shield stamps in hand, to do our basic shop. We pass Pollyanna, the children's clothes shop, and look through the window at a bright green boxy shaped jumper. Laura is an artist but she demands nothing. She has a sketchbook on the go, and one of those black metal boxes of Winsor & Newton watercolours, not the one with the flat top: the lid has compartments. She opens the lid and inside are intriguing little boxes of colour, and she mixes up familiar shades, like burnt umber, raw sienna, yellow ochre, burnt sienna, ultramarine and Chinese white. She is very frugal, but always splashes out on sable brushes. She never demands silence or space to concentrate, and puts down her brush to get supper together. Her art is never a 'get out of my way' thing or a 'you must admire me' thing.

In the orchard, we picked the apples in misty sunlight. Lydia came walking up the path in a wide, white skirt and bare feet. She looked mythological and proud. I called her to join us but she went on in haughty silence with her drawing book and pencil. Sometimes she was like that, proud and virginal. At other times she prattled with an artlessness which I thought must be an innocent pose. It became her. Perhaps she knew that.

Laura's sketches and watercolours are of us all; of the house, of flowers, of Tara the dog and of the Heath. We go for a walk on Hampstead Heath and she brings her sketchbook, a Daler, or a knobbly watercolour pad from Cornelissen. With a 6B or even an 8B pencil she draws tree after tree which get more abstract as she goes on, until they are just a collection of beautiful lines. Wild trees in a dream. Occasionally she puts people in, but this is not her best suit; sometimes they have an Edward Ardizzone charm to them – just an oval head and a shape for the body. She has a fine instinct for putting the pencil on the paper and producing the line that is somehow the right, the unmistakably right place for the line to be.

> The train drew in… and I walked down through the crowd that poured out of it, very slowly, so as not to miss Lydia, the stranger, wrapped in a dream of Florence. I saw her before I reached her. She smiled at me sadly. She was wearing what had once been my green coat and skirt. She had bleeding feet and her eyes were remote with sorrow. I looked at the green coat and skirt. It had become the sackcloth of all pilgrimages. Lydia looked like the Gioconda.

Laura had told me about this trip, in a vague and sketchy sort of way, and I knew it was important to her, as a coming of age just before she went to art school. She had stayed with Communists; was that Rosemary's doing? How did she know Italian Communists? Laura never named or described them. During the trip she had visited San Marco. I went there myself a few years later and vividly remember the little cells, each one with a Fra Angelico angel. The visit seemed to have shaped her artistic development, and she brought back boxes and boxes of postcards.

> Lydia's voice came over the telephone, fresh and lilting, the voice she used when she was happy and excited. I could see how she looked, I could see her ravishing green and brown colouring, her awkward movements, her rapscallion appearance, the soft straight fall of her beautiful untidy hair. There she was at the end of the line, an awkward, hopeless, graceless, obstinate, lovely girl. My daughter.

I am feeling a little overwhelmed. Here it is in black and white. My airbrushed grandmother, Rosemary, *adored* my mother.

Chapter 13

$\mathcal{H}$ ampstead was an old-fashioned place in the 1970s. We frequented the fruit shop, the butchers on Flask Walk, Boots, a haberdashers and a toyshop, and expeditions were just as likely to be in the company of Tony as Laura, for Tony loved shopping. I remember gazing covetously at an array of tiny and realistic things for dolls' houses – miniature ironing boards, perfect little pieces of wallpaper and little joints of meat on plates. They reminded me of Hunca Munca trying to eat the fish that was fixed to a plate and of Tom Thumb losing his temper and smashing the ham with tongs, only to find that it fell to pieces, 'for underneath the shiny paint it was made of nothing but plaster!' Only one or two clothes shops had found their way onto the High Street – Colts and Monsoon were the only ones that interested us (these days of course it is heaving with clothes shops, a brash and characterless shopping street for rich people). About halfway up Hampstead High Street on the left-hand side was a down-at-heel community centre, where we used to fight our way to the front of jumble sales on a Saturday, searching for treasures.

Downshire Hill itself was full of interest. An 'Any Old Iron' man trundled up and down our street, an old tinker with a tray full of junk. Sometimes a young, blind woman rode her horse past our house; I was fascinated by her beauty, her cool and her unseeing white eyes as she turned to address her companion. A French onion seller would ring the bell on his bicycle to call us, and he really did have a beret, a stripy Breton top and a silly French accent. One day I opened the door and before I could see what was happening, Tara, our golden retriever, had dashed out of the door and sunk her teeth into the onion seller's knee. He shook her off, instantly dropping his jovial act in favour of a very nasty sounding invective; I grabbed the dog and ran inside, slamming the door behind me.

During the week, life for Ant and me was a steady rhythm of school, homework and family spaghetti suppers. Merlin was quite a few years younger and no longer the adorable little baby, but starting to develop his own personality. We had very few visitors and a few 'pets'.

'So-and-so's an absolute *sweetie*,' I can hear Tony saying, which was really just shorthand for less sophisticated and educated than us, and thus posing no threat at all. There were also some regular and much-admired favourites. Foremost amongst these was Ant's friend, Raph Mizraki, an Israeli, a comic genius who drew our family around him like moths to a flame. Raph played the cello, very brilliantly – 'It just plays itself, doesn't it?' he would say to me, and I would think, no it doesn't, it takes all my concentration. With an outsider's ear he noticed that Tony had developed an obsession about the Merovingians. I used to be thrilled that Raph would catch my eye every time the word was mentioned, and he and I would be overcome with helpless laughter, sharing a private joke.

Our Sunday walks on Hampstead Heath were as inevitable as the tide. Our route, after crossing East Heath Road, took us past the ponds. These were considered a bit wicked and it was understood that you certainly never went swimming there, full as they were of broken glass. People *died* in there. Fools staggered drunkenly out of the Freemasons Arms at the bottom of Downshire Hill in midwinter and went for a walk on the ice. Once in a while one of these drunken visitors to the sacred ground of Hampstead would fall through the ice and drown – the Heath claiming another victim. 'You have to be a writer or artist to come here', it would gurgle as it swallowed them, 'didn't you know that?' 'I think drowning would be ok,' my brother announced as we contemplated the idea of the drowned philistine scrabbling desperately for a hold on the edge of the treacherous ice only to find his fingers could not get a grip on it. 'No it would not!!' I shout. 'It would be horrible!!' The only family member to attempt a swim there was Tara, our golden retriever, and almost immediately she proved our parents right by cutting her foot on broken glass, bringing on a great rigmarole of unwound bandages and plastic lampshades.

In the sexist world of the 1970s, Ant did woodwork classes at school, while I did something called 'Home Economics'. I made a brown wraparound skirt with a wide waistband, of quite spectacular ordinariness. On one occasion Ant made me a pair of stilts in his woodwork class, and walks on the Heath were transformed. Instead of tramping sulkily in the footsteps of my parents, I was a fast-moving alien, all spiky elbows and stick legs moving fast across the landscape. I carried them under my arms as we walked down Downshire Hill, turned right into Willoughby Road and crossed onto the Triangle. I kept patience as we crossed the steep and uneven grass of this little islet of Heath, separated from the mainland by East Heath Road. Once the big road was safely crossed I stepped up to the footholds and accelerated off on my own adventure.

Sometimes we walked up Lime Avenue (later decimated by the hurricane of 1987) and paused at the football field. We would sit on a rug on the grass, talking, while Tara helpfully dug a really deep hole – so deep she disappeared right inside it. I can't imagine why nobody stopped us. At other times we approached via Nassington Road and Parliament Hill. Here was an intriguing house lived in by an old lady which had the most gorgeous, intricate and beautiful white lace curtains. Or *appeared to*. There was always speculation about whether they were in fact painted onto the glass. Did they ever move? we asked ourselves, intrigued as we walked past. Nassington Road ended on a slightly alien part of the Heath – Parliament Hill Fields. Here was a running track, an adventure playground, a bandstand and people flying

kites. It was a whole different walk coming this way; the running track was always a foreign and unvisited thing, but the adventure playground was open to us and dangerously fun – involving racing chimpanzee-style along high, rough poles with no safety nets.

Whichever route we took, Tony would often sling a huge army issue pair of binoculars around his neck; I can feel the solid heaviness of them, the sensation of the lens end pressed against my eye, the faintly frantic shifting of the stiff dial, trying to find the point of perfection when the blurred image sharpened. Tony loved tools. He treated them with reverence; the handing over of the binoculars was almost ceremonial.

Usually, if the binoculars came out of their case, it meant we were heading for the 'far ponds', to look at the great crested grebes. I found the little sailing boats rather more fascinating – there were some beautiful, trim little vessels, every detail so perfectly reproduced, tiny cleats, little coils of rope, sails with little pockets for batons, varnished mahogany decks. Their owners lying on their fronts at the edge of the pond would push them out and off they would go, catching the wind, picking up speed, while the boys sat up and watched.

Tony and Laura wanted to watch the birds. There were coots, moorhens and swans to be seen, but for some reason for us it was all about the great crested grebes. For a while this was quite fun; I can see them very clearly, with their slim, elegant necks and theatrical, highly coloured crest swimming out across the pond, then disappearing with magical suddenness, an elegant and efficient dive taking them out of vision. I would scan the surface closely through the giant binoculars, trying to work out where the grebe was going to surface. As time went on, grebe watching became shorthand for boredom; *every week* we had to go and visit them and I would have happily wrung their little necks.

The Heath was only for Sundays, however, and for the rest of the week everything revolved around Laura and the house. Our feet were usually hurrying in the other direction, towards South End Green to catch the bus, or to the Hampstead Classic Cinema, or to go shopping. One day Laura was out with her shopping basket, wearing a blue Liberty's scarf over her head and knotted at the chin. She was making her way along Rosslyn Hill, her thoughts all concentrated on her shopping list and supper that evening. She was startled out of her reverie when another woman, a little younger, of similar build, fair hair and blue eyes approached. Their eyes met for a moment and the fair woman made as if to say hello. There were years of intimacy behind the movement. Laura averted her eyes and swerved to avoid the woman with fair hair, head down. Her whole being was focused on not making eye contact. The woman looked after her, her face etched with hurt and incomprehension. Laura hurried home, feeling disturbed and upset, but didn't mention it to any of us. Life went on, uninterrupted.

The author with Tara on Hampstead Heath

Chapter 14

*L*ike a photograph in a darkroom, my Unknown Grandmother's image is becoming imperceptibly more distinct; this little paperback Robin has given me is the photovoltaic fluid. The main text, written by Alastair, starts to sketch in details of her life, and the incomprehensible void where she should have stood is gradually filled with colour. I find I have started to dream about my grandmother: she is trying to say something important to me, but begins to fade and soon is gone.

When Rosemary was nine years old her father, Ivor, was appointed Lord Lieutenant of Ireland, and there the family lived for four years in a state of grandeur in the Viceregal Lodge in Dublin. On their return to England life shuttled between Wimborne House next to the Ritz and Ashby St Ledgers, and Rosemary's 'wicked fascinating parents', as she later called them, set about their careers of seduction.

One of Uncle Robin's letters sets out the consequences of this for their daughters:

> It is certainly true that when her only son Ivor Guest (the future Lord Wimborne, the one who inherited all the money) was growing up and inviting his young male friends to stay, [Mimi] banished her two daughters to live in a cottage at the end of the garden (with their governess) so that their youthful looks would not outshine hers!! Evidently she was very disturbed.

As the only boy, and the heir, Rosemary's brother, Ivor, had privileges heaped upon him. Mimi was related to John Buchan by marriage, and Ivor was a page at Buchan's wedding, where he is described as 'the very image of a little lord Fauntleroy in his pink and silver brocade court suit with lace ruffles and paste silver buckles'.

For Rosemary and Cynthia, however, in the 1920s years of emotional drought set in. The two girls were sent to live in a cottage in the village with their nanny and governesses and only occasionally summoned to see their parents when they were in residence at Ashby. Rosemary later wrote, in a fictionalised account, that they 'came home by invitation only', and that Mimi 'endured their brief and infrequent visits with impeccable manners and charm'. As for their father, 'when the weekend guests arrived, the young and pretty ones would play bridge with him, after which he would invite them separately to walk in the garden'. It was Mimi who was spending time with the bright young things who were her daughters' contemporaries, while Rosemary and Cynthia were shut away and denied proper interaction with their peers.

The girls' life was pretty bleak: they had no fun and games with the other children; Sunday lunch with the parson was a regular event, as were walks down the lane with nanny. They saw no one at all their own age, except for one girl who came to tea once a year. As a consequence, the two sisters clung to each other, forming a club of two, called 'The Firm'. Rosemary's nickname was 'Wag'.

Their main pleasure was learning 'yards and yards of poetry'. Rosemary was passionate about literature, and throughout these formative teen years when she was developing her own identity, she lived almost entirely in a world of her imagination. Not only was she cut off from the big, grand house and the lives of Mimi, her father and her brother Ivor, but she was rather deaf. She read obsessively and her favourites stayed with her throughout her life. Thomas a Kempis' *The Imitation of Christ* was seldom far from her side, and her Beardsley edition of Malory's *Morte d'Arthur* contains a number of passages relating to Lancelot and the Holy Grail carefully copied onto the flyleaf and endpapers in her beautiful governess-constructed handwriting. Above all she loved Bunyan's *Pilgrim's Progress*, the great Christian allegory written in 1660. Perhaps she was introduced to it early through the family connection with John Buchan, who himself used it as a constant reference both in his novels and in his life.

Apart from their devotion to literature, the girls did have one important and grounding area of activity – horses and hunting. They were completely fearless, riding sidesaddle and known for jumping over 'bullfinches' – wild hedges with the top growth uncut, which forced them to shield their eyes with one arm as they jumped. An album snapshot shows Rosemary sitting in a butt, smoking a clay pipe with a loader poised beside her. She looks cool, I think to myself.

Perhaps in part because she herself had been married at twenty-two, and she thought this was the correct thing to do, Mimi steered her eldest daughter into marriage at the first opportunity. Robin thinks that the idea of being a very young-looking grandmother also appealed. So when Rosemary was twenty, and Gilbert Hay proposed, her mother was very clear that she ought to marry him. Mimi added that she was *unlikely to get any other offers* because of her deafness (Rosemary was always made to wear large and ugly hearing aids). Her brother Ivor commented: 'How is it that my plain, deaf sister has netted the best looking eligible bachelor in London?' In fact Rosemary was always very attractive to men, despite some insecurity about her looks. A photograph of the wedding, in 1926, shows Gilbert holding Rosemary's hand in his as she steps forward, clad in what looks like a bath-hat which

Rosemary and Cynthia

Gilbert and Rosemary – man and wife

practically covers her eyes, brimming with vitality and trying to see beyond her strange veil.

To begin with, the newly married couple lived a pretty normal life for people of their class. They had a town house in Cornwall Terrace in Regent's Park, and their son Alastair was born a very respectable year after their marriage. My mother came along seven years later, in 1934. They were comfortably off, but not rich. Ivor got most of the Guest fortune, while Rosemary and Cynthia, just as they were denied a proper education, were also denied a decent share of the loot. On Gilbert's side, the Hays did not have money.

Along they jogged, Gilbert and Rosemary, seemingly managing well enough for the fourteen years of marriage that they had before the war, although Robin comments that 'as a couple, I doubt they were ever happy'. There was plenty of contact between Rosemary and her sister Cynthia, who was happily married and lived close by in Regent's Park (Chester Terrace on the east side), and they visited the family home of Ashby St Ledgers, the comforts of which they had both been denied as teenagers. But Rosemary was not content. As soon as she could, she began making moves away from her husband, developing a circle of her own, including Margaret Douglas Home, Gwladys Gordon Ives and 'the mysterious Zita'. Who knows? Perhaps everything would have continued reasonably normally if it hadn't been for the war. The war changed everything, for everyone.

I think back to the few almost imperceptible hints I ever had about the shadowy figure of my almost grandmother during my childhood, and it always hung in the air that she must have been distant and reactionary. Here she was instead, I was beginning to understand, creative, romantic and, despite her privilege, burdened with many insecurities. Such bleak formative years were bound to lead to some vulnerability.

Chapter 15

Lars Porsena of Clusium
By the Nine Gods he swore
That the great House of Tarquin
Would suffer wrong no more!

Tony declaims the words with ferocity, his eyes alight, and thuds his fist down on the table, his whole face twisted up with the effort. His favourite poem – he loves to attack the words. We all listen, or get up and drift off into another room, having heard it a thousand times. He moves through to the sitting room to light the gas fire, put a record on to the enormous hi-fi unit, and open a book. He mutters as he reads.

Laura comes in from the garden and says, 'I'm just going round to see Gill.' Laura goes next door to No. 38 and steps into a vortex of drama.

Gill was the person that Laura spent most time with – her next door neighbour and close confidante. She was married to Tony Greenwood (who was Wilson's Housing Minister), so there was a lot of talk of 'your Tony and my Tony'. Gill relied very heavily on my mother. She was extremely good looking, with fantastic cheekbones and a rich theatrical voice, full of precision and confidence. She dressed well and elegantly, having been a window designer for Jaeger. I remember being told that the job had been fixed up for her at a party.

Gill's presence was always glamorous and elegant. She sat in our sitting room with beautifully pressed trousers along with elegant polo necks and jackets. Once I bought myself, with eyewatering extravagance, a white alpaca coat from Nicole Farhi which I adored, and I can remember Gill coming into our wood-panelled Arts and Crafts hall where the coat was hanging ostentatiously among the waterproofs and greatcoats; she ran her hand appreciatively over it, saying 'that's a nice coat'. Gill's approval was something that mattered.

Perhaps I responded to this sense of style in Gill because it was lacking in our house. My parents fetishised and desired certain garments, items that were considered real, in the way that brown bread was considered real. Breton shirts, oiled wool fishermen's jumpers, sheepskin slippers, white Aran cardigans, Birkenstocks (I'm not mad on them now – I can see my own vanishingly thin ankles disappearing inside them – more dodgem car than shoe), and later 'gear' – Gore-Tex (worshipped), weird cycling shoes that looked like aliens' feet, lycra (not sexy). Laura was prepared to employ some surprisingly low tactics at a jumble sale to get her arms around an Aran jumper.

No. 38 reflected the character of Gill, its mistress, as clearly as No. 38A reflected my mother. Mum and I often went round there, charged with looking after the house when the Greenwoods were away, and shared some delicious hours watching *Dallas* on Gill's television. The house was closer to the road than ours, approached by a steep flight of stone steps. Inside, the hallway was narrow and wallpapered in some very fancy embossed paper; the sitting room, immediately to your left, was long and narrow, with a window giving onto the street. Compared to ours it was extremely smart, with a luxurious and new carpet, smart polished furniture, expensive armchairs, fancy glass lamps and cats. So many cats – I think she had about seven, who crouched on windowsills staring unsettlingly or rubbing themselves against your legs. I never went upstairs, but we did descend to the kitchen, which was in the basement. It was not a place to feel relaxed in; we always trod carefully and felt constrained. As I describe it, I realise that although the Georgian houses had greater snob value, No. 38A was roomier, lighter and rather beautifully designed for living.

Tony Greenwood, the Minister, we hardly ever saw. He must have been busy in the House of Commons. The only detail I can remember is being told that the Greenwoods threw a party at No. 38 when Harold Wilson became Prime Minister. Harold Wilson's wife was so distraught at the prospect of being 'first lady' that Gill spent the entire party comforting her in the back garden.

Years later, my parents told me a story, which may or may not be true.

They said that they visited Gill for tea when she was living with her daughter. They were chatting away, when gradually all of Gill's cats gathered around her, arranging themselves in various positions around her shoulders and over her armchairs. She said to Laura and Tony: 'I wonder what will happen to all of this when I am gone?' waving her hand to indicate her furniture. Then, right there in front of them, she died, with her cats arranged around her like an Egyptian preparing to enter the next life.

Sketch of a cat by Laura

Chapter 16

*H*ow was it that my mother had a sister that she never spoke of? This played on my mind as an even stranger circumstance than an unknown brother. Sisters are so close, so significant. I understood all about brothers, but my very lack of experience made sisters fascinating. I watched them at work, sensing that it gave them an extra dimension of female confidence and energy, a deep understanding of female secrets, which were mystifying to me, beyond my frame of reference, but which I needed to understand and to possess. If only I had sisters! How much more knowledge would I be a mistress of? The vivacious energy of the Bennett sisters, and the beautifully rendered picture of sisterhood in *Sense and Sensibility*, absorbed me for days on end. Eleanor and Marianne behave so absolutely in accordance with their characters – Marianne so passionately carried along by her own feelings, Eleanor so self-denying; they have every reason to find each other infuriating, and yet they are the most important people in the world to each other, and their deep level of mutual understanding sustains them in a bleak, superficial world of socialising and matchmaking. Neither would be whole without the other.

My close, close bond with my mother was a thing in itself, perhaps becoming so important because I did not have a sister. But our closeness existed on quite a lofty, artistic, ethereal plane, and we did not open up to each other about anything earthy, troubling, personal. I was very much left to make awful mistakes and find it all out for myself. As I became an adolescent I felt her angelic, self-denying loveliness to be something of a burden, feeling my own style of womanhood was not admired in the family. But now a new female presence was entering into this relationship that I had with my mother, so central to my life. For my mother *did* have a sister. Robin had been mentioning her in his letters since we first corresponded. It took a few years of knowing Robin before I finally came right out and said, 'Do you think I could meet your sister?' It was all so absurdly everyday and ordinary, the way he replied: 'Sure, yes, I'll invite her to dinner in London.' Coming from Devon to that dinner with Robin in London was quite an undertaking. Tension began to build during the two-hour train journey and I felt that my conversation was overly bright and artificial as my husband, Charles, and I negotiated the tube followed by an obscure bus picked up round the corner from Finsbury Park station. We made our way down the road, identified the flat, and stood looking up at it for a few moments. I felt quite shaky.

I rang the bell at street level. Robin's wife, Hilly's breezy voice came through the intercom. 'Oh, Hi Fanny! Come in,' and the intercom buzzed. We edged our way up the narrow staircase and the door was flung open. 'Hi! Hi! Hi!' cried Robin. 'Welcome to The Lost Boyds!'

We stepped into a large, light, open-plan flat, tasteful and minimal with interesting pictures on the wall. Hilly came forward – she was very slim, with dark, straight hair and a husky voice, and extremely chatty. She was a psychotherapist and I sensed that she was absolutely committed to the enterprise, experienced in situations of high emotion. Robin was hostly, self-deprecating, laughed a lot, enquiring about our journey, fixing us strong drinks. Some chat about buses flew about the room – which one had we caught? The high charge of the situation made me chatter some inconsequential nonsense, laughing too much, admiring things.

I turned to be introduced to the woman who rose from the sofa. She was calm, well-spoken, in her early seventies, wearing a blouse and skirt; she had short fair hair and blue eyes. Mum's sister, Juliet. 'Hello Fanny,' she said in a low, well modulated voice. Before I knew it, I was seated opposite her, resting my drink on the low coffee table and hoping I didn't spill it. This lady was a stranger, completely mistress of herself. She drew out a ring with a large green stone from her pocket and handed it to me, saying it had belonged to Rosemary. 'You can have it altered.' This was followed by a handful of photographs of my mother.

My husband sat down and began chatting to her husband, Alan, a large rugby-playing figure with huge shoulders and magnificent Denis Healey-style eyebrows. This was the man who had queued behind us in the bakery all those years ago.

Hilly summoned everyone to the dinner table. Alan rose awkwardly, as

Laura

he had bad knees. Soon the six of us were seated round the table. Thank the Lord for Charles' social skills. We were outsiders in a close family party: the four of them knew each other inside out – Juliet called her brother Robin 'Tiger' or 'Ti'. Drink flowed and talk flowed too – we talked of topics of general interest, of politics, of medicine, of life. Juliet began discussing teenagers and how much you should talk to them about sex. Alan was intimidating – extremely clever, with a very dry sense of humour, and I felt all the more that I was talking absolute rubbish. Robin was easier, always charming and quick to laugh at a lame attempt at a joke. 'Charm and brains,' he said to me, looking across at Charles. 'So rare to find them together in the same person.' 'Of course your children are all so wonderful, I predict bright futures.'

I asked about his children. 'Oh well... the artistic calling so difficult, and the other son – the mad, mad world of advertising, he bounces off the walls. And no girlfriend at the moment, he very much goes *"de fleur en fleur".*' (Much laughter.) 'My daughter – she hasn't quite found her direction yet.'

I could tell he was immensely proud of them, though, and self deprecation was a charming habit. I had brought out some sketchbooks of Laura's and we all poured over them at the dinner table. They made admiring noises.

'Has anyone inherited the artistic gene?' Juliet asked politely.

'Not really,' I said. 'Maybe me, a bit.'

At last we got onto the subject of *what had happened.* Robin pushed back his chair and declared, with a glint in his eye, 'The emotion!' I tried to get them all to understand the extent to which we had known absolutely nothing at all about them. Everyone mulled it over, sighed, and shook their heads.

Robin told us that he had boldly come round to Downshire Hill in 1978 when their father, Gilbert, died, in order to impart the news to Laura. Had he? What would have happened if one of us had opened the door? Would that have brought the whole secret house of cards down? Apparently Laura had turned round and called out: 'Tony. What shall I do?' Robin laughed uproariously, and said he had commented: 'Whatever the spirit moves you.'

'Rosemary adored your mother,' continued Robin, refilling my wine glass. 'She used to follow people in the street. She kept thinking she saw Laura and would follow them, only for them to turn around, revealing that it was not her beloved daughter but a stranger. Each time, she was so sure.'

This was the woman who searched for my mother through the streets of Hampstead as we lived our lives so unaware.

I found my eyes drawn over and over again to Juliet. She bickered good humouredly with Ti, teasing him for being a hypochondriac – 'That's why he became a doctor'. She had short hair, fairer than Laura's; she was well brought up, interested in all subjects under discussion, talkative, a little cleverer than Laura in terms of intellect, rather more direct and less artless. It emerged that she had taught special needs primary school kids in New York City for a number of years. There is no way Mum could have done that. She and Alan were a very longstanding alliance. He called her 'Julia', and told her off for being 'Pollyanna' about things; she called him a 'bloke'. It was just very small things, the tilt of her head, the set of her mouth, the shape of her eyes, that made me pause in the conversation, unable to speak for a moment; in that moment I wasn't at a dinner of strangers – an ancient connection passed across the table.

I was quite drunk by the time the dinner came to an end. We sat around the coffee table for a while, chatting and drinking our herbal teas and coffees, and then, with social inevitability, Alan and Juliet rose to leave. Charles and I were shown to our little room that looked out onto a London roofscape. Everything was well ordered and comfortable. In the morning we breakfasted with Robin and Hilly, nursing mild hangovers, hitting an easy rapport with them and making one another laugh, before taking our own leave.

Robin drove us with great *élan* through the back streets to Paddington Station. We waved goodbye, and Charles and I were left on the station platform. I stood still for a moment, surrounded by the metallic voices of train announcements and the hum of pedestrians. 'What the hell?' I said to Charles, tears springing to my eyes. 'What the hell was everyone thinking?'

∿

Over the next few weeks Juliet and I exchanged letters. 'It is the future that matters', she wrote, and before long she had invited us to stay with her and Alan in their home close to the coast in the south of England. We found a well presented, spacious house, part of a well-designed modernist development in a clearing in the forest which was so like our house in Ornan Road as to be almost disturbing – rather neat, minimalist, organised, tasteful, filled with art and books and with a garden whose format was almost identical to ours at Downshire Hill. Juliet showed us to our room, and after gathering social courage we descended to be offered drinks in the sitting room. The whole of one side of the room was a huge window, giving the impression of being right in the forest, although their house was in a little close. Our attention was drawn to a small clay sculpture of a girl, with long hair and rounded shoulders, playing the guitar. I knew immediately it was of my mother.

Sculpture in bronze of Laura by Seth Cardew

'It's very like her,' declared Juliet. 'She used to sit just like that.'

While we all sipped our drinks and ate olives, looking closely at the sculpture, each one of us thinking our own private thoughts about Laura, all aware that the sculptor had caught something of her spirit and invested it in the clay, Juliet picked up a postcard that sat next to it – by design, not accident, I was sure. The postcard was written in Laura's handwriting, It was an invitation from Laura to her sister, asking her to visit Downshire Hill, but specifying that it must be after the children had gone to bed. A simple little postcard, but fraught with significance and carefully preserved by Juliet all these years, placed next to the sculpture of her sister.

'I think she wanted to talk about our mother,' said Juliet, 'but when it came to it, she couldn't bring herself to.' That, it became clear from further talk, was the last time Juliet ever saw Laura.

Alan was the chief cook in the family and we all sat down to a good meal. Juliet was extremely chatty, just like Laura, and Alan would cut through her chatter with dry humour. It occurred to me that he would surely have got on rather well with Tony. Robin had described Alan as an *'homme du peuple'*. A Russian specialist who had worked at the UN, he would have been on Tony's intellectual level and his political analysis would have interested him. It was all so stupidly natural. Juliet talked quite a lot about her mother, in a rather detached and critical way.

'I began life,' she told us, 'called Caroline' (I remember my mother writing about her sister Car in her childish letters.) 'But one day my mother came into the nursery and said, "From now on, you will be called Juliet!"'

As we talked, I found the sisterly relationship between Juliet and my mother to be elusive. Simple things rose to the surface, such as Juliet's slight envy of my mother's pony, called Grey Squirrel, and the fact that they were at different boarding schools for much of the time. But I couldn't work them out as *sisters*. Juliet didn't really talk about Laura that much over dinner. Talk was all of other matters and I began to see that Juliet was very capable. We were both determined that any awkwardness between us would soon be banished. Gradually things felt more comfortable; I found my aunt to be very nice indeed and highly intelligent. She was not artistic like Laura, but I recognised my mother in her lack of interest in abstract thought, and the way she was so good at concentrating on the practical job in hand – plants, her garden, birds, her nieces and nephews all absorbed her. There was no trace of self pity in her.

It was only after supper, when Juliet and I were in the kitchen, washing up, that the depths of her feelings about her sister rose to the surface. 'I saw her,' she said, 'my sister.'

'You saw Mum?'

'It was in Belsize Park. I was walking towards her, right up close, and she just walked right on past me as if she hadn't seen me.'

Juliet was the fair-haired woman whom my mother had swerved to avoid in the 1970s in Belsize Park Gardens. Before we knew it we were both in tears and hugging.

'Mum just couldn't cope,' I said. 'She didn't know what to do.'

The next day, Juliet took us to hear a nightingale. We walked softly through the post-apocalyptic landscape of the New Forest, scrubby heathland cut through by huge, busy roads, outsized electricity cables and power stations, until we got to the edge of the forest. She asked for hush and switched on her tape machine; we all stood still and listened. Nothing. We thought we were going to be frustrated, when it began. The song of the nightingale is so mythic, one wants it to be heavenly, but in fact I found it to be a strange mixture of sounds, sometimes a lorry backing, sometimes an endless burbling stream. The occasion was strange, dislocated, alienating, with an undercurrent of sadness. Juliet insisted that her passion for birding had nothing to do with her mother, but Rosemary's diary is full of birds.

When the visit came to an end I found I was exhausted. The sad little postcard resting on Juliet's bookshelf lingered in my mind, and I wondered why everyone had to torture each other so much, and pondered the enrichment of knowing those that are close by blood, the infinite value of a sense of belonging, the damage caused when pieces are missing. I thought about Laura's transformation into clay, and the sadness of those who loved her relating only to her image and not to the real woman. It reminded me for a moment of William collecting portraits of Mrs Jordan – the family gazing lovingly at brushstrokes on a stretch of canvas, while she herself was far away, dying in exile far from everyone she loved.[4]

---

[4] The next year Juliet and I met up again, this time in London at the British Museum. After a little bit of angst when we couldn't find each other, we went around the Hokusai exhibition, followed by a bus across to Tate Modern and a Giacometti exhibition. This was the first time I had spent time with Juliet without Alan, and I felt I got to know her better. I began to see the same magic that my mother had possessed – a gift for easy and happy relationships, for seeing things that others don't see. Outside Tate Modern there was an ice cream van. Juliet insisted on buying me a cone, and we looked slightly wanly at each other. What a strange situation. She was doing just as an aunt would do. Just as she would have done, had... things been different.

Chapter 17

The phone went one evening in 2011, bringing Tony's voice to my ear.

'Hello darling. Dad here.'

'Oh hello, Dad, how are you?'

'I'm fine. I have something to tell you'… pause for effect.

'Oh?'

'I have found you a cousin.'

'What?'

'I have found you a cousin. He lives in Barcelona and in fact he is very nice.'

'Oh! Really? Who is he? You've been to Barcelona?'

'Yes, and he's met Ant.'

He kept that pretty secret; I felt vaguely nettled that he'd met my brother first.

'Does he have a name?'

'Francis.'

Tony knew very well that the trickle of disclosure that had started with Robin was fast becoming a torrent. He couldn't stop it and all he could hope for now was damage limitation. A week or so later, sitting in Tony's garden in Christow, having lunch, we asked more about this Francis.

'What does he look like?'

'Weird,' said Tony emphatically.

'In what way weird?'

'He has one bulbous eye and a Berber nose.'

A few months later I finally received a cheerful email from a Francis Ghilès, introducing himself. He attached a photo and some recent articles. He was apparently a journalist working in Barcelona for an institute called CIDOB (the Barcelona Centre for International Affairs), and was formerly of the *Financial Times*. The black-and-white photograph showed the head and shoulders of a rather distinguished figure, a young-looking seventy, not weird at all, with a keen intelligent look, curly grey hair and glasses. The articles concerned Tunisian politics and were of fiendish complexity, so I quickly laid them aside. He finished his email with the words: 'You bear the name of the woman I admired most in the world...' These words felt subliminally unsettling.

Not long after receiving that first email, Francis called – 'Francis Ghilès speaking.' He spoke in an authoritative, distinguished and very educated broadcaster's voice. A matter of weeks later he would come to stay, and once again we were thrown into a frenzy of preparation for the visit of another close relation of whose existence I had been completely ignorant all my life – this time from Tony's side of the family.

And there he was, standing in our kitchen, dispensing gifts of jewellery and red leather Moroccan slippers. At a glance he was very like Tony. The same tall, thin frame, glasses, sharp intellect, an eye that was so keen it was like a laser beam playing over us, and the same tendency to talk and talk and talk without ceasing. But he was a lighter presence, slimmer, quicker in his movements, less portentous in his manner of expressing himself, and fully equipped with a sense of irony.

Francis settled in. An unstoppable force of articulate energy, he blasted into our quiet West Country haven, my own particular version of Mrs Jordan's Bushy idyll, and took over our lives. We provided him with good food and drink, and he talked without stopping about his fast-paced life as a journalist, regaling us with stories of this, that and the other – dinner with ambassadors, meeting Margaret Thatcher, his job at the *Financial Times*. All the while his keenly penetrating gaze seemed to look right into me. I felt his enquiring intellect working on what he found, slotting me into his world view and rewriting his own story.

I have to admit the truth – I was fascinated. He did have a problem with one of his eyes, he explained, and it was a little magnified through a very strong lens. He wore expensive but simple clothes, of carefully chosen brands, neatly packed in a smart suitcase, the product, I felt, of a very careful upbringing. He cast his eye over our homely thatched house with a strong measure of satire. Charles provided an outsider's calm perspective, cooking and stage-managing, understanding and putting us all at our ease, conjuring up lethally strong dry martinis to lubricate the process.

Francis's overwhelming love and admiration for our shared grandmother, Fanny, became immediately apparent. They had been very close during his childhood and she had influenced him profoundly.

Fanny Rubenstein.

'I mean you know she was Circassian – the most beautiful women in the world. P-e-r-f-e-c-t face, with a square jaw, and an excellent bosom. I mean she was just to the manner born, people thought she was a film star. I was once walking with her, and she was well into her sixties when someone wolf whistled. Uh?'

His eyes rested on my face, placing it in the cannon of family beauty, or lack of it. 'She was a depressive, of course,' he said, which put me in mind of the pencil drawing in Downshire Hill, her huge eyes looking sadly into the distance.

Francis and I were both engaged in a task of reconstruction, and it involved a generous and open attempt to understand what had been going on in the other family. As with Robin, it was hard for him to understand the extent of the blackout that we had lived with all these years. He reported that it had been almost impossible to persuade Tony to give him our names and addresses.

'What about your daughter?' Francis had asked, over and over again. Tony would only speak of his sons. He had told him that we were 'very English of a certain sort', and that Francis would be 'too exotic a bird' for us to meet. He had spoken dismissively of my husband as 'a pillar of the local church...' It felt uncomfortable to hear all this. The real truth was that of all my father's children I was the one who questioned his carefully constructed narrative most closely. I was the one with whom his relationship was the most strained and difficult and he feared and dreaded what would happen if I came together with Francis and we started comparing notes. But he had not reckoned with Francis's determination, and in the end Francis overwhelmed Tony's defences and got his way.

Francis Ghilès

After a long day chewing over family matters we moved on to other topics at dinner. Francis talked without ceasing for hours. As a specialist in North African affairs, the Arab Spring meant that all of a sudden his analysis of events was very much in demand. He was scathing about the endless recycling of journalistic cliché.

After ten days the visit drew to a close and I took my cousin Francis to the station. He had behaved, a friend of mine suggested, not like an Englishman, or even a Frenchman, but like a North African Berber pitching his tent.

Chapter 18

*I*t is curious the way adolescence creeps up on you, uninvited and inevitable. Time does not release you from the pressure to grow up, even if you are not ready for it. There was no one particular day I could point to on which I withdrew into my bedroom, started to spend too long looking in the mirror, and began to fight with Tony. I would find it hard, too, to identify the moment he stopped being reassuring, clever Dad, and turned into unbearably irritating Dad. I couldn't tolerate his habits, and had to leave the room if he was eating oranges. Always lecturing, never communicating, and seemingly uninterested in my own thoughts and feelings. As the only girl in the family, I was caught in the midst of some very confusing pressures: all he seemed to care about was my academic achievements, which he pushed as if nothing else mattered, not noticing that I could not really see the point. At the same time he was utterly crushing, positively misogynistic, towards female academics, novelists, politicians. It was as if I was being pushed, with all the force of his huge personality, towards a destination which, if I ever got there, could never evoke any reaction from him other than derision. He put my mother on a pedestal, which was a place she found herself very surprised to be occupying.

I think in fact that his relationships and approaches to women were extremely complex. There *were* strong women whom he admired fervently, in particular (strange for an ex-Communist) Mrs Thatcher. His approach to his daughter was constantly coloured by this complexity. Tony loved me, I am sure of it, in his own overwrought and complex way, and wanted to do the right thing, but had no idea how to cope with a full-on teenage girl. I have a vivid memory of the time he took me shopping in Hampstead High Street and bought me a mini-dress. I see it now: it was bright blue cotton, with buttons right up to the neck, a rounded collar, and quite short. It was probably pretty stunning and quintessentially late 1970s, but I couldn't rise to its challenges. I was still at the stage when, if I wore a mini skirt to school, everyone would laugh and point out my 'matchstick legs'.

My brothers and I listened to our father's stories with diminishing relish, and since our parents never went anywhere or saw anyone the stock was never added to. The stories were mummified. My father still breathed not a word of any family, beyond an occasional anti-Alastair rant, or a descent into hellish brooding about his father. He and my mother both kept going with their policy of careful curating the past. Our questions were met with exchanged glances, silences and secretiveness. Their position was impregnable and, I felt, rather conceited. They were so perfectly satisfied with each other that everyone else was excluded. But what about us?

The five of us were bound together by a cultural position that amounted to an orthodoxy, and a series of judgements about one another that were at best clichés and at worst damaging. We were all slotted into pigeonholes. 'The trouble with Fan is…', 'Merlin's really tough…', 'Ant's a sweetie…' I felt I could not move for Tony's neurosis, fearfulness, criticism and crushing intellect. I can feel his long, bony fingers at the back of my neck in the midst of a quarrel during a family meal. He had named me after his mother, and when he looked at me he had a tendency to see her. I was up against a ghost, so the odds were stacked against me.

I lost my temper with him often at the dinner table – challenging his demeaning, reducing and infuriating view of women. It is said that it takes a community to raise a family, and with the drawbridge so firmly raised family life became much too intense. There was simply not enough on offer from outside the family: the kind of necessary corrective that comes from parents' friends, cousins, aunts and uncles, did not penetrate the walls of No. 38A Downshire Hill. Family life was at times suffocating and certainly emotionally weird, for all my mother worked to keep it all happy.

In those days Merlin always seemed loftily in receipt of parental admiration, regarding me in my denim jacket with a packet of Camels in the pocket, and my lost life roaming around London with unsuitable friends, with detachment. Searching for something outside the family, I joined a band of gloomy lost girls, levered myself out of my bedroom and crept out into the night into a half-life of grimy tube trains, of joyless parties in kitchens, of rich-smelling chestnut brown tobacco laid across rizlas, of standing in weakly lit streets looking up at a window while a foul-mouthed girl I half know leans out of a window and shouts, 'Alex is licking my bum!' One friend is anorexic, moonfaced, with a soft voice, seems old, ancient, and smiles tolerantly at us. Another is addicted to weed and rolls her first joint early in the morning to take the edge off the day.

Hampstead itself began to lose its savour. Instead of a leafy paradise full of fascinating characters, it appeared dysfunctional, snobbish and limited. Walks on Hampstead Heath began to fill me with loathing. The stresses on our little family gathered force. The truth about my parents' life is that they were running out of money. Laura trained as a secretary and went out to work for the NHS, and the pressures towards selling our beloved house began to mount. With money dwindling, we borrowed our neighbour Gill's house on Mersea Island in Essex for a family holiday in the long hot summer of 1976; wading into the sea, we swam through wave after wave thick with dead ladybirds. The early days of unshakeable love, stability and eternal happiness were fast being eroded. Laura cried more often. Tony muttered and strode about and chewed his hand more than ever. His internal agonies seemed enormous, as he tried to suppress things that kept threatening to overwhelm him.

Chapter 19

The war brought change to the family on many fronts. On Laura's side, for my maternal grandfather, Gilbert, it brought excitement and success; his war took him through the Italian campaign, where he joined the staff of General Alexander, whom he much admired. He was mentioned in dispatches, promoted to lieutenant colonel, and awarded the Territorial Decoration and an MBE (mil). For my mother it brought weeks, months, years of lonely waiting for her father to come home.

On Tony's side, the highly perceptive Fanny saw exactly how dangerous things were in the 1930s for Jews. One of the Bernstein cousins, Fania Fénelon, despite her mother moving to France, changing her name and converting to Roman Catholicism, was caught doing resistance work and ended up in Auschwitz. This tiny, dark-haired, charismatic lady survived; a talented musician, she was recruited to the camp orchestra and wrote an extraordinarily moving book about her experiences, called *Playing for Time*. It was later made into a film starring Vanessa Redgrave. (Fania didn't approve of this, as Redgrave was tall, fair-haired and blue-eyed, and a supporter of the Palestinian cause. She thought she should have been played by Liza Minelli.)

Back home in England, it was decided that Fanny should take her son Anthony (he wasn't known as Tony until later) to Canada, for safety, while Alec stayed at home. Mother and son sailed out on the SS *Duchess of Richmond* to Montreal, and Alec moved to a new house near Kew Gardens.

When they arrived, Fanny arranged for her son to go to summer camps and then to Montreal High School. But he missed the paradise of Dartington Hall and quickly began to behave like a delinquent, joining in with a gang who roamed around the city heaving snowballs through car windows. Fanny acted fast to save her wonderchild: she took him out of that school and sent him to Pickering College, a Quaker school, the closest thing Canada had to a private progressive school. Things improved somewhat.

Fanny Rubenstein. Pastel on paper, by Emmanuel Levy

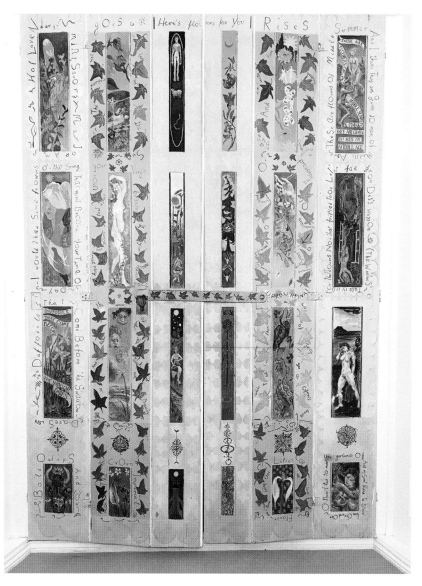

The shutters at Saligo. 'The Winter's Tale' painted by Laura Boyd, Renato Guttoso,
Peter Peri and Peter de Francia

*Mrs Jordan as Viola in Twelfth Night
painted by John Hoppner*

*The Leger print
that formed such an
arresting image as
you entered the sitting
room at No 38A
Downshire Hill*

*Alice, Viscountess Wimborne, née Grosvenor, wearing a diamond and
ruby tiara by Chaumet, 1928. Photograph by Cecil Beaton*

Tony used to tell me stories of his time in Canada, of enormous boys, of skating down frozen rivers, and of a teacher who used to scratch his arse while walking up and down, saying, 'Now look-a-here boys, now look-a-here.' I am sure that Tony was many levels ahead in whatever subject they were trying to teach him, and a teacher's worst nightmare. 'I wonder what Anthony will become when he is older?' muses Fanny in a note written on an envelope from this time.

In Canada, Fanny began to confront the results of her neurotic hothousing of her son. The pediatrician had said that she was 'pathologically attached' to him and should not spend too much time with him, and yet here they were thrown together with all the anxiety and tension of wartime, in an alien environment – in a freezing cold country, with young Anthony on the brink of adolescence. The result was disastrous; the wonderchild was proving hard to handle. Fanny wrote letters home describing him as a 'little Hitler'.

When Tony told me about his time in Canada, the one thing he never mentioned was that one day he found his mother in the snow outside the house, having thrown herself out of the window in a suicide attempt. This was the second major emotional collapse of her life, some twenty years after the first. In 1944, Alexander dropped everything and got special permission to travel to Canada. He fetched home his wife and the sixteen-year-old Anthony, whom he had not seen for four years.

Chapter 20

*H*aving discovered us, Francis was not going to let us drift away again. This work of reconstruction was of deep personal significance to him, for although my cousin had created a colourful, energetic and rewarding life for himself, his family relationships were at times a little tortured. He did crave some sort of deep family peace. He was also an extremely curious journalist, so he enjoyed sniffing out a story.

Visit followed visit, as well as invitations to go and see him in Barcelona, which I accepted out of curiosity and a similar desire to examine and rebuild my own foundations. He always brought something with him – a necklace from Barcelona which has the power to lift any outfit, one of our grandmother's chiffon evening dresses, an exquisite chinoiserie mirror of hers, and an antique Algerian Berber pendant set in silver. His sojourns with us were always full of interest, bringing with them a ceaseless flow of talk. I've never met anyone who could talk so much. Oh yes, actually – one other, my dad. At the heart of Francis there was an intelligence and great kindness; I felt the relationship was an important one.

'Three times I tried to make contact with your family,' said Francis.

Once I came to your place in Belsize Park. Your mother was extremely shy; your father did all the talking. The second occasion, I ran into your father in the delicatessen in Hampstead High Street. He said, 'One day I will tell you everything.' I mean, what was this nonsense? The third occasion was at St Anthony's College in Oxford. I used to go to high table there once a year, usually bringing guests from London.[5] Once, in 1979, I was astonished to bump into your father at the beginning of the meal. We were both extremely surprised and just

---

[5] Francis completed his thesis on Algeria 1830–1834 at St Anthony's College Oxford between 1969 and 1972.

about exchanged greetings. Later, over port, a fellow of St Anthony's, an Egyptian/Lebanese academic who had witnessed the scene, asked, '*C'est qui?*' '*C'est mon oncle,*' I replied. '*Non, il n'est pas!*'

'I never came to Downshire Hill,' he added. 'I didn't know what sort of reception I was going to get.'

Early on, Francis proffered a photograph album; he pushed it across the kitchen table and awaited my reaction. I drew it towards me. For the very first time in my life I was about to get a glimpse of his mother, Tony's 'wicked sister'. I almost experienced a moment of grief, for my childhood imaginings were about to be replaced by some sort of implacable reality. I had always pictured her trailing through the bazaars of various North African cities, her clothes dirty, a wrecked woman who could not be spoken about in polite society. Now with my cousin's eyes firmly upon me I opened the album, a red one with photos slipped in under plastic sheets.

'This is your mother?'

'Yes, her name was Margaret, although she was often called Margot.'

The kind farmer's wife who helped me around the house stood by and watched the extrovert, unstoppable force that was Francis; he might have landed in Devon from outer space. 'I think you've found yourself another brother,' she said wisely. She looked over my shoulder at the photographs of Margaret and commented, 'She looks very like you.'

Oh yes, I think to myself. There had always been, somewhere in my consciousness, although I did not give her much direct thought, a fantastical image of Tony's lost sister. Without realising it, I had draped her ethereal absence with clothing of my own invention, with all the distant exoticism which the words 'North Africa' had always conjured up in my mind. She had always *been there*, in negative form, a concentration of energy that drew my thoughts in and gave nothing back.

I study the photograph album. A schoolgirl. Thin, with a lively face and dark hair gathered behind her neck, a mouth full of crooked teeth grinning, a rounded, striped collar. Here is a photo of her in a family group on holiday in Devon, a slim girl with masses of curly hair, smiling at the

Margaret Ghilès (nee Hyman)

camera. Then, a little older with short, dark hair carefully ringletted, a teenager now, with fashionable soft, white shirt collar. Here she is as a gorgeous, curvaceous young woman in a '30's bathing costume, looking confidently at the camera with a slight hint of irony in her smile.

I look up again at her grown-up son, delivering a stream of talk, a transforming beam whose effect was to convert her into a real person, although one seen through the prism of his own huge and restless, admiring eye.

'And she died when?' I ask.

'Just last year,' replies Francis emphatically, as if it was obvious.

There is no holding back the real woman now. A confident and engaging person has entered the room, who has none of the glowering introversion of Tony. She is light, talkative, extrovert; she never looks back, agonises, or questions her decisions. Certain phrases – 'a very strong woman…', 'beautiful…', 'looked like Gina Lollobrigida…' It is clear that Francis admired his mother as much as he did our shared grandmother.

A couple of details now. She was educated at Channing School. A little bell went off in my head as I remembered Tony reserving special scorn for Channing, when the decision was being taken as to where to send me. Next – she was very clever and a brilliant linguist. Her father had some ideas of a semi-arranged Jewish marriage: he had in mind Abba Ebban, who came from South Africa and went on to become Israel's most famous Minister of Foreign Affairs. Margaret declared that he was too pompous by half and too ugly. She had no intention of falling in with her father's plans. She knew that she found English men stuffy and boring, and the suburban Jewish life she encountered at school insufferable.

Even a bright spirit can be worn down by the prosaic, unimaginative realities of everyday life, and how very prosaic they could be for a Jewish girl in Finchley in 1938, when Margaret's schooldays came to an end. Then two things happened. The first was a love affair. She met a Hungarian student on a summer course in France who came to visit her in Finchley in 1939. The second was that great disrupter – the outbreak of the Second World War. Margaret enrolled at UCL to study French and Italian, only to find that her course was evacuated to the distant Welsh coastal town of Aberystwyth. Her Hungarian boyfriend wrote her letters and poems which paint a haunting picture of the curtain of Nazi barbarism falling over Europe, and then he disappeared somewhere on the Russian front.

Being of exactly the right age, and the perfect temperament, as well as having a strong sense of duty, Margaret was determined to offer her services

Margaret with her Hungarian boyfriend in 1939

to the war effort. She graduated, looked about for a wartime job that would allow her to use her language skills, and was offered a prestigious position as translator to Richard Crossman, deputy head of the Psychological Warfare Unit overseeing propaganda against the Axis powers.

Margaret did not look back. She found herself at Woburn Abbey for a brief and intense period of training, and before she knew it, she was being dispatched to Algeria in the immediate aftermath of Operation Torch, the Anglo-American invasion of French North Africa. So she *did* run away to North Africa, in a sense, but not in the way I had imagined.

So in 1943, she found herself packing for a trip, the duration of which was unknown, and with head-spinning speed she was on board a ship bound for North Africa, showing a youthful disregard for the real possibility that a stray torpedo could have ended her adventure before it had begun. And then, there in the distance was the skyline of Algiers, coming closer. From a cold, grey British February, the exotic and vibrant life of North Africa enveloped her. As soon as she disembarked, the chaos and excitement swept her up and carried her along with it. She was billeted at the Aletti Hotel, living out the dream that her mother had conceived as a brilliant student just before the First War in rainy Manchester.

Allied soldiers were everywhere; Margaret, clad in a white, short-sleeved shirt, a cotton skirt, flat sandals and a military cap on her curly, dark hair, an army rucksack slung on her back and a rifle over her shoulder, was right in the middle of it all. Francis shows me a photograph of his mother in a storeroom with a metal cupboard, a broom and a few more rucksacks and tangles of barbed wire against the wall. Something is written in black pen on the photograph, rather hard to discern, but it looks like 'TAKE THAT EGG OUT OF MY HELMET' signed *Bill Stapleton*. A private joke suffused with wartime camaraderie. Her job kept her very busy right from the start, and as a very attractive twenty-two-year-old her time off was a whirl of dances and semi-serious marriage proposals, all of which she laughingly turned down.

Algiers in 1943 – there was much work to be done, which meant that Margaret's skill with the French language was put to immediate use.

The situation was complex: before Operation Torch, the region had been

under the control of the Vichy French – officially Nazi-controlled, but with mixed loyalties. Preliminary intelligence work established that several French officers would be willing to support the Allies. When the American and British forces invaded on the 8 November 1942, under Operation Torch, the level of French opposition was low, all coastal batteries having been neutralised by the Resistance, and one French commander openly welcomed the Allies.

Algiers surrendered, and Eisenhower, with the support of Churchill, made an agreement with Admiral Darlan, commander of the forces in the region. Darlan ordered all French forces to cooperate with the Allies, in return for being made 'High Commissioner'. The agreement meant that Vichy officials would remain in power, with no role provided for the Free French, France's government in exile. But the tide was turning. Many Algerians declared Free French allegiance, and on the 24 December 1942 a French resistance fighter assassinated Darlan. His successor, Giraud, was also inclined to maintain the old Vichy administration. Margaret's immediate task was to assist in the propaganda effort – putting pressure on Giraud to replace Vichy officials and rescind its most offensive decrees. Gradually the regime shifted towards the Free French and their leader de Gaulle.

With Algiers secured for the Allies, the next focus was Tunisia, where Hitler had sent reinforcements, leading to an urgent flurry of propaganda work. For Margaret this meant composing propaganda leaflets in French to be released in the air over Tunisia. She was instructed to emphasise certain topics – the certainty of Axis defeat, the Axis military leaders' knowledge that Tunisia is doomed and the battle lost, the promise that 'if you surrender you will be well treated', the undermining of the deep German belief in Rommel as one of the great generals of all time, a dramatisation of the Sicily–Tunis Death Run, a report of all sinkings and disasters on this route, and an emphasis on the horrors of death by drowning.

Heavy fighting followed, with the Allies victorious, and Tunis fell on 13 May. With this victory, the first phase of Margaret's posting came to an end, culminating in a transfer from Algiers to Tunis. After a long journey by Jeep she willingly exchanged one vibrant North African city for another. The focus of much of the work of the propaganda division shifted to Italy, with Margaret's Italian now called into service. Although based in Tunis, and still required to help stabilise the French situation, most of her leaflets were now in Italian, ready for airdrop over Italy.

The Germans, her leaflets emphasised, could only be beaten through resistance. '*Popolo italiano! L'ora di agire!*' (Italian people! It's time to act!) One leaflet depicted an Italian woman with long, dark hair, her hand to her head, and a black-bordered paper in her hand, her little daughter throwing her arms about her. '*Quanto tempo ancora la Guerra tedesca fara versare lacrime italiani?*' (For how much longer will the German war make Italian tears flow?) Another shows some thuggish-looking German soldiers with swastikas on their hats preventing a group of Italian soldiers boarding a train back home: '*L'OSTACOLO ALLA PACE ED AL RITORNO A CASA – I TEDESCACCI!*' (The obstacle to peace and to going home – the Germans!)

Margaret soon developed a routine in Tunis and adapted to life there with all the ease of her youth and outgoing personality. One day, a day like any other, she was sitting in a café near to Allied HQ when two handsome brothers caught sight of her. One of the brothers made a little ball out of the soft inside of a baguette and threw it onto her table. She turned and saw the two young men. How could she have known that in that brief instant her life was about to change forever? The brother that caught her eye was not the one who had thrown the little bread pellet, but the other one, Marcel. A sort of electric charge flashed between the two of them, and nothing could stop the two brothers joining her at her table. Marcel was overwhelmingly charismatic, dizzyingly attractive, and in that moment of seeing each other for the first time a passionate affair had already been set in motion.

Margaret's easy social life, full of fun and friendly interactions with men, was replaced by the heightened intensity of an all-absorbing love affair. Marcel Ghilès was half Sicilian, half descended from North African Berbers, and the opposite of what she saw as the stuffy English men who had so bored her back in suburban Finchley. His face was pale, and his eyes glittered; he was newly released from imprisonment by the Vichy Government of Tunis in a small cell in El Kef near the Algerian border, and suffering from both TB and malaria. He was a born hero – a union man, left-wing and a natural rabble-rouser, all of which had brought him to the attention of the Axis-supporting authorities and led to his arrest.

In wartime, however, no state of affairs is allowed to rest for long, and the lovers were soon parted when Margaret was moved from Tunis and posted to Naples, the new focus of Allied attention, leaving Marcel behind in Tunisia. She found herself in yet another city as full of interest and personality as Algiers or Tunis. She arrived at High Command in Italy's most colourful chaotic and rough city, set in its position of breathtaking beauty on the Bay of Naples, and as weirdly dislocated as anywhere at the centre of the fighting. She would have found a city demonstrating a quintessentially Neapolitan response to the situation it found itself in – a crowded city where ancient grandeur and poverty existed cheerfully side by side, where hawk-eyed boys roved around restaurants looking for scraps, where bands of citizens took trips to the outskirts to strip the land of any vaguely edible vegetable matter, where black markets thrived, piles of rubble lay in the street, and bombs left behind by the Germans might suddenly explode, leaving a scene of pale dust-covered people, dead or just stunned.

Not long after Margaret's arrival in Naples, when she was becoming absorbed by her new life, she began to realise that she had not left her North African life behind quite so emphatically as she thought. She discovered that she was pregnant. Moreover, there was the inconvenient fact that Marcel was in fact already married. Married, it turned out, to a trapeze artist. Although Marcel and the trapeze artist were separated, and Marcel professed complete love and loyalty to Margaret, this was certainly a complication. There was little that she could do, other than writing about her situation to her mother in Canada, but carry on. She was at least in Italy, where an unforeseen pregnancy would have elicited fuss and concern, but not judgement.

The Italian campaign moved quickly, necessitating a new posting for Margaret to Rome – another romantic city, an advancing pregnancy, more translation work and the platonic devotion of Gino de Sanctis, a famous Italian journalist, who fell in love with her. On the 13 November 1944, aged twenty-four, Margaret gave birth to a son, Francis, without any family support. With enormous resourcefulness she set about looking after her new baby, while making sure her job was not neglected. She was a very strong woman, Francis said emphatically, as he told me this part of the story.

Peace came at last, and Margaret's great adventure had inevitably to come to an end. She returned to England after more than two years' absence, during which she had lived more intensely than many people do in a lifetime, with an 'illegitimate' baby in her arms. The humdrum life of single motherhood and postwar Britain became Margaret's new reality. But what an adventure she had had. The real living person of my father's sister had a story that was quite as romantic as the imaginary North African waif that had taken up home in my imagination, although she turned out to be a woman with real agency, impressive and independent, and not the lost soul of Tony's mutterings.

Chapter 21

'Darling', declaims Dad. 'Just say to yourself "I'm bloody good and the rest of you are a bunch of fools!" That's the way to get through things.'

'But Dad, is it the way to make friends?' I'm thinking to myself, feeling awkward. I probably just say nothing. 'Life is all about capturing little bits of territory. A-Levels, just a little piece of ground, University, just another conquest.'

One day he brought home a strange device, excitedly extracted it from its cardboard box, and tried to interest us in what it did. It was called a Sinclair Spectrum. It was the first time I had ever heard of a computer. It was a strange plastic object into which you typed things and the machine responded. I didn't have the haziest idea of what it did, or what the point of it was, but I could see that for him it was a thing of wonder. The event took its place in a family tradition of trips to science museums and science fairs, birthday presents of encyclopedias of bird and plant life, and sessions with Tony on maths and physics which he was very brilliant at explaining to us. Those subjects didn't especially interest me, but he made sure I easily got through my O levels, after which I finally ditched them.

Tony's scholarship to read maths and physics at Cambridge had reflected an extraordinary and natural ease with those subjects, and a penetrating depth of understanding of matters abstract, scientific and numerical. He should really have sailed into a university career and spent his life illuminating and explaining things to eager groups of young acolytes, to whom he would have been a sort of guru – dressed in his fishermen's jumpers, sandals and his trademark '60's black-framed glasses. He would have explained everything with startling clarity and littered his lectures with 'shit', 'fuck', and other expletives, or perhaps just stuck to his favourite 'round objects!' But something stopped him. Why did he fail to concentrate on his degree and come away with a Third Class, of which for some reason he was terribly proud? He would have said he was too iconoclastic to fit in with the narrow and dull expectations of the academic establishment. Was it his poor degree or his Communist Party membership that really got in the way of his moving on in academia?

He spent the rest of his life trying to return to it in some form or another. His early years working for ICL were more or less fine for him – he was on the research side of the business which interested him, quite liked putting on a suit and going to the office, and the job paid the bills and allowed him to set up home in Belsize Park. He was also sponsored by his employer to do a PhD at Reading University, which he did on the subject of selenium. When he threw it all in to 'become a writer' that was really his attempt to set up a mini university in Downshire Hill, with his children as his little students, and his determination was simply to think and to write.

His first book, *The Computer in Design*, published in 1973, breathed his desire to marry his scientific background and cast of mind with the semi-worship of the arts that he had picked up at Dartington Hall school from Breon and Laura. The book opens with the sentence: 'In Renaissance Florence men such as Brunelleschi and Da Vinci were at once artist and engineer.' The prose is exactly like Tony's spoken phraseology: clear, explanatory and slightly patronising. The style of the book, published by Studio Vista, reflects its times exactly – a square hardback with black-and-white pictures of glowing neon computer-generated images and nerdy-looking men or beautiful women gazing intently at computer screens. The first chapter, called 'What is a Computer?', opens in classic Dad style: 'A computer is a thing that does what you tell it to do.' He then elaborates: 'It is a decision-making system which can alter its own decision-making system as it proceeds.' He goes on to explain how the computer draws a line:

As soon as lines are well defined, the problem is solved. The difficulty arises with hand-drawn lines: the essential features of hand-drawn lines have not been properly analysed and are not well understood. It is always possible for a line to be subdivided into a very large number of dots giving both direction and thickness.

Then he moves on to the third dimension, and this chapter is very revealing. For all his attempt to unify science and art, he cannot help attempting to impose systems and patterns onto everything. His restless mind wanted to encompass everything in those systems.

> Painters have for a long time studied the problem of representing three-dimensional objects, animals, landscapes, tools, or whatever was the subject of interest, in three dimensions. The problem arose when the first cave artist drew an animal. During this time a great deal has been discovered about the possible means for achieving verisimilitude with different media and for different purposes. There is really no single solution to the problem: any method implies selection and must be suited to a particular situation, problem or set of problems.

I am very struck by the number of times he uses the word 'problem'. What is revealed in this passage is a mind that tries to reduce everything, including art, to a set of mathematical *problems* to be solved. The mind and sensibility of an artist usually works quite differently. It can exist comfortably in a state of imperfect knowledge, an idea most beautifully expressed by John Keats. In a letter to his brothers he introduces the idea of 'negative capability, that is, when a man is capable of being in uncertainties, mysteries, doubts, without any irritable reaching after fact and reason'. Keats means that a poet is entirely content with half knowledge; he or she is flexible, receptive and open, content to live in the world, to experience its chaos, to intuit its truth, and not to explain it; a sense of beauty overcomes all other considerations.

Irritable reaching after fact and reason was *exactly* the character of Tony's mind. Keats would absolutely have placed him in the bracket of people who did not understand poetic truth – just as he ridiculed Coleridge for his obsession with a philosophical, higher order truth. Keats's ideal of the perfect artist was Shakespeare, whose poetry articulated various points of view and never advocated a particular vision of truth.

Tony's next book further developed his desire to explain the computer to a non-technical audience. It was called *The Coming of the Chip*, a prediction of the transformational effects of the silicon chip on society. The only copy I have is an Italian version (it did well enough to be translated into several languages). It has prescient chapter titles like '*L'ufficio eletronico*' (The electronic office), '*Lo shopping del futuro*' (Shopping in the future) and '*Nel ventunesimo secolo*' (In the twenty-first century).

His magnum opus, however, to which he devoted many years of research and writing, was a highly respected biography of his hero, Charles Babbage, the inventor of calculating machines which were the forerunners of the modern computer. So obsessed did he become by his subject that my brothers and I couldn't bear to be in the room when it was discussed. We perfected the art of rising silently from the table and melting away when we heard the words 'Charles Babbage'.

It is a detailed and academic biography, published by Oxford University Press, a labour of real love. Tony's admiration for his subject shines through every page, and his grasp particularly of the technical side of Babbage's life and work is absolutely thorough. His prose is clear and full of his personality – in fact, I can almost hear him speaking as I read. Tony admires Babbage as a polymath ('How easily an educated man could pass from one profession to another at the time!'). He was a man of science, a political theorist, a creative thinker, an energetic and determined manager of engineering projects, a reformer, a writer and a man of excellent, upright character.

> Babbage said that it was his aim, before he adopted an opinion, whether in morals or in politics, first to collect the facts, and then apply all the powers of his reason in order to arrive at the correct conclusion. If he was shown by facts and by clear reasoning that his opinions were wrong, then it was his duty as well as his determination to alter them.

Tony saw in Babbage a sort of idealised version of himself, or more accurately, the sort of man he would like to be. Although he admired his subject so intensely, in reality his subject appears to have possessed levels of energy, organisational power and steadiness of character that Tony could only dream of. He saw Babbage as a kindred spirit, with the pure fire of intellectual truth burning within him, battling against the corrupt influence of a British Establishment educated only in the Classics. 'The central message of *The Economy of Machinery and Manufactures*', he writes, 'was that the future of industry required a consistently scientific approach to all aspects of its problems, both technical and commercial.' Throughout his life Tony railed against what he saw was the consistent undervaluing of science by the Establishment.

Charles Babbage –
Tony's alter ego

It must have been a joy to Tony that his other great hero, Karl Marx, was also an admirer of Babbage. Marx read Babbage very carefully, recording no less than seventy-three excerpts. Babbage's influence on Marx, Tony tells us, can be seen in the chapters of *Capital* on 'The Division of Labour and Manufacture' and on 'Machinery and Modern Industry'. He quotes Babbage:

> When from the particular nature of the produce of each manufactory the number of processes into which it is most advantageous to divide it is ascertained, as well as the number of individuals to be employed, then all other manufactories which do not employ a direct multiple of this number will produce the article at greater cost, here arises one of the main causes of the great size of manufacturing establishments.

It followed as a corollary that as technology advanced, and also as more auxiliary commercial and industrial functions (such as development laboratories) were required, the size both of factories and of commercial organisations would continue to grow. Marx and Engels were particularly influenced, Tony tells us, by Babbage's exposition of the union of theory and practice.

Tony's biography contains exhaustive detail of every advance of Babbage's thought, every meeting of the Royal Society, every blueprint for his calculating machines, every man of science he met, every trip abroad. But his marriage is glossed over in an instant: 'On 2 July 1814, shortly after coming down from Cambridge, Charles Babbage married Georgiana Whitmore in Teignmouth. They went for their honeymoon to Chudleigh. The marriage was to be very happy and while it lasted provided a secure and stable basis for Charles' life.' Then, thirty pages later, her sudden illness and death are described in one short paragraph. 'By the end of August, Georgiana was dead. A newborn boy also died.' He goes on to say that Babbage was devastated, that he flung himself into his activities with peculiar passion, but that there was an inner emptiness. In between these events there are a few letters and the odd reference to her, but precious little. They are in Tony's eyes an idealised couple – Babbage rugged, manly, courageous and rational, Georgiana pretty, supportive, and very much in the background.

The merciless march of the power of reason, impatience with established ways of doing things, sweeping change, a tendency towards authoritarianism, dividing of humanity into systems and patterns – these were overriding preoccupations which run through all of Tony's writing. You just have to *grip* everything, to be perfectly rational about everything, and all would be well. However, unfortunately for Tony, the 'crooked timber of humanity' has a way of resisting being corralled into anybody's systems. There is not always a 'correct conclusion'. Keats enlarged on the theme of negative capability in another letter: 'We hate poetry that has a palpable design on us – and if we do not agree, seems to put its hand in its breeches pocket. Poetry should be great and unobtrusive, a thing which enters into one's soul, and does not startle it or amaze it with itself but with its subject.'

In relation to my own development, I collided constantly with this academic, scientific, authoritarian approach. In the confusion of my late teens I knew at least that I wasn't interested at all in science or maths, that I was passionately immersed in literature, and considered talented by my art teachers. I plumped for English Literature, Art, History and Latin as

A levels. As a creative teenager I was inclined to embrace chaos, to desire human experiences, even if they left their mark on me, and not to respond well to pressure towards academia. I couldn't see the point of it. Tony as usual wanted to control everything. He arranged for me to do six months' work experience at IBM, the computer company. This bordered on cruelty, as I had no interest whatsoever in computers and was utterly bored and miserable. I was parked in an office on my own on a top floor, given some tedious tasks to do, and subject to some sexual harassment by a man in his forties who realised that there was a nineteen-year-old in an office on her own with no idea about anything at all.

The next task Tony set himself, with all the force of his huge and controlling personality, was to drive me towards what he considered a suitable academic subject. He conducted a campaign to steer me away from English literature, declaring: 'You will learn the things you least want to know about the books you most want to read.' How confused I was! And how I wish I had had the strength at the time to resist. History was the subject that *he* was interested in, and he showed no understanding of what was going on in my head at all. I got into Oxford to study history, but always felt like a fake. I struggled and struggled to try and force an interest, but it was really never any good.

Tony's judgements about people were often crude, and his judgements about women particularly so. In his attempts to place me into some comprehensible model of womanhood he had decided that I was like his mother, who was both fascinated by and brilliant at history – a natural academic. As usual, there was a dear old ghost moving about in the background.

Chapter 22

$\mathcal{R}$osemary was a young mother of three in her early thirties when the war broke out. Suddenly she was extremely busy, and the crisis brought out her strengths. She and Gilbert had moved just before the war to the Lutyens Dower House on the Lytton estate at Knebworth.

In common with many people of her class, Rosemary had real things to do for the first time. Her pre-war life of privilege, dependent on servants, collapsed; she taught herself to cook, took over the care of her three children, four after Robin was born in 1941; she even got to London to deliver 'meals on wheels' in Camden Town from a depot in Eversholt Street, a prime target area for German bombs close to the main termini of Euston and Kings Cross. Rosemary was very capable and never lacked courage. She shared the sense that spread across the whole country that there was a real threat of imminent invasion, which led to serious discussions with Gilbert as to whether the children should be sent to Canada. They decided against it.

When war finally came to an end the Boyds found, like so many other families, that nothing was quite the same. A new era brought a new government and a change of address. They moved from Knebworth to No. 45 Eaton Terrace, with a countryside residence too, Kintbury Lodge, a charming, small, Queen Anne house with a generous lawn shaded by a huge cedar tree, running down to the Kennet Canal in Berkshire. It all sounds idyllic for Rosemary, on the cusp of turning forty, two delightful addresses, a husband returned from the war, four children – Alastair, Laura, Juliet and Robin. But unfortunately it wasn't idyllic. 'It is still a wonder to me', writes Alastair, 'how life in so pretty a place became such a nightmare.'

The truth was that Rosemary and Gilbert's marriage had run into serious difficulties.

The war, so often a catalyst, had radicalised Rosemary, so much so that she no longer had any tolerance for the world she was expected to occupy as Gilbert's wife. After all this was the girl, sensitive and isolated, who had developed a vivid imaginative life during her emotionally stunted adolescence, her mind filled with 'yards and yards of poetry'. The everyday life of their county neighbours could only seem dull by contrast with her rich inner world, and she set herself against it. At Kintbury she had a room to the right of the front door, with her typewriter, gramophone and books, to which her children had the right of entry, but her husband never crossed the threshold. She point blank refused to take any part in his perfectly reasonable life of social engagements, considering it all predictable, self-satisfied, sanctimonious and boring. Gilbert as usual was trying to patch things up and keep everything on an even keel. Years of maintaining a dignified steadiness in the face of his brother's excesses now applied to his marriage.

'I've invited so and so for a drink on Sunday. Of course you remember Hal and Hermione?' Gilbert would say.

'Oh God, you haven't,' followed by retreat and slammed door.

When she threw one of her monumental sulks the children would say to each other 'Ma's got the pip'. Rosemary would refuse to speak during meals served by the absolutely enormous butler, Elton, who was comically out of scale with the dainty house, and reserved special scorn for the fact that Elton picked Gilbert up from the station, a mere fifty yards from their house, in the company Bentley. Her two pleasures were her beloved car named Pilotis, a Ford V8, a chunky sort of cops' car – she *loved* to drive, the faster the better – and birdwatching with her youngest son, Robin. They would take off up to Inkpen Beacon together and nobody else would be invited.

After the war, Rosemary was in her prime. Intelligent, capable and imaginative, she possessed the energy and ability for a career, but she had married at twenty, been busy with four children, and her education had been patchy and eccentric. The children were her everyday preoccupation and challenge. The three who contributed to the *Memoir* all report a lack of close physical rapport with her when they were small children, but her increasingly central place in their lives as they grew older. She was not easy, with a tendency to self-dramatisation, poor diplomatic skills and a way of casting life so that you were either for her or against her. She concealed her feelings, and on the surface was well defended emotionally. Robin describes her as exceptionally courageous. 'She was a stoic with a greater capacity to endure chronic physical pain and suffering than any other person I have ever come across – including all my patients.' This stoicism I recognise from my mother – it was her defining characteristic.

Rosemary's feeling that something was missing, more a sense of unspecified yearning for she did not know quite what, found its expression in somewhat over-passionate relationships with her children and their friends, as if the younger generation would somehow provide the magic missing ingredient that would give meaning to her life. She had, Robin tells me, a sort of love affair with each of her children in turn.

Alastair writes that as he became an adult he started to enjoy her company. He reports being aware of her sexuality and her capacity to pull people into an orbit around her. Her third child, Juliet, found her a bit of a distant and difficult figure; their tastes were rather different, and she was not Rosemary's favourite, but they shared French lessons and a love of birds and grew closer. My mother, Laura, she was devoted to. They were 'like sisters'. Robin she adored with such a passion that he felt suffocated and later had to distance himself.

Aside from her children, after the war the problems in her marriage only grew worse. Rosemary histrionically took all the blame on herself, and kept praising Gilbert's 'nobility' and 'goodness', and castigating herself for her own weaknesses. This is probably more or less how things were, but it didn't help. Eventually the inevitable happened and there was a *de facto* separation, with Gilbert taking rooms in Curzon Street for his working week, and inhabiting Kintbury at weekends, along with Elton the outsized butler. Rosemary took over Eaton Terrace. Here she established what can only be described as a *salon*, an echo of her mother Mimi's, filled with people of her own choosing. Alastair describes her as coming into her own: she 'positively glowed' and was 'gracious, arch, earnest, flirtatious by turns, and sometimes all at once.'

Rosemary did not share her mother Mimi's ruthlessness or her absolute certainty of her own beauty, but she seems to have absorbed her mother's habit of requiring the devotion of young men. Alastair in the *Memoir* speaks of 'being promoted to the role of escort' and even of 'supplying her gatherings with fresh blood'. Apparently she was most delighted with a one-eyed, handsome, bearded Guards officer called Michael Scott. He had lost an eye in the war saving a soldier who was trapped in a minefield. Rosemary, in her forties, was starting to approve, at last, of the way the narrative of her own life was unfolding.

Released now from what she saw as her suffocating marriage and milieu, always devoted to literature, Rosemary was determined to develop herself as a literary figure in her own right. Without a university education she fumbled her way, working in the dark, but she was extremely determined. She had a new social circle which excited her, a postwar sense of liberation – why shouldn't she? She bought a typewriter and set about writing her first novel. It was called *A Hill called Error* (a direct reference to *The Pilgrim's Progress*, one of the books she had clung to during her lonely adolescence), released into the world by a small gentlemanly publisher called Peter Davies. Rosemary published under the name 'Evelyn Jordan' – Evelyn because it was androgynous, and Jordan after Mrs Jordan, the abiding myth in her

husband's family. 'I shall never forget the ring of triumph in her voice when she rang to tell me the news,' reports Alastair.

When I talk to Robin or Juliet about *A Hill called Error* they respond with good-humoured family satire, mixed with embarrassment. 'She was beta plus,' laughs Robin. 'The cover is pretty dramatic. Probably the best thing about it,' says Juliet. 'The treatment,' writes Alastair, 'is fey and fanciful, almost ridiculous.' To be fair to Rosemary, she did win the *Daily Graphic* prize of the month for 'best young author'.

The novel takes the form of a Quest for enlightenment. Rosemary's heroine, Maureen, something of a self portrait, starts her Quest in a leafy English garden, where she is part of the audience for a children's outdoor production of *A Midsummer Night's Dream*. Maureen is frustrated, as the author lets us know with the following sentence: 'All over England in gardens such as this, people rather like herself allowed their lives to tick softly on till the clock stopped.' At this gathering Maureen fixes on one single hapless man called Robert. This is how she introduces him: 'He came over to her, walking quickly from the shadow out into the sunlight. He was a heavy man, but moved lightly with grace and confidence, and it was as if he came not alone, but in the company of friends and guardian angels.' He seems to be just a fairly ordinary member of Maureen's social circle, but from this moment is charged with fully fledged guru status.

Maureen then sets about following her vessel of enlightenment, first to London, followed by Stonehenge, and then the Austrian Alps. After Robert disappears from her life she has a vision revealing to her that he is in Tibet. Reports start to reach her of a certain Cedric Fortescue, who is living among Tibetans in a monastery, and whom she is convinced is in fact Robert. She tracks down this Cedric Fortescue to the Outer Hebrides. There is a great palaver of mistaken identity: 'Robert!' Maureen calls out desperately, only to be gently corrected – his name is Cedric Fortescue. But Maureen *knows* in her heart, because of the richness of his voice, that he is in fact Robert. As they part, 'Cedric' gives her a gift from 'Robert', although he never fully admits to *being* Robert. Somehow this encounter puts everything right in Maureen's life, and she goes back to her ordinary existence and lives happily ever after.

I can't help finding myself extremely touched by my grandmother's first novel, not least because she reveals herself so absolutely within its pages. This is as close as I am going to get to time travel. Perhaps the most revealing part of all is delivered in the prologue, in which a minor character called Liz describes her first meeting with the novel's chief protagonist, Maureen. Liz remembers two very strange sisters from her childhood, called Maureen and Rosalind de Vere. This is Rosemary telling us about her own teenage years. Amongst all the gymkhanas, treasure hunts, tennis parties and dances that were organised in the district, no one ever saw the 'de Vere girls'. There was a very large house set in its own grounds, called Hartley Manor and one day Liz happens upon her 'hitherto unsuspected neighbours'.

> I shall never forget my first sight of them. They were curiously dressed in black riding breeches and white silk shirts, and they had loose, absolutely straight hair hanging half way down their backs. They were solid girls of about my own age, but in some extraordinary way they contrived to look like dryads. Their appearance was always quite unaccountably romantic.

They were locked up in one wing of the great house, with a governess and an army of servants; when questioned, their mother, Mrs de Vere, a thinly disguised portrait of Mimi, explained that she wished her daughters to maintain a sort of primeval innocence until they were married. The monotony of their daily lives was shocking, but 'at the same time there was a distorting illusion of spiritual grandeur about it. I mean, that it was an etherealised picture of an upbringing, rather than any real process.' While their peers socialised and participated in vigorous and 'normal' activities, the de Vere girls wandered about the confines of their grounds relating a never-ending story 'which became their real world so absolutely that they were almost dead to what actually went on around them'. Mrs de Vere eventually woke up to the cracks that were beginning to appear in her 'carefully constructed Palace Beautiful', and tried to procure them some education and social life. But for Maureen it was too late: she was fatally attached to the parkland around Hartley Manor, giving 'to that too familiar environment the idle, passionate, langorous adoration of lover for lover, steeped in the ache of longing, unappeased and unappeasable'. She saw herself as a Circean figure, drawing her power from the magical kingdom she inhabited quite alone.

In the novel Rosemary gives her heroine Maureen a husband and daughter who are versions of Gilbert and Laura. She does not even change the names very much, calling the husband Roland (Gilbert's middle name was Rowland), and the daughter Laurian. As with Rosemary's diaries, I find it unsettling to come upon the first scenes of mother and daughter.

> Her vexation at being disturbed melted at the sight of Laurian in her crimson skirt and ragged blue shirt, her thin brown legs scratched by brambles. Her arms raised in an unconscious graceful gesture to the low branch of the birch tree in front of her; there was a glorious, careless, almost pagan loveliness about her.

None of the characters can understand why Maureen is not perfectly content with her husband and daughter. The latter two have a special connection, a feet-on-the-ground practicality, from which Maureen feels excluded. 'Mother thinks everyone ought to live on air,' Laurian says. When Maureen, following her Quest, announces that she is going away to the mountains, her husband and daughter look on somewhat reproachfully. 'Have you thought of Laurian?' Roland asks, adding 'I don't understand why you want to leave your home,' and 'one day you will even be glad of me.'

> As she rose, she saw Laurian standing in the doorway in the half darkness.
> 'Are you going away?' Laurian asked in great surprise.
> 'Yes, to the mountains.'
> 'Will you be away for long?'
> Maureen looked at the immature, heart-shaped face, the long eyes, the soft straight fall of hair.
> 'I don't know,' she lied.
> 'Will you be back for my birthday?'
> 'Oh Laurian...' Her heart began to die inside her, 'perhaps not. I'll send you things. Postcards and cowbells and...' She cast about in her mind for inspiration '... a cuckoo clock.'

'A cuckoo clock,' Laurian repeated. 'That would be nice.' She came further into the room. 'But I would rather you were here, all the same,' she added.

'Laurian, you must always take care of your hair,' Maureen said, feverishly. 'Don't neglect it.'

'My hair? Why?'

'It's so pretty.'

My first thought is that *The Third Man* was the new film on the block when Rosemary was writing, coming out in 1949, with Orson Welles' immortal delivery of the line making the phrase 'the cuckoo clock' very much more famous than it deserved to be, and my second is that Rosemary is obsessed with Laura's hair. She did have lovely hair. Then, of course, I realise that what makes me sad is the foreshadowing of disaster that is woven into this exchange.

I read on, pausing every now and then to consider the context for my grandmother's novel. It is 1950, five years after the end of the war. Mass politics were the order of the day. Socialism was dominant, and England had embraced social engineering on a grand scale – the welfare state, the National Health Service, and town planning, the building of supposedly idealised environments for living, mass education and red brick universities, modernism. Other books published that year included *Lolita* and *Lucky Jim* – these were on the cutting edge. But here is Rosemary working in a more old-fashioned tradition, half digesting material from books that she found on the bookshelves at Ashby St Ledgers, or which she had been given to read by her nannies and governesses. Her novel is stuffed with literary references, to *The Pilgrim's Progress* and to the *Morte d'Arthur*, but also to Shakespeare, Webster, Dostoevsky and the Bible. Her subject matter and style are reflective of John Buchan, Somerset Maugham, James Hilton; she shares the milieu that they inhabit, and their interest in a sort of spiritualism-lite.

Rosemary's story has in fact very strong parallels with Somerset Maugham's *The Razor's Edge*, which features its own version of Rosemary's Robert, called Larry. Larry has a sort of inner radiance, a depth, which serves as a contrast to the shallow, gossipy (American) milieu he inhabits. 'I see vast lands of the spirit stretching out before me, beckoning, and I'm going to travel them.' Larry is described as possessing an extraordinary voice: 'it was only now that I became conscious of the melodiousness of his voice. It was very persuasive. It was like a balm.' In just the same way Rosemary described her Robert as having 'an irresistible voice, a voice without rough edge to it'. *The Razor's Edge* in fact came out two years after *A Hill called Error*, so Rosemary cannot have borrowed from her much better-known contemporary; perhaps it was the other way round, or there was just something in the air.

Surely Rosemary must have had a copy of *The Lost Horizon* by James Hilton on her shelves. This was the smash hit bestseller that created Shangri-La, the fictional utopian lamasery high in the mountains of Tibet, whose inhabitants enjoy unheard-of longevity, and where a member of the British diplomatic service finds inner peace and a sense of purpose. It was written in 1933, but might have been fresh in Rosemary's mind if she had heard a repeat of the BBC's original broadcast of the story in 1945, or a new version broadcast in 1948, starring Ronald Colman. This must have been lingering in her imagination when she transported her fictional guru to Tibet. Reports start to circulate of a man living among Tibetans in a monastery 'tanned and weathered and wearing Tibetan clothes... One of the lamas told these friends of mine that it was assumed that he would become a convert to Buddhism.'

Of all of these literary influences, it is *The Pilgrim's Progress* that is most consistently present in the novel, which often has a Christian flavour, despite its flirtation with Buddhism and other spiritual ideas. Soon after her initial revelation about Robert, Maureen meets him by chance or design in the local church. She 'opened the church gate, grey and fragile with age, walking slowly up the brick pathway through the solid dignity of leaning graves'. As I try to resurrect my grandmother, here is her fictional alter ego, living forever, walking amongst gravestones and meditating on the eternal.

When Maureen's Quest takes her to the Austrian Alps she christens the nearest mountain 'Error', taken directly from *The Pilgrim's Progress*. The mountain gives her a moment of transcendental beauty: 'As they watched, a blood-red splash stained the immaculate snow and spilled itself over the sheer side of the mountain. "Christ," said the American. "Christ".' I can feel Rosemary's imagination straining to the highest pitch as she sat at her desk in her study at Kintbury. 'Over to the East, the peaks were still as red as tiger lillies, but even as they stared, the sun gave a great leap, and wide, ragged rivers of gold came flooding over the ramparts of the immemorial amphitheatre.' There are very clear echoes of Bunyan's classic in her description of Maureen's trip down the mountainside to get medical help for her friend's son. Deep fog descends, obliging her to get down on all fours and crawl so that she does not stray from the path. 'Maureen groped, hesitated, paused, advanced a yard, stopped, groped again, dragging her knees, feeling with cold and ever colder hands the ground directly in front of her. Her back began to ache and her hands to bleed.'

Rosemary's landscape descriptions reveal a sensitive, romanticised response to the natural world, which she possessed all her life. When her heroine arrives in the Outer Hebrides she sails around with her companion, finally arriving at a distant island which she knows is the right one.

> Seen in this radiant hour, it seemed like something only just created, Arcadia, glowing in the fragile mist, blue shadows and shining water, the sharp hills delicately cut against a mysterious sky, the green valley sloping to pale cold sand and sea drenched rock. There should be mermaids, Maureen thought, and coral reefs.

A great Celtic cross stood in front of them. As I read my grandmother's descriptions, I cannot help melting into my teenage self – an English lesson with my favourite teacher who became passionately caught up in the ups and downs of my literary development. She once read out a story that I had written, set amongst the bulrushes, the rivers cut out of peat, the windmills and vast skies of the Norfolk Broads. When she had finished she put my exercise book down and let out a deep, long-drawn-out sigh, raising her eyes to the ceiling, teasing me for my romanticism. I think, too, that whatever the success or otherwise of Rosemary's novel, here was an artist at work. Laura derived some of her artistic sensibility from her mother.

Lest I am carried away by my grandmother's romanticism, however, Rosemary also shows us a different and very characteristic side of herself through her heroine's upper-class, worldly, debunking practicality almost at the very moment of spiritual revelation. 'I suppose you were misunderstood,' says Maureen to an effete poet, fellow resident in the Austrian chalet. And when they arrive on the Scottish island, one moment Maureen is caught up in her reverie of 'simple and mysterious stories of long dead saints and archaic kings', and the next she is suggesting they set off to find Robert, and commenting 'We don't look very tidy do we?' Rosemary's governessy education is never far away.

I have to confess that it was hard not to find the whole Robert/Cedric part of the novel a tiny bit funny, but it is also true to say that Rosemary's life and work are threaded through with changing names and shifting identities. It makes me think immediately of Rosemary going into the nursery and saying to her daughter Car, 'From now on you will be known as Juliet!' Perhaps Rosemary is trying to tell us that the enlightenment that she searches for so desperately is a fluid thing, moving between persons, impossible to pin down, and far from the implacable solidity of her husband and daughter.

Rosemary's novel ends with one of the characters saying that the Quest had 'put right all of Mrs de Vere's miscalculations', and there is no doubt that an underlying force in the book is the sharp critique it contains of her mother. Alastair writes in the *Memoir* that he feels this must have provided her with a catharsis: 'The wicked Queen laid to rest.'

Mimi, it is clear from the descriptions contemporaries have left of her, was a figure of charm, grace, sensitivity and judgement. But Rosemary's treatment of her mother in fiction reveals how very differently her own eldest daughter felt about her. In Rosemary's eyes her mother's narcissism seems to have been her overriding quality; and she, Rosemary, felt that she had lived in its shadow her whole life. Mimi had died two years before the novel was published, having spent the previous fourteen years wrapped up in her romance with William Walton. Rosemary placed the blame for the neglect that she suffered, which she describes so vividly in this novel, and her own sense of incompleteness, squarely on the shoulders of her 'wicked, fascinating' mother. However, Alastair, ever balanced, writes that her feelings were not quite as negative towards her mother as her fictional portraits might suggest. The phrase is 'only partly a rebuke, and also a tribute to her parents' style. In later life at least she appears not to resent her parents, appreciating them for what they were, rather than hating them for what they were not.'

Two years later, in 1952, Rosemary published a second novel, called *The Nature of the Beast*. It is set in France (she was a great Francophile, speaking the language very well), shuttling between an island and the mainland linked by a ferry. It is peppered with French phrases – '*Mon dieu!*', '*Vous allez prendre un café?*', from people wearing berets and blue cotton blouses and padding about in espadrilles. But how French is it really? Are they really more reflections of Rosemary's own set?

This novel is quite satirical, with an Evelyn Waugh flavour at times, featuring some convincing monsters: a controlling father-in-law called 'Poppet' – 'a beautiful old man, daisy fresh and a little sly under his papery lids', his wife Coco 'straying in brown velvet towards the breakfast table', a female character called Liza who 'opened her mouth and said mechanically "Darling" and shut it again, making agile movements of the shoulders'.

The meat of the novel, however, is as earnest as her first book. Once again her heroine, Pauline this time, is a version of herself. Pauline is a waiflike figure, much less capable than Rosemary, but she is a well-born rebel, which is exactly how Rosemary liked to view herself. Pauline is an aristocrat, a gamine who wore 'the black cloak and beret of the district, her hair fell in a plain, dark curtain to her pale-blue collar and her swinging skirt was carelessly strapped into her rough leather belt'. This was Rosemary's wardrobe exactly.

Once again, Rosemary's heroine seeks salvation in a man. Pauline's meeting with Liavrec, an 'immense man', a former naval officer of humble birth with an important mission to tackle the problem of malaria in the marshlands, is described almost as if Cupid had fired an arrow. It happens very suddenly and near the beginning of the book: 'She turned and the movement was so beautiful that it drove the blood from Liavrec's heart. Nothing about her was ever again to move him so deeply as this, the first gesture he ever saw her make.'

The wicked characters conspire in an attempt to de-rail the romance, and eventually succeed in engineering Pauline's lover a job far away. Pauline goes almost mad with grief. When her lover finally returns, it is too late, and they cannot pick up where they left off. My grandmother's very un-feminist conclusion seems to be that 'Liavrec understood the indisputable truth that women are replaceable, and jobs are not'. It puts me in mind of one of Laura's little aphorisms: 'Men must work and women must weep.'

Rosemary seems to have held back her romantic longings in both her novels with a degree of realism, an understanding that salvation cannot always be found in a single man. But in an epilogue to *The Nature of the Beast* it is the romanticism that gets the last word: 'It would be pleasing to be able to believe that, in spite of all signs to the contrary, Liavrec got his princess in the end, having at last learned to love her as she had every right to wish to be loved.' This is revealing of Rosemary's inner feeling that she had a *right* to be loved as truly, completely and passionately as she dreamed of. This is teenage stuff, yet Rosemary was forty-six when she wrote this. Rosemary and her creation were on the brink of becoming hopelessly entangled in a way that was to become momentous for her own future. Her step would have profound consequences for the future, both for herself and for her family.

Chapter 23

Towards the end of the 1970s, with money fast running out, Laura and Tony began to sell things – old friends that had always been a part of our Arcadia. First to go was the beautiful oil painting of sunflowers by Mark Gertler which had hung above the fireplace at Downshire Hill. Then Laura left her artistic paradise on earth and went out to work; she did a short secretarial course and found a job in the NHS.

She went off without complaint every day to her job, typed everything very slowly, and soon became the heart and soul of the office. She was also very good at saying 'no' when she thought she was being asked to do something unreasonable. She just very charmingly said, 'No, I don't think I can do that.' There was something in the aristocratic finality of the way she said it that shut everyone up and made people leave her alone. Tony stayed at home and, isolated from any sort of academic world, his ideas became increasingly esoteric and his attempts at greatness more desperate. Laura's talent was sacrificed without a second thought.

Laura's calm practicality kept the family going for several years. Like a faint echo of Mrs Jordan at Bushy Park, she fought for her idyll. She was never a good secretary, but nobody ever wanted to get rid of her, and she became a proper worker, with a strong sense of her rights, perhaps true to the early left-wing ideas developed together with Tony.

My brother, Ant, underwent a butterfly-like transformation from nerdy teenager in National Health glasses and spots to a sort of suntanned god. This transformation happened quite suddenly over one summer holiday in about 1980. He went off with his good-looking friend, the friend's gorgeous girlfriend, and a girl who was really… well, less good-looking shall I say – for himself. By the time he returned his hair was short, he was bronzed, he seemed more muscly, he had ditched the girl and found himself a *Dallas*-style red-haired beauty from Texas. I had a friend round when he walked through the door after this disturbing evolution. My friend and I were at the top of the orange-carpeted stairs at Downshire Hill. She stared at him and said: 'Your brother's quite good looking actually.'

'No he's not. Don't be absurd.'

He had no intention whatsoever of stopping there. Having buried his teenage self, he did not intend to exhume him. From that point onward we all had to be interested in his serial monogamous parade of girlfriends. I became closer to Merlin – trusty sibling in the face of this seemingly endless promotion of our older brother. Merlin and I started calling our brother God (satirically of course).

After the Dallas beauty there was a doe-eyed South Sea Islander, a pale-skinned, fair-haired New Englander, a small Japanese girl, a butch Portuguese woman, each one brought home and endlessly discussed. I can remember sitting in the front bow-windowed room at Downshire Hill, which was no longer Tony's study and had been transformed into a dining room, entertaining the Portuguese girlfriend. She was much older than him, had a deep, husky smoker's voice, and the face of a woman who had already lived hard. My mother was charming and polite to her, although she said afterwards to me, 'What's wrong with a nice English girl?'

Ant, having emerged from his awful spotty years, became an absence in my life. When he did come home he was overflowing with confidence, grew his hair into a pony tail, and wore leather jackets. He pursued a career in science and became Tony's pride and joy. When he came home he didn't stick around for long, but was on his bicycle and off into the night. Before long he went to America and I was left to bear the full brunt of my parents' growing divergence from reality. We didn't see each other or speak much after he took off. Recently a tragedy occurred in his life, and I went out to Germany where he lives to spend time with him. We spent five days together and for the first time in his life he took time off work to be with me. We spoke incessantly of everything and began to see things a little more from each other's point of view. We went round the Christmas markets, buying amongst other things a strange wooden figure of a rotund man who blows scented smoke from his mouth, and we drank *gluhwein*. I realised that his life in Germany hadn't been as perfect as my father's encomium had suggested; in fact it had been strangely secluded. The life of scientists had a peculiar cult-like quality. I also realised I had been seeing my brother through the prism of my father. When we hugged at the airport we couldn't let go for ages, and when I said, 'I've missed you' I really, really meant it. At every turn in this story, there are deep feelings, love even, denied, ignored, neglected, hurt.

In Downshire Hill, once my brother had gone off to live his own life, Merlin and I were still at home and continued to accompany our parents on their Heath walks. In those later years we started to vary our route. Every now and then we would walk to Primrose Hill, unheard-of in the early days. This route took us down Belsize Avenue, along Belsize Park Gardens and then on to Primrose Hill, and would usually prompt Tony to a muttering rant, often containing the phrases 'Laura's brother', 'absolutely pathetic', and 'Kingsley Amis' butler'. The shy ghost of my Uncle Al, usually resident only in the fawn duffle coat, began to inhabit a house on Primrose Hill. I would gaze up at the house, my imagination filling in all the blank spaces, my curiosity unsatisfied.

∿

I never really had a clear figure in my mind when I tried to search for the ghost in the duffle coat. 'He used to knock about with your mother in London,' Tony would say. I had a vague idea of an arrogant and unpleasant, reactionary figure; certainly any mention of his name led to a frenzy of hand biting and muttering, the word 'Alastair' expelled with a rush of dark, mysterious loathing, often followed by a half-articulated 'He betrayed us' or 'He turned everyone against us.'

So who was the man behind the sash windows of that house in Primrose Hill? The first clues came with my meeting and correspondence with Robin, who seemed to be very much in touch with his older brother, and visited him quite regularly. When I tried to explain Tony's ferocious hatred towards their brother, Robin and Juliet just looked confused and wondered in amazement that anyone could react to their brother in that way. For some reason the suggestion was never made that I should meet him, but when I received my copy of his book, *Rosemary: A Memoir*, another section of the wall of silence fell away, and a real human person started to appear.

The phrase 'he used to knock about with your mother in London', I realised, contained an important truth, which was that Laura's brother, Alastair, was really the man in her life before Tony came along. He was in fact a *rival*. I soon realised, as I began to read the *Memoir*, that the characterisation of him as reactionary, an upper-class fool, or a person who plotted, or tried to turn people against his sister and Tony, was not truthful.

Alastair, known by friends and family as Ali, sketches in a brief self portrait in the *Memoir*. He describes himself as a difficult adolescent who tried to be 'cock-o-the-walk' at school, formed a gang, and was considered pretentious by his headmaster. At thirteen he was sent to Dartmouth to become a naval cadet, where he became obsessed by an older boy with an arrogant pock-marked face and a knowing air, who dared him to pilfer a watch from someone's locker. Anxious to stand well with this raffish figure (who later became a dealer in narcotics), Ali stole the watch. When detectives arrived the next day he confessed, was sent into 'ethical quarantine', and then sent down. His corrupter, meanwhile, denied all knowledge and got away with it. Rosemary was sent for. 'She was the ice queen, refused to upbraid me in front of third parties, and simply drove me away, still maintaining her icy calm.' After that Rosemary took charge, managed to get him a place at Bradfield, and set his life 'humming along in a more fruitful direction'.

The next step in his life is a surprise: Ali went to Cambridge to read English. Tony certainly never hinted that Laura's siblings were clever. That would certainly not have fitted the narrative. Tony must in fact have been at Cambridge at the same time as his future brother-in-law, although Ali was at King's, famously an aesthetes' college. Dadie Rylands was a fellow there at the time, and an absolute institution. He was a renowned Shakespeare scholar and director, much admired for his good looks – his thick, canary-coloured hair and pastel blue eyes. His lectures were inspirational, conveying his passionate belief that literature should move the heart. Ali's tutor was Noel Annan, another flamboyant figure, who had been in intelligence during the war. Among his contemporaries was the writer Simon Raven, who as a young man had the 'looks of an angel' with an abundant mass of Titian red-blond hair. He consumed vast quantities of drink, seduced men and women with equal enthusiasm, often behaved caddishly, ran up huge debts, and was probably a bad influence on Ali. In other words, Ali's 'set' were posh aesthetes, who would have been very distasteful and intimidating to Tony, who hung out with the nerds and earnest historians. Rosemary was a frequent visitor and was charmed by King's College. Unfortunately, Ali was only there for a year; he too had incurred debts which his father offered to settle provided he would start work in the City. This time Rosemary did not bail him out.

After a thorny early path, beset by struggles to find the right way, Ali, having got married, struck out on a great adventure. He and his wife, Di, decided they would start a new life in the town of Ronda, in Andalucía, Spain. In November 1957 (not long, I note, after my parents met), Ali and his wife took berths on a liner, 'which rolled and pitched its way to Gibraltar'. They then loaded their possessions into a first-class compartment of the old express train which was hauled up to Ronda by two steam locomotives. Not an unbending and unimaginative reactionary figure at all, Ali was beginning to reveal himself as a romantic.

And where could he possibly have chosen that was more romantic than Ronda? A stunning Spanish town set astride a deep gorge, with a dizzying bridge joining the two sides. He and his wife installed themselves in the Villa Paz, where Ali settled down to finish his second novel. When this was rejected for being too libellous of certain City interests, they tried opening a rowdy tapas bar. But this was closed, perhaps because the locals didn't like the competition, or perhaps because of a brawl. Finally they settled on teaching English and Spanish, opening what was to become a famously charming language school. For this purpose, they rented Mondragon Palace, an enchanting Moorish place with little cloistered courtyards decorated with tile work, pretty rounded arches springing from delicate pillars, and beautiful rooms with wood-panelled ceilings. A small garden rich with greenery is threaded through with little rivulets and fountains, with only a delicate fence to separate you from the precipice, plunging many thousands of feet below. Ali was in search of his own version of the Bushy idyll as much as any of us.

In Spain, Ali held court at his language school. A pupil describes arriving there and being met by Ali, a languid Englishman who impressed him enormously with his easy command of Spanish. When he wasn't teaching, Ali, like Rosemary, took to writing, and his subject lay all around him. It was the craggy vastness of the mountainous district in which he made his home, the high plateaus which shifted under the ever-changing light, the circling vultures, the white villages and towns climbing up steep little streets, the Andalucian people and their politics, the drama of the bullfight.

Ali set off on Chico, a small, elderly, bay gelding, to explore the landscape all around Ronda, following rough tracks which led him to farms and villages and through picturesque ruins. He loved the physical pleasure of riding, taking advantage of the ease with which one could find almost nightly stabling. Laura too had a special connection with horses. I can picture her in her duffle coat stroking the pale, soft nose of a horse with its head over the gate of a field, and feeding it with a carrot offered on a flat hand. 'Funny,' she says, 'how ponies were the centre of my world for so long.'

I acquire a copy of Ali's book *The Road from Ronda* from somewhere deep in the internet – a hardback, with an orange cover showing two figures on horseback with the Ronda bridge in the background. I turn it over, and here is a picture of my uncle, seated on his horse with one hand on the reins. His stance is relaxed, his clothing is dapper, and he looks calmly at the camera. His face is very like my mother's, calm and self-contained. I open the book, with some admiring words written by Jan Morris fresh in my mind: 'I will never ride down to Toledo again without a Boyd in my saddlebag.'

Ali followed inaccessible, rocky paths through the high sierra to little villages, finding himself amongst mountain dwellers, whom he immediately charmed. I find myself being rather touched by a little detail of his saddlebag, of thick grey material with a slit in the narrow part between the

Alastair

two bags to fit it over the high charabanc of the saddle: 'it held my extra sweaters, shoes and most of my clothing'. I am searching for the physical presence and reality of my uncle, somewhere amidst all the words.

Ali clearly inspired amused and tolerant devotion among the Andalucians. They admired him for his education and his breeding, for his fluent Spanish, and for his deep knowledge of everything about Ronda and the surrounding district. He describes in his book being fleeced in the purchase of his second horse, Babi. Frasquito, his factotum, looked on despairingly: 'You are very soft,' Frasquito would wind up pityingly, stubbing his cigarette out on the carpet. 'That is your trouble. You are very soft.'

As I read, Ali is coming slowly to life before me. I can start to dream up a vision of the four siblings, a sort of presence, despite their invisibility, in every interaction I had with my mother. They had always been there, in a way. I can hear them laughing, quarrelling and chattering away. They are self-deprecating and shy, brought up not to talk about themselves, but to express their views confidently and lightly, with reference to those around them. They have a fresh charm, they are cultivated, intelligent, and inclined to be soft and whimsical. You might wish they would take a grip on things sometimes, but full of warmth and human understanding, and they have a gift for relationships. They enhance the lives of everyone around them. My mother's ghost siblings have all taken flesh now.

Turning to the next phase of Ali's story, he and his wife enjoyed ten happy years in Ronda, much of it running the language school, but eventually the difficult parts of the idyll – the lack of money, the alienation of an ex-pat life – got too much for Di, and in 1968 she left Ali and returned home.

Not long afterwards, through the doors of Mondragon Palace, to take up her place as a pupil at the language school, walked an attractive fair-haired woman. This was Hilly, ex-wife of Kingsley Amis. Ali immediately fell for her. In the family she is known as Hilly Major to distinguish her from Hilly Minor, Robin's wife. Hilly was the love of Ali's life. She joined him in Ronda and together they had a little boy, Jaime, born in 1972. All seemed set fair for a continuation of the idyll, except for the fact that their lives were increasingly impoverished. In 1975, however, everything changed. My grandfather Gilbert died, which meant that Ali became the 7th Baron Kilmarnock, and with it a seat in the House of Lords.

With his increasingly precarious financial position and new fatherhood to consider, the language school years came to an end, and Ali formed a plan for Hilly and little Jaime to stay in Ronda while he moved back to England and took his seat in the Lords. Once again Arcadia is disturbed by reality. In 1975, when I was twelve years old, my uncle was about to swim right back into the same pond as us. My parents knew very well that he had returned to England, but never breathed a word about it.

Two years later, Ali was still struggling to find a job and a home in England and realised that the stipend for belonging to the House of Lords didn't go very far. Nonetheless, Hilly and Jaime eventually came to England to be with him. They all lived in a tiny cottage in Buckinghamshire. Whenever the Lords was in session Ali stayed with friends in London. With all those earldoms, baronies, viscountcies, who was it that left him this absolutely tiny cottage in Buckinghamshire? His nanny.

Ali, Hilly and Jaime were now seriously impoverished and, in a bid to stave off disaster, Hilly and a friend set up a hot dog stand by the side of the motorway. At this worrying moment in their lives, Hilly's sons, Martin and Philip Amis, came up with a plan. Their idea was that their mother Hilly, together with Ali and Jaime, should move in with Kingsley, her ex-husband.

Martin Amis, in his autobiographical book *Experience*, writes:

When canvassed, the principles appeared keen. An introductory dinner was scheduled. Everyone else, by the way, considered the idea both bizarre and impracticable. Like an Iris Murdoch novel, they kept saying, Yes, and it would have been more like an Iris Murdoch novel if Kingsley had been called Otto and Hilly had been called George. It was an unconventional proposal, true; but they were an unconventional crowd. Philip and I thought it might work for a good six months, even a year. We all gathered in the house in Flask Walk (where else but Hampstead?), and the inaugural dinner began.

The arrangement was that their living expenses would be taken care of, so Kingsley arranged to pay Hilly £50 a week to keep house for him.

The actual move took place in January 1982, just as my schooldays were coming to an end. The three of them moved into a small house in Leighton Road in Kentish Town, not very far from us – a short walk to Parliament Hill Fields and then another ten minutes' walk. It is linked in my mind with the school my brother went to in the sixth form, *the* trendy Hampstead school for boys, called (all one word in my memory) Williamellis.

Leighton Road is just a couple of streets away from Caversham Road, a name which immediately accesses memories of childhood for me as this meant the doctor: the Caversham Clinic. Here were long-drawn-out waits which seemed endless in a shabby waiting room, feeling ill, observing others – the doctor, an aged lady who kept gin bottles stashed under her desk, or the brisk, sensible one. And it also meant my cello teacher, Janet Coles, with her very long, fair hair and floor-length skirts, who lived at the far end of Caversham Road nearest to Kentish Town Road. I got off the bus just there, awkwardly managing my cello in its soft plastic case. I *must* have passed Kingsley, Hilly or Ali in the street. Ali and I would have had no idea we were related.

According to Martin Amis, in 1985 the unusual ménage moved to 194 Regent's Park Road, on the edge of Primrose Hill. While the three of them were living their lives so beloved of the gossip columnists, we would skirt round the address, Tony would mutter, and I would gaze up at the house with curiosity. I had no idea that a scene something like this might be playing out within:

> 'Kingsley's whims were indulged. He had Hilly to run after him, he had Lord Kilmarnock … I remember once going to the pub, and then we settled into Kingsley's sitting room, and Ali came in with a tray and gave us our supper. … Just before the door closed Kingsley deliberately said, 'Not bad for a boy from Norbury, eh, to have his supper brought to him by a *peer of the realm*!' When the door was shut I asked him, 'Are you turning Ali into a Monkey figure? In other words, are you making him the butt of your jokes?' He looked rather taken aback … I once asked Hilly how she was doing and she replied, 'Oh not bad, dear! Down to about thirty tranks [tranquillisers] a day!'[6]

Living with Kingsley Amis was clearly putting some strain on my uncle and his little family. Quite often Ali and Hilly would hear the sound of Kingsley falling over from upstairs 'like a chest-of-drawers jettisoned from an aeroplane'. This 'happened so often we don't even go up. Unless he's wedged. Then he bangs on the floor and sends for Ali.'

It must have taken huge reserves of tact, patience, practicality and love to make the Kingsley situation work. Laura used to hide her own feelings,

---

[6] Artemis Cooper, in her biography of Elizabeth Jane Howard, reports that Julian Barnes wrote this about his visit to the menage.

put her own needs second to everyone else's, and so, I think, did Ali. These self-appointed geniuses need to be careful about how their actions affect the good people who serve them.

During the time that Ali was living with Hilly and Kingsley he became deeply involved with the newly formed Social Democratic Party.[7] At exactly the same moment in Downshire Hill my own father also became a fanatical SDP devotee. But while we talked about it, just a stone's throw away my unknown uncle Ali was actually doing something, putting himself at the heart of the movement. With all that talk of Laura's family being caricature British ruling-class reactionaries, how much more complicated they were.

Ali was as conflicted about his heritage as my mother was. He loved the SDP's vision of a classless society, as set out in their founding Limehouse Declaration of 1981, as well as the concept of the social market economy as promoted by David Owen. In fact Ali became the first executive director of the Social Market Foundation, and became so involved with the movement that he was appointed party whip (1983–86) and deputy leader of the SDP peers (1986–87). He wrote a book about it, *The Radical Challenge*, in 1987. Was Tony alive to the irony of the situation?

The Amis brothers had predicted that the ménage would last six months, but in the end it lasted about thirteen years, only coming to an end with Kingsley's death in 1995. Ali apparently said the idea of returning to Spain was 'something we keep alive in a dream'.

In the end, the little family of three did return to their beloved Andalucia, and Jaime still lives there. They found it sadly changed. When I hinted to Robin that it would have been nice to go out to Spain and meet Ali, he replied, with sadness entering his countenance, that his brother was much altered after a long and messy dispute with greedy property developers. He died in 2009, seven years after my first meeting with Robin, and I never met him. I read my uncle's obituary in the *Guardian*:

---

[7] A new centrist political party founded in March 1981 by four senior Labour Party moderates, dubbed 'The Gang of Four' – Roy Jenkins, David Owen, Bill Rodgers and Shirley Williams.

His untidy life had one enduring quality – his sweetness of nature. Unfairly damned by curmudgeonly Kingsley Amis as an 'upper-class fool', Kilmarnock was not half as vague as he sometimes appeared.

And the one in *The Telegraph*:

In later years he was a slight, faintly elfin figure, ruddy-faced and silver-haired, as well as a snappy dresser with a matching green paisley tie and pocket handkerchief. He inspired real devotion among his many friends.

Why did Tony feel such obsessive hatred towards Alastair? So overpowering was this feeling that he ranted about it for three hours on the very night that my mother died. 'Laura's family never lifted a finger to help us.' The truth is that Tony projected a persona onto him that did not reflect his reality. He gave him the label of a chinless wonder, and built a narrative of betrayal and wickedness around him that was, to use a modern phrase, fake news.

I had discovered that this bad, bad uncle whose name could never be mentioned, led a chaotic and romantic life, that he pursued lost causes, and that he was in fact sweet-tempered to an absolute fault, so soft that people constantly took advantage of him, and he never had any money. I expect Tony found him languid and a bit hopeless, but he was too clever, upper-class and socially confident to be adopted as one of Tony's 'pets'. Did he make Tony feel socially insecure? I expect he did. Did he tease Tony? Tony hated being teased.

There was something deeper here, though, than just an antipathy of class. Alastair, and later the Amises too, took on a sort of symbolic significance, embodying *precisely* the opposite qualities to those that Tony admired. It is interesting, when it comes to Martin and Kingsley Amis, to note that Tony really despised their writing. He hated *Lucky Jim*, and he hated all of Martin's novels. It was one of his slightly unreasonable antipathies, rather like Channing School, which had a hidden and intensely personal underpinning – things that were just too close for comfort and people he just couldn't bring himself to think about. He couldn't bear the world-weary, sophisticated humour, the chaotic private lives that the Amises touted so unashamedly. As masters of narrative they struck at the heart of his own carefully constructed version of the truth. As brittle and chaotic literary figures they represented the opposite of everything he admired: 'tough' controlling men who *really sorted everything out* – Tito, Mao, even Stalin.

Tony, with his obsession with *strength*, despised relativism, weakness and flaws. There was a lack of humanity in the way he viewed weakness. I certainly remember as a child feeling horribly that my own flaws were contrasted with my parents' perfections. I think that Tony felt this way towards Ali (who is very candid about his own periods of foolishness), damning him as *very weak*. I think this led to a lack of understanding, a failure to see Alastair's charm, his diffidence and his good nature for the strengths that they were; a failure to see that in struggle and disorder you can find depth, humanity and redemption.

All that muttering about Ali, *'absolutely pathetic'* – I can still hear Tony spitting out the words – seems to speak of a strange narrowmindedness and lack of imagination in my parents. All that was going on, after all, was an alternative lifestyle. My parents cast themselves as the radicals, the ones who had rebelled and got away from a reactionary background, but the reality was that they had retreated into a positively Victorian ideal of the nuclear family – a heavy-handed father figure and domestic goddess of a mother. The family we weren't even allowed to mention were all leading crazy, unusual, adventurous lives of one sort or another.

At the heart of this, I think, lay *fear*. Alastair made Tony feel unsettled not because of difference but because of similarity. Tony may have admired tough, controlling men who really sorted everything out, but he himself was not one of them. He found it very hard to settle to anything, did not have a sustained career, and was always short of money. He had an exaggerated respect for men with careers, but couldn't make it happen for himself. When he looked at Alastair he felt all of those things in himself, and could see them in his mother too. Alastair confidently embraced and celebrated insecurity and chaos, a true artist, like Laura (who once said to me 'learn to love your overdraft, darling'). But Tony was terrified of it. He reacted by building an entirely false narrative around his brother-in-law, in an attempt to keep it all at bay.

And what of the duffle coat? It was a rough, beige, and very large one which had belonged to a naval friend of Alastair's. He must have given it to Tony when everyone was still friends. How strange that it should have become so much a part of Tony's persona; he carried the discarded shell of his enemy upon his shoulders for years.

Alastair

Alastair in Spain

Chapter 24

Francis continued to be as keen as ever to keep up our new friendship, and since he is a prolific communicator I soon had an entire folder in my inbox devoted to his emails.

He organised an exhilarating trip for me to visit Tunisia. I had never set foot in Africa before, and there, after trailing after Francis for a very long time, under a bright blue sky, we stood outside the white Sicilian house in Salammbo where my aunt had lived for seven years. We had dinner with some friends who had known Margaret. '*Elle avait beaucoup de personnalité,*' one of them said, '*comme Francis.*' Francis talked a great deal of his mother, describing her as a free spirit – a highly educated and intelligent woman who was 'sweetness personified', but at the same time taught him to live dangerously. A friend said of her that she was 'a gentle feminist who showed us all the way'.

As time went on, Francis was warm and generous in sharing his wide circle of friends with us, introducing us to a rich cast of journalists, writers, financiers, film-makers and thinkers. And he took a keen interest in the progress of our children.

Once he brought a Romanian friend who had expressed an interest in visiting Devon – a linguist and musician. 'No, not Silvio – Silviu!! He's Romanian, not Italian!' I parked our old car at Tiverton Parkway station, and there they were. Francis, thin and distinguished-looking, in clean, well-presented clothes of superior fabrics, holding onto a carefully packed, neat, black wheeled suitcase, and this must be Silviu – in a characteristic Homburg, skinny trousers and jacket. Francis begins: 'I mean it's quite extra*or*dinary' the stream of talk… 'I mean what is this? Mind your bags, tell the conductor if you see a suspicious package, speak of nanny state – the English love to *nanny* everyone.'

'Hello,' said Silviu in a strong Romanian accent. 'Good to meet you.' He's funny, quick, and charming.

Silviu is very confident and makes himself right at home, asking for WiFi codes, plugging in his devices. A Peter Pan figure, he is boyish, constantly on the move and overflowing with energy. 'Ah, the piano, may I?' He dwells, it turns out, in a multicultural Eurozone, brilliantly multilingual, a crooner. The evening comes and Silviu sets up his iPad as a backing tune and begins to sing 'My Funny Valentine' and 'Fly me to the Moon'. Charles and I sit in armchairs wondering what has happened to our sitting room, half seduced, half embarrassed. Our little dog has fallen entirely under his spell. She lies on the sofa on her back while he sings to her, breaking off to say: 'I'm sorry, Bella, in another life what might have been?'

We move to supper and Silviu turns out to be almost as loquacious as Francis; they are magnificently, gloriously, epically self-confident. Our British reticence means we feel they never ask and do not care much about anything that we might be doing. But their culture is that you shouldn't wait to be asked. Silviu is a good foil for Francis; where my cousin is intellectually talkative, Silviu is relaxed and emotionally intelligent, quick to get a joke. They are lively company.

My son comes into the kitchen.

'Kiss my shiny metal ass!' Silviu is saying. 'Hey Sam, how's it going? You've been to a festival I hear.'

'Yeah, that's right. Boardmasters.'

'Boardmasters, cool. That's on the beach, right?'

'Cornwall, yeah.'

'Your Dad and I've been cooking up a *storm*. You want some, Sam?'

'Yes please, great.'

'Sam's been in a *moshpit*. Am I right, Sam?'

'Yeah, one or two.'

'Moshpit?' asks Francis. 'What is this moshpit?'

'Francis doesn't know what a moshpit is,' says Silviu.

'I believe a whole lot of people gather in a big circle and sort of run at each other.'

'Oh,' says Francis, ever highbrow, 'I suppose the people must be entertained.'

On one visit I notice that Francis, when he is thinking, closes one eye and looks intently at the window, slanting his head this way and that as if trying to bring something into focus. My brother Ant has an identical mannerism. Later that evening, very unusually, Ant rings. 'D'you know,' I say, ruefully, 'sometimes I feel as if I'm just a collection of the worst bits of both grandmothers.' He laughs and says loyally, 'I think you don't take yourself so seriously as them.' Through the course of the visits I began to piece together the story of the family after the war.

∿

As the war drew to a close, Fanny and Alexander's family returned from their various adventures to resume their lives in London. Of course nothing would ever be quite the same again, for them, or for any other family.

Britain in 1945, seen from our own times, is a distant land. It lay in ruins, people had lost their homes – about three quarters of a million of which had been damaged or destroyed. In his book *A World to Build*, David Kynaston gives us a brilliant picture of a Britain emerging wearily from the Second World War: 'No supermarkets, no motorways, no teabags, no sliced bread, no frozen food, no flavoured crisps, no lager, no dishwashers, no Formica, no vinyl, no CDs, no computers, no mobiles, no duvets, no Pill.' He goes on to describe a world where everyone wore suits or dresses and hats, for there was no leisurewear: 'Heavy coins, heavy shoes, heavy suitcases, heavy tweed coats.' The clean lines, highrises and shopping malls of modern cities did not exist yet, and people would have hurried through narrow streets between nineteenth-century terraced houses. About seven million homes, Kynaston tells us, lacked hot water, and there was such a thing as a wash day, when clothes were washed in a tub before being wrung out in a mangle. Teenagers did not exist, and divorce was a scandal. 'Abortion illegal, homosexual relationships illegal, suicide illegal.' An exhausted and deeply conservative land.

A group of left-leaning, tweed-suited, pipe-smoking members of the intelligentsia thought, argued and wrote with enormous earnestness about how to shape a new Britain after the war. The freshly authentic comments captured by the researchers in the Mass Observation described in *A World to Build* show that many of the people to whom all this intense thinking was directed were rather skeptical about the utopia that was being imagined for them. The Beveridge Report was published in 1942, identifying the five giant evils of want, disease, ignorance, squalor and idleness, selling a truly amazing 630,000 copies, astonishing for a dry government publication. In 1945, the Labour Manifesto *Let Us Face the Future* came out. It outlined plans for nationalisation, an urgent housing programme, the creation of a new national health service, and the construction of the welfare state. It was extremely high-minded, and authored by a graduate of my father's alma mater, Dartington Hall school, named Michael Young.

As they surveyed bombed-out cities and homes reduced to rubble, glorious visions of new, clean, brilliantly engineered new cities took shape in the minds of architects and planners. 'There must be no uncontrolled building and no more ugly houses and straggling roads,' said a commentator in a wartime documentary. MARS, the Modern Architectural Research Group, was full of well-intentioned, modern men like Ernö Goldfinger, who followed the lead of the French architect Le Corbusier and began to plan modern cities with high-rise flats set in grassy estates as 'the pleasantest possible conditions of living'.

When the Labour Party won the election many people were shocked by the lack of respect shown to Churchill, their heroic wartime leader. But they were in retreat, and there was a real feeling that with the shift towards Socialism old habits of deference were changing. Kynaston reports a telling incident from these times: 'My man!', called out a blazered, straw-hatted fourteen-year-old public schoolboy called John Rae, as he stood on Bishop's Stortford Station with his trunk that late July. 'No,' came the porter's quiet but firm reply. 'That sort of thing is over now.'

In 1945, Fanny and Alexander and their family reassembled in London, somewhat battered and bruised by their wartime experiences. Fanny arrived home from Canada with her doted-upon son Anthony, now a young man of seventeen. Anthony had been taken away from a school that he loved, an unusual place with pioneering ideas about how children should be treated, dedicated to very high standards of artistic expression and scientific enquiry, then thrust into an environment in which he was much less likely to thrive. The family had been warned by their doctor that above all they should avoid a situation in which Fanny would be spending a great deal of time alone with her son. Their wartime experience, thrown together in Canada, was likely, in the doctor's view, to be damaging. The doctor was right – without a supportive environment, away from her friends and with insufficient social intercourse of a sort that would suit her very refined and brilliant mind, the toll on Fanny's mental health was serious. Alec, meanwhile, had stayed in London, despite the bombing, and continued working.

Margaret had had the best war of the four of them. She was twenty-five years old and had had two intense and eventful years. The family must have been proud, and perhaps a little bit envious, of her brilliant wartime record. However, considering the conservatism of Britain in 1945, to return home with an illegitimate baby in your arms, as Margaret did, cannot have been an easy thing. She moved into No. 19B Belsize Park Gardens (the family's first Hampstead address) with her mother's best friend Marion and Marion's daughter Fiona. Alec, in particular, was not pleased that all of his plans for his marvellous daughter to make a glittering marriage were in ruins. He engineered a trip to South Africa to make sure he was not there for her return. Francis' version of the story is that when Alec did come back from his trip he had imagined that his daughter's baby was going to be black, and refused to come and see them. 'He was a racist,' declared Francis. 'When he finally visited, he discovered I had copper blond, curly hair. That surprised him.' Whether this is true or not, Alec certainly had not envisioned single motherhood for Margaret. He was an organised and methodical man and did not enjoy the chaos.

It is perhaps not surprising that before long Alec would be on a collision course with his son. Anthony (not known as Tony within the family), was coming of age at the exact moment when the new postwar spirit of modernism, of shaping the future, was sweeping the land. He was a graduate of Dartington Hall school, just like the author of the Labour Manifesto, extremely bright, and starting to embrace, with all the force of his considerable developing personality, a very left-wing, high-minded outlook. Anthony participated fully in the debates of the time, about how society should be re-engineered and built by people of intellect such as himself, how lives could be progressively improved, structures of privilege dismantled. A strong sense prevailed that nothing that had gone on before mattered much, that one's parents were atavistic. Anthony rejected the whole *style* of his parents' life – the dependence on servants, the smart clothes and hotels – and took instead to wearing fishermen's jumpers and sandals, to sitting cross-legged on the floor listening to folk music and admiring the music of

Tony – angry young man

black America. He learnt to play boogie woogie piano and had a great stack of the sheet music of Pinetop Smith, Jimmy Yancey and Jelly Roll Morton. He was a modern man, a Jimmy Porter figure who read the *New Statesman*, sat around in his flat talking endlessly to his even-tempered friend, refused to get a job in line with his abilities and education, dodged National Service, and glowered angrily at the world.

Anthony was keen to paint his father as the polar opposite to himself – as right-wing and backward-looking, dressed in a pinstriped suit, and perusing the stocks and shares at breakfast. It is true to say that Alec was an integrator, a conservative. Britain had served him well; he had suffered none of the extremes of persecution of his father, Rabbi Aaron; the knowledge of what life for Jews could be like drove him to work hard. He achieved success, respect and material comfort in the country where his father had chosen to seek sanctuary. He would have reacted to everyday and petty anti-Semitism for what it was – irritating, but not life-threatening. These differences in outlook were real, but in fact much of the reason for the increasingly nasty clashes between Alec and his son were rooted in the similarity of the two men. Both had an unbending quality, an inclination to be hard and unforgiving. Both were heavy-handed patriarchs who undervalued the intellect and contribution of women, despite having two examples of exceptional female capability right in front of their noses.

Anthony claimed for himself a commitment to and understanding of the arts, and a broad vision of how the arts and society were interrelated, designating his father as a reactionary philistine. However, this was really an unfair characterisation of Alec. When many of Alexander's things finally came to me, I found that they were full of interesting first editions, beautiful carpets and paintings. Here was a man who was given a complete set of Thomas Hardy as a wedding present from Shell, who bought the beautiful Mark Gertler painting of sunflowers that had been so much a part of my childhood, and who built up a remarkable collection of autographed manuscripts and first editions, a lot of it early twentieth-century literary works. One of these has come down to me. Sourced for him by Rare Books of 123 Bond Street, it is an advanced proof copy of the correspondence between Bernard Shaw and the actress Mrs Patrick Campbell. It contained some unpublished typescripts of Shaw poems and photographs of Mrs Campbell as loose inserts. The letters are charming and intensely romantic: 'You are so beautiful that all the stars are not too fine to make a necklace for you, and there are secret places in the world where there is nobody else but you.' No, this seems to reveal that a very much more interesting sensibility lay somewhere in Alec. Moreover, my father too had an enduring love for Shaw as a playwright, and he must surely have been influenced in this by his father. In Alec's close personal relationship with artist Robert Gibbings, it is again possible to see that there is very much more than just a professional necessity, but rather a real and deep reverence for artists and their creations. If Alec admired the calm, un-showy beauty of Mrs Patrick Campbell, this style of beauty was much in the same mould as my mother, and of Arletti, who played Garance in *Les Enfants du Paradis*, the film that captured my parents' imagination so completely, for so many years.

Fanny must have been a driving force, too, in her husband's patronage of the arts. This was the woman, after all, who chose Dartington Hall as a school for her son, who had her portrait painted by a leading Manchester artist, and a studio portrait taken in the Surrealist style. She placed herself instinctively at the cutting edge.

Despite Alec's unhappiness at Margaret's situation, his fury was towards the man who had got her pregnant but was now nowhere to be seen, and despite the rows with Anthony he did not banish his children, but entertained them and their radical friends at his table, liberal with his wine and generous with his hospitality. Perhaps he could see that the world was moving on and he had limited powers to control the things he disapproved of. A huge sprawling cast of bickering and squabbling characters gathered. It reads like a Jewish, left-wing version of *La Ronde*. Marion's daughter, Fiona, was madly in love with Tony's best friend Harry Poole, a physicist at UCL who lived 'way out on the Northern Line', but she was 'too fat', and Poole fell in love with a Polish Jewess who had escaped through France during the war. Myrtle Solomon, known as 'Moke', a lesbian, daughter of a wealthy lawyer and barrister, Secretary General of the Peace Union, was madly and unrequitedly in love with Margaret, who was still in love with her Berber war hero. Tony hated Moke. Fiona's half-brother, Ben Weinreb, ran a print shop near the British Museum where everyone would gather. And finally there were two beautiful Communist twins called the Manukin sisters, and everyone was in love with them.

As for Fanny and Alexander themselves, it is unknowable what goes on between a couple, even if you have frequent contact with them, or are very close. Fanny came back from the war in a fragile state. Francis tells me that not only did they cease sharing a bedroom after the war, but that Alec, when he was abroad, was photographed with women 'who were clearly tarts'. Francis insists that Alec adored his wife, but perhaps he was not the man to respond with sensitivity to her fragility. Family life was tense; nobody could relax, nobody was as happy as they had been before the war. The scene was set for some titanic clashes of the ego. Every move any one of the mightily intelligent foursome of Alec, Fanny, Margaret and Tony made would, with absolute inevitability, provoke and inflame the others. The whole family found itself caught in a fiendish trap.

After the war, Margaret and her little boy, Francis, were very much a part of her younger brother Anthony's life. The father of the child was but a shadowy figure living in Tunisia. But then in 1948, Marcel Ghilès, the war hero, actually appeared in England. He paid a brief visit to see his beloved and laid eyes on their son for the first time. There is a photograph of Marcel in the garden at 18B Belsize Park Gardens. Finally in 1952, eight years after their first electric meeting in Tunis, Marcel and Margaret were reunited. Marcel had finally secured a divorce from his trapeze-artist wife, opening the way for Margaret and Francis, who was now seven years old, to join him in Tunis, and for the two of them to be married at last.

As his mother had nearly ten years previously, the seven-year-old Francis experienced Tunisia as a glorious freedom, excitement and opening up of life. 'Is this a Babar book?' he asked on arrival. He remembers a great

Margaret and Marcel

*Marcel meets his son for the first time
– number 18B Belsize Park Gardens*

Francis as a schoolboy in Tunisia and Margaret and Francis

storm in the Mediterranean, riding in horse-drawn open carriages and a new school where he made friends easily. Then as he became a teenager there was Tunisian independence, Suez, a half-Lebanese girlfriend called Monique, and a thrilling new dance called Rock 'n' Roll, made all the more enticing by his father's reaction: 'What is this dance of black savages?'

From that time onwards Fanny would visit her daughter every year. Alec, who could not reconcile himself to Marcel, even when he became Margaret's husband, did not accompany her. Fanny, on the other hand, loved Tunisia. Thanks to her daughter's sense of adventure, she could now live out the dreams she had had as a young woman when she had developed her intense interest in North Africa. She must have felt, I am sure, that her influence had had a bearing on Margaret's choices. She was never happier than when wandering around Classical sites under a brilliant blue sky, picking up Roman coins. She enjoyed a sense of liberation here, away from the heavy hands that had constrained her – both her tyrannical son, whom she had described so vividly as a 'little Hitler', and her patriarchal husband, away from the hated Canada. The wealthy Sicilians who lived opposite Marcel and Margaret laid on a dinner when Fanny came to stay. Fanny took her time getting ready. Marcel grew impatient.

'We're late!'

'No, we're not late,' said Fanny sweetly.

She emerged wearing an eye-stopping necklace of green Murano glass and a green dress. They walked over the road and every single eye turned on her. Offered a stage, she was incapable of refusing it.

Things weren't completely straightforward in Tunisia. Fanny found her daughter's domestic life to be tempestuous; Marcel, she learnt, had an almost uncontrollable temper, and she found him to be rather insecure. But at the same time Fanny could see that Margaret was passionately in love with this man, and volatility simply had to be accepted as the way things were. When another baby arrived, a little girl called Micky, Fanny was on hand to provide grandparental love and support.

Back in Britain, the political scene that the intellectually curious Anthony was emerging into had moved decisively to the Left, but there was much that was complex about it, particularly in relation to the international scene. The new Labour Government was divided on its response to Communist Russia and its relationship with the US right from the start. Many Labour MPs on the Left, including Michael Foot and Barbara Castle, warned that American capitalism was 'arrogant, self-confident, merciless and convinced of its capacity to dictate the destinies of the world'. The *New Statesman* wrote: 'the United States is nearly as hostile to the aspirations of socialist Britain as to the Soviet Union'. But the bullish, blunt and powerful Ernest Bevin, a crucial figure during the war as Minister of Labour, deeply distrusted the Soviet Union, and felt that British policy towards Moscow must be one of suspicion and mistrust.

In 1947, President Harry Truman proclaimed his fiercely anti-Soviet policy, promising the free world an 'enduring struggle against it'. In response, three youngish Labour MPs, Richard Crossman (who had been Margaret's boss during the war), Michael Foot and Ian Mikardo, published a pamphlet called *Keep Left*, critical of Bevin's dangerous dependence on the US, and demanding that British and French Socialists form an alliance strong enough to hold the balance of world power, halt the division into Western and Eastern blocs, and make the UN a reality.

In the end, however, they veered right, and in 1947 began to fall in behind Bevin. Two things made them change their minds – the enormous economic assistance offered by the US (Marshall Aid), which could only be welcomed in the face of Britain's huge reconstruction task, and the Communist coup in Czechoslovakia. In response, the British Communist Party hardened its line and attacked the Labour Party at every turn for its dependence on America. Many people such as the young playwright, Robert Bolt, started feeling uncomfortable in the Party and became defectors. The Cold War was beginning.

Anthony was nineteen at this juncture, and caught up sharply in these political currents. He was doing well academically, securing himself a place to read maths and physics at Trinity College Cambridge. He felt the exhilaration of being part of the new generation that was shaping Britain, but went beyond the prevailing Socialist position when he became a member of the British Communist Party, even volunteering for an expedition to Yugoslavia, supposedly to help lay railway line. This was not so surprising at the time. There was still considerable pro-Russian sentiment at the end of the war, there were two elected Communist MPs; the BCP's membership had tripled to about 50,000 during the war and it included Iris Murdoch and Kingsley Amis. The latter's early novel *Who Else is Rank* featured a sensitive lieutenant who says that 'these common men, from whom we're separated only by a traditional barrier – we're no more than common men ourselves – benefit from the work that has been done, and if the system won't let that happen, we shall just have to change the system'.

Anthony was very much drawn to the Communist vision. He had always tended towards extremes, and had an almost overpowering need to create a narrative for his life. As he set about forming one he tried to fit everyone and everything into it. His Jewish heritage, although he rejected it, played into this, as Jews live in the shadow of the most overpowering narrative in history. He was strongly drawn to Karl Marx's unfolding determinist story, with its certainty, its relentlessness and its simplicity.

There were some personal reasons too for his stance. To begin with, what could he possibly do that would disappoint, taunt and annoy his father most? And perhaps there was a deeper reason, too. The Communist movement was steeped in male chauvinism; Tony's feelings about women were complex to a high degree – what could be better for his ego than a creed that said strong, earthy women should dig the soil and admire the intellect of their menfolk? What an escape from his mother's brilliance and fragility. In response, his mother disapproved of his Communism. For her it was just the underside of Fascism; -isms, she felt, were excuses to dissolve the individual in the collective, making it easy to deny their humanity and to allow tyranny to flourish. Fanny spoke acidly of 'communist frumps' and disapproved of her son's choices.

Anthony graduated from Cambridge with a disappointing degree, having 'never turned up to a single Physics practical', he boasted proudly. He did quit the BCP, but was convinced that thereafter he was turned down for many jobs because of his Communist past, and convinced too that his phone was being tapped. It was certainly true that by 1948 the government had established an anti-Communist propaganda unit called the IRD, and Attlee announced that members of the CP and those associated with it would henceforth be forbidden from undertaking work deemed 'vital to the security of the state'. Civil servants were investigated, academic appointments were closed for Communist sympathisers. Anthony's suspicions may not have been pure paranoia. Certainly his particular cast of mind, his attacking, restless intellect and mania to try and explain everything, would have suited him to an academic career, far better than one 'in industry', which he tried to pursue, and it is possible that the early Cold War did hamper his progress and inhibit his achievements.

Margaret had not disappeared off to Tunisia for good, and in 1956 events again brought her to London. The trigger for her return was Tunisian independence. When Margaret, Marcel and their two children arrived back in England, the whole colourful and bickering scene, including Tony, turned up to welcome the War Hero. They all gathered at Moke's beautiful late sixteenth-century house in the New Forest with views over the sea. I ask Francis what my father thought of his sister's husband Marcel. After all, their politics were very similar. 'I think your father couldn't make him out. Marcel was exuberant, over the top, out seducing women at sixteen, a great gardener, artist activist and naval officer. He wasn't an intellectual. I think your father did admire him.' But he never mentioned him once, I think to myself.

This was to be a brief visit for Marcel before he left to try and find work in France; Margaret and the two children moved into her parents' flat in Richmond. After about a year, Margaret and the baby, Micky, again left England, to settle in Grenoble, in the south-east of France. Francis, now aged thirteen, was left behind in England to live with his grandparents; he was enrolled at the London Lycée to continue his education.

Francis describes this period of his life as 'perfect', recalling with pleasure Rolls Royces, dance lessons, skating lessons, riding lessons from a Polish captain, and above all things, front and centre of his musings on this idyllic time, he remembers his grandmother. She was not only a complete inspiration intellectually, who opened up vast worlds for Francis, but she was a nice and sweet person, he tells me. There was something about her – she just couldn't stand pretence, bullshit or hypocrisy, and she instinctively punctured it when it came her way. When she got excited, her Manchester accent reasserted itself.

He remembers as if it were yesterday the first dinner party he attended at his grandparents' house, to which the great and the good of Shell had been invited. He sat paralysed in front of a bewildering array of cutlery. 'Where should I start?' Fanny leant over and said, 'Darling, in life you must never hesitate.' She had laid out a set of glasses, one of which had a small, secret hole drilled below the rim. One unfortunate guest took a swig of his drink only to find it dribbling down his chin. The next morning Alec remonstrated his wife gently: 'Fan – you shouldn't have done that.'

Lovely Mitzi, Fanny's Austrian pastry cook, had been 'found a husband' – a rather boring man who lived somewhere near Hull. But she still dropped by and created wonderful cakes. She was very talented, making Francis a Tudor court costume for some school event, complete with ruff.

At a prize-giving for the Lycée at the Festival Hall, Francis remembers Fanny in an orange bell hat and green dress. 'I mean she was just a born queen. She had excellent legs and a wonderful bosom, and her face, well, Circassians are the most beautiful women in the world.' She turned the heads of his friends. *'Mon dieu, c'est ta grandmère??'*

Chapter 25

 $\mathcal{B}$ y 1952, Rosemary had two published novels under her belt. The first had put into print her childhood, her strong sense that Mimi had neglected and damaged her, allowing her to live more easily with it. In both novels the author went on the attack against what she perceived to be the emptiness of her own milieu, and both novels featured a heroine, closely modelled on herself, engaged in a desperate search for something. The heroine has a fierce need to become a whole person, but instead of looking within herself she places her longing for salvation squarely on the shoulders of a single man. The course of her own life was soon to take a dramatic turn, and she became hopelessly lost in the borderlands between fiction and reality, as she cast herself as the heroine in her own romantic story.

About a year after the publication of *The Nature of the Beast*, when Rosemary had achieved some contentment and sense of fulfilment, mistress of her own 'salon' at Eaton Terrace, her son Alastair made a fateful introduction. He brought home a young artist he had recently met, and introduced him to his mother.

Alastair had met John Berger at a gallery in Regent Street in 1953, several years before he left for Ronda; Berger was exhibiting his paintings, and Alastair, with his usual charm, breezed up to the artist, introduced himself, and invited him back to Eaton Terrace. 'Fresh blood' for his mother. The attraction between Rosemary and John was immediate. Rosemary had shown in her second novel that her romantic hero had to be a man of the people, with physical presence and overwhelming confidence in himself, disapproved of by the Establishment. Suddenly, standing before her in her salon, was this good-looking, young, charismatic, serious-minded, anti-Establishment twenty-eight-year-old. 'He had that enviable capacity to convey total absorption in whatever you were saying. This penetrating focus on you and his carefully pondered response – as if life depended on finding the right word – were devastatingly effective.'

In *The Nature of the Beast* Rosemary's heroine, Pauline, found her charismatic man of the people, Liavrec. Now Pauline's creator had found in John Berger her own version. Entangled in her mind with her heroine, she was absolutely primed to surrender to Berger's personal magnetism. Berger, for his part, confessed later that the well-born rebel – always the aristocrat however extreme the rebellion – was the wellspring of his attraction to Rosemary, who was nineteen years older than he was.

I watch a film clip on YouTube, pausing and going back to it to try and recapture a few moments of what Rosemary experienced. With his broad brow, strong eyebrows and nose, and his powerfully expressive manner, Berger's qualities were the very opposite of the hesitant charm of an upper-class Englishman. He was, if you like that type, as my mother would have said, 'a knock out'. For him, Rosemary was prepared to risk everything – her children, her home and her happiness.

Throughout my childhood it had been hinted that if I did have a grandmother, her anti-Semitism brought her to reject my father. Here was another blow to this theory, for John Berger was himself Jewish.

Alastair was used to his mother's crushes, and to begin with Berger must have appeared to be just another addition to her salon, another adoring swain who was drawn into her orbit. But behind the scenes things were moving fast. Rosemary had decided it was time to turn her longings into reality. She and the young artist were embarking on a passionate affair. It must have felt like a dangerous adventure for Rosemary – a real-life Marxist intellectual! A blow right in the solar plexus of her family, and her husband's tedious circle, and what's more he seemed to be completely in love with her. Now she was really starting to live.

As their affair began, just as Rosemary was lost in the wild border country between fiction and reality, so was John. He committed it all to fiction in his mind, writing about it many years later. In a story called 'The Szum and the Ching', written in 2005, long after Rosemary's death, John writes about her. They gave each other pet names (why am I not surprised to find this out?) – he is 'Met' (or 'Mit') and she is 'Liz'. They are driving to Poland in separate cars.

Do you think you are driving fast enough to get away from me? She asks as she draws up beside me at the first traffic light in Kielce.

I notice she is driving with her shoes kicked off, her bare feet on the pedals.

No question of leaving you behind, I say, straightening my back and putting both feet on the ground.

Then why so fast?

I don't reply, for she knows the answer.

In speed there is forgotten tenderness. She had a way, when driving, of lifting her right hand from the steering wheel so that she could see the dials on the dashboard without having to move her head a centimetre. And this small movement of the hand was as neat and precise as that of a great conductor's before an orchestra. I loved her surety.

When she was alive I called her Liz and she called me Met. She liked the nickname of Liz because during her life up to that moment it would have been inconceivable that she should answer to such a vulgar abbreviation. 'Liz' implied a law had been broken and she adored broken laws.

Met is the name given to a flight navigator in a novel by Saint-Exupéry. Perhaps *Vol de nuit* brought us together? Superficially it was curiosity – almost everything about us, including our ages, was undisguised different. Yet more profoundly, it was an unspoken acknowledgement of the same sadness that brought us together. There was no self-pity. If she had perceived a trace of this in me she would have cauterised it.

Our two styles were *Nuit*. She was much better read than I, but I was street-wiser, and perhaps that is why she named me after a navigator.

The traffic light turns green. I overtake her and she follows. After we've left Kielce behind, I give a sign to announce I'm going to stop. We both pull up along the edge of another forest, darker than the last one. Her car window is already down. The very fine hair by her temple, sweeping back behind her ear, is delicately tangled. Delicately, because to untangle it with my fingers would require delicacy.

Back in the real world, things were not so straightforward. Rosemary committed her feelings to paper in page after page of furious typing. Those pages reveal a mind in turmoil. Her secret affair was constantly on her mind; the relationship very quickly became the central one in her life, but she could not reveal it to anyone, particularly her teenage children. Ali had already left home, and Laura was just about to go off to art school in London, but Juliet was thirteen and Robin eleven. The great step, she writes. Will they like it? After a few years of separation, Gilbert wanted to remarry. He did the honourable thing and went to a hotel in Russell Square with a prostitute.

Every minute she spent with her children was charged with the knowledge that *she must tell them*. It must have made her appear distracted. Days passed, life with the children continued, while Rosemary tried to work up her courage. She watched a film with her two eldest: 'Orlando and Lydia were sitting together at the side of the room. I looked at their fine, unusual profiles in the flickering film light. I was lucky to have them there with me, to have them at all, I thought. I have them, I repeated to myself.' Always I am struck by the way in which she romanticised and idealised her children. Right from the beginning she realised that, at forty-six years old, she was at the centre of a web of duties and relationships, all of which were going to be profoundly affected. She was a postwar woman with responsibilities and did not share the casual ruthlessness of Mimi.

Finally, after pages and pages of agonising, Rosemary tells the children. It is in the open at last. She drops the bombshell that she and their father are getting divorced, Kintbury would be sold, and she is buying a house with this John Berger, not so very much older than them. Here she is, telling Robin (known as Lyon in her diary): 'I closed my eyes and told Lyon. He became very still. Then he wept. When I drew him to me he did not resist.' I have a strong sense, reading her diaries, that it was the *narrative* that preoccupied her. Even as Robin was sobbing at the breakup of the family, she was turning it into a storyline. And Laura? I think she was profoundly upset by her parents' divorce.

Completely unmentioned in her diaries, perhaps because she seemed to Rosemary to add nothing to the narrative, is poor Cynthia, Rosemary's devoted sister, who loved her so much and shared in her lonely adolescence, and called her 'Wag'. Together they were 'The Firm' – wasn't this so solid that nothing would shake it? Cynthia was somewhere in the background while all this was going on. She adored Rosemary throughout her life and was completely bewildered and devastated by her sister's behaviour after she met Berger, and by their growing estrangement. 'With Wag she had shared all the ghastliness,' writes Cynthia's daughter, Meriel, 'and it was Wag that she really loved.' Cynthia came to see Rosemary's postwar life as a sort of 'Cultural Revolution'. 'When it was at its height, all icons of the past were simply smashed. When Rosemary was in her own words "kicking over the traces" of her past, everyone in the carriage was going to get hurt.'

∿

In the twenty-first century my relationship with my Uncle Robin continued to be sporadic but deeply important. We didn't see each other all the time, but I received, and continue to receive, regular updates by email. His long emails are works of art, which never disappoint. He writes fluently, naturally, brilliantly and so funnily that I have never received an email from him that doesn't make me laugh. I am always drawn to this – Charles is also a comic of genius. Robin Jordan Boyd was twenty-two when I was born and walking the streets of Hampstead, just round the corner at any moment, probably seen unknowingly by me, hurried away from by my parents, was this funny, charming, self-deprecating uncle. We swapped emails, updated each other with news, and he listened with avuncular interest, unaffected by all the lost decades, to my tales of family life and the progress of my children. He was supportive and kind, but not interfering.

I looked forward to an email landing in my inbox with keen anticipation. One described a flat owned by one of his sons as having a staircase held together by a line of worms holding each other's hands. My most recent mail from him records that his new dentist peered into his mouth and asked, 'Was your last dentist very old?'

Robin understood everything. He is 'a shrewd observer of the *comédie humaine*'. Rosemary's diaries are steeped in her love of this quality in him, to the point of outrageous favouritism. In her slightly pretentious way, she writes:

Knives dangle at his belt. He wore them unselfconsciously, and not as toys. In the raw cold we tracked the green sandpiper with whipped faces and frozen feet and hands. Lyon was a clown of unstressed genius. Like all clowns, he understood life, he was immensely old and immensely aware of sadness. He was Orwell, Joyce Carey and St Ex. He listened without comment to conversations.

Or this –

Lyon came in. He was an urchin and a vagabond. A good home was not necessary to him. He was tiny and could have led juvenile cockney gangs. Lyon liked to graze on the edge of danger. When there was no danger, he created it, in order to have an edge to graze. Lyon wore his cap at a flash kid angle. He was so golden as to be suspect; but he never gave trouble; only anxiety because of the danger.

Robin dressed in his page's livery
for the Coronation in 1953

And on the front page of the
Evening Standard

~~~

When Gilbert and Rosemary divorced in 1955 they sold both Kintbury, their pretty red brick house on the Kennet Canal, and their London house, 45 Eaton Terrace. Seated in an empty room at Kintbury, Rosemary drank coffee and watched the removal men tramp through, carrying tables and beds like coffins.

Rosemary did not mourn her old life for long. She set about finding a new house, which would be a fresh start, a chance to share her life with John Berger. The one she settled on was a solid stone place, the Dower House, in the village of Newland, near Monmouth, in far, far away Forest of Dean. She immediately gave it a new name, 'The Dark House'. Informally, though, it was often known as 'Saligo', though no one can be completely sure why. There is a suggestion that the name came from the French *saligaud*, meaning 'swine, son of a bitch', or from *salopard*, synonym of *saligaud*, which also means 'rebel fighter'. The family think that the name was a sort of symbolic clenched fist – revenge on her own past, solidarity with John's revolutionary politics, and an expression of herself as a romantic rebel, a most cherished part of her own self-image.

And it was a romantic place that they chose. The Forest of Dean was an ancient landscape, remote and wild, the preserve of primitive woodmen who seemed to grow out of the forest floor. This held great attraction for

The Dark House or Saligo

John, who throughout his life said that 'peasants' were his most important teachers. Rosemary's old life – the semi-sophisticated, respectable, vapid world of English country motherhood with its petty social life of the 'surely you know so and so' variety, its bridge-playing and its flower-arranging, swiftly receded to a distant memory.

Above all, Rosemary's new house was to be a love nest – a hidden place where her future with her new lover and partner could blossom. For Rosemary, love was the thing. During her unnatural and isolated upbringing a yearning for romantic love had taken root deep within her, nurtured by her immersion in literature. She saw it as her escape route, and as the ultimate fulfilment, searched for with the reverence of the quest for the Holy Grail. She was nurtured by Shakespeare; his plays and sonnets were seared deeply into her imagination – 'Love is not love which alters when it alteration finds, or bends with the remover to remove.'

Here she was then with John. Her existence was to be built around this one magnetic twenty-seven-year-old. 'I have never known anyone with so dazzling a presence as Mit',[8] she wrote in her diary, adding: 'Dominating and flamboyant, [he] straddled my life like a Colossus.' Pouring out her feelings in her diary, she is almost breathless with the exquisite delicacy and beauty of her new situation. 'Can I take responsibility for this man's enormous passion, his dependence, his absolute love?' She was forty-six years old, in her prime, and what is age anyway when there is love? Rosemary was a magnetic force too. She was charismatic. Her gently critical eldest son writes in the *Memoir* that if we are to define charisma as 'a favour specially vouchsafed by God, a grace, a talent', he has no hesitation in saying that 'whatever its source, there is no doubt she had it. She spread around her an aura of her own, sometimes glittering invitingly.' She drew people to her with her deep, husky, seductive voice. Two magnets, then, exercising a powerful attraction over each other. Outsiders commented that they seemed very much in love.

---

[8] It is not clear why Rosemary uses the term 'Mit' for John in her diaries rather than 'Met' as in Vol de Nuit.

There were, however, also practical matters demanding Rosemary's attention. She set to work with energy on the house and garden, while John came and went, still busy with his literary and artistic life in London. Her niece, Joanna, had an abiding memory of Rosemary pushing back her hair as she removed dark green paint from the window frames using a blowtorch. Then there was the wider landscape to explore. If she climbed from the potting shed into the loft and looked through the round window with its glass missing, she could see the church spire, hung from the sky, its base hidden by the hill and the house. When she downed tools, she would wander across the countryside, sit down on the drinking trough in the field with the huge, twisted, Spanish chestnuts, and enjoy 'the scoured spacious look of pasture land in high summer'. She might go further, through the Spey Valley to see crossbills, wandering through the emptiness of the forest with pine needles underfoot. One day she heard a high wild crying, 'a stream of sound ascending from the bubble to the sobbing, from the sobbing to the cry of ecstasy'. It was curlews, she reported excitedly in her diary.

In the locality the new, somewhat ill-assorted pair was observed with curiosity. People sensed Rosemary's power of command and John's incipient celebrity. However, Rosemary, determined not to be drawn into a new web of dull social obligations, would open the door a crack if anyone called round unannounced and say 'Yes?' rather forbiddingly. Thus frozen off, they would scuttle away. She did, however, find some kindred spirits, as one always finds in such a place: there was the doctor, whose life John was later to describe in his book *A Fortunate Man*, there were 'the Wogs', grand Communists Wogan and Tamara Phillips, later Lord and Lady Milford, whom Rosemary had known beforehand, and an old colonial servant called Wilson Plant. She enjoyed the company of the chosen few.

Then of course there were the children, always so passionately at the heart of the diaries. They all came to live with Rosemary after the divorce, together with 'nanny', although they were at all stages of their lives, which meant they were not there all the time. Their presence helped her to make the move seem normal. Alastair was twenty-six, with his own life in London, but was a regular visitor, to be seen walking through the house in red Moroccan slippers, with his shoulders hunched. Her beloved Laura was just starting art school. She would come home, steeped in her new world, wearing a scarlet skirt with a guitar slung around her neck. (How strange that my mother is so often described or depicted at this time with a guitar, and yet she never had one, nor played one, to my knowledge.) During the holidays Laura lazed about doing anything she felt like doing, and nothing she did not feel like doing. Wearing a wide, white skirt and with bare feet, she helped her mother pick apples in the orchard.

Juliet was at boarding school, but came home and hung out with her big sister during the holidays. She seems to be the one of the four that received least attention from her mother. Rosemary records in her diary that "Jillie" made the lightest of marks on the house. She gave the impression of being in transit to somewhere else. Adolescence seemed to leave her exceptionally healthy minded.' Rosemary felt that Juliet had the best all-round intelligence of all her children, and that her self-sufficiency meant that she could more or less bring herself up.

Always the apple of her eye, her beloved youngest, Robin, was twelve when she moved, on the cusp of being sent off to Eton. For him, the Forest of Dean opened up a boy's adventurous world of excitement and interest, whether it was going shooting with a group of men from the village, working in the mushroom tunnel and sharing jokes with two locals called Stan and Ernie, or perched on a stool in the entrance to Stan's pub, listening with rapt attention to their reminiscences. Rosemary writes at length in her diaries of the anguish she felt at yanking him from this magical, free and wild existence, putting him in a suit, and taking him to the station to send him off to school. He hated it too; the night before he went, his face would be white and strained, with blue circles around his eyes. There was corresponding joy when the holidays come round. The knives would come out, he would be back in his holiday clothes, and Rosemary could listen to 'the complex of sounds which meant that Lyon was getting up directly over my head'. It seems that his golden charm worked on the locals too; Rosemary found when she went to pay the bill at the pub that Mrs Bream seemed to know that Lyon's arrival was imminent. 'Does he really come Wednesday? I must tell Stan. Oh and Stan's damaged his gun, he'll have to borrow one so that they can go shooting.'

Life at Saligo soon developed its rituals. Rosemary set up a small private sitting room, dubbed the snuggery, to which the children were not invited. She would retire there with John, to read, to write letters, to listen to music. Often the slightly gloomy strains of Carl Nielson, whose music was fashionable at the time, could be heard emanating from within. In the evenings before supper everyone who was in residence would gather in the main sitting room to listen to classical music on her wind-up gramophone with its enormous horn – Bach cello suites or partitas, Mozart piano and violin concertos, and Haydn's concerti grossi. At other times it would be just Laura who came in for music. 'She sat opposite me in the chair that had been green. We never spoke. She read. I changed the records. It was a ritual that had gone on since she was sixteen.' In these descriptions of life at Saligo I discern the genesis of our life in Downshire Hill.

With tiresome people banished, and her children starting to live their own lives, Rosemary was free to enjoy her new relationship. But however grand Rosemary's conception of love, which she saw as the meeting of souls as well as bodies, writing of 'all the extraordinary power charging

Rosemary, Laura and John Berger at Saligo

the idea', Rosemary hints that her excitement was already mixed with some uncomfortable realities. She found John difficult and did not enjoy the way he projected his moods onto her. She realised that John loved the life in Saligo, but he was 'perpetually restless, anxious to be off, to be on the road. And he travelled, not for relaxation, change, pleasure, though these things came into it, but for experience.' For his part, he commented, 'You have no pleasures, no excitements.' 'He wanted us to share everything, but we were temperamentally so different that it was almost impossible.' 'Perhaps the main difference between us was that he throve on movement, whereas I felt myself grow in stillness.' However, Rosemary reassures herself: 'But he knew, all the same, that in some mysterious way, my life was full to the brim and happy. And this was largely because of himself.'

If Rosemary was preoccupied with love, it was definitely not the only thing on John's mind. He did not share Rosemary's reclusive tendencies, her self-sufficiency, or the Circean way she drew her strength from the earth, the landscape, her wild kingdom. He was a man of ideas, passionately exercised by the great questions of his time, well connected with his peers through organisations and editorial positions, and he thrived in an atmosphere of debate. He was a convinced Marxist and his friends were of a like mind. The need for a critique of the destructive power of capitalism held the sort of urgency for them that climate activists might feel today. John brought his Communist friends back to Saligo.

Rosemary is picking apples in the orchard with Laura in bare feet and a wide hat. They spot John approaching. He hails them to announce that Renato Guttoso, the Communist painter, has arrived. 'Coming!' they shout back. In the room with the pink carpet and aubergine-painted doors a solid, stocky Sicilian with a large head and powerful arms and shoulders is seated in the green chair. He smiles as Rosemary and Laura come in – a woman of strong presence and her daughter with her soft, straight, fall of beautiful untidy chestnut hair, wearing a fisherman's smock. They are soon followed by Juliet, who sits by the window, wrapping her arms around her knees. What does he make of his young friend's instant family? He smiles and exclaims how charmed he is in strongly accented English. Rosemary puts on a record, and as a Mozart concerto fills the room John and Renato fall to discussing art and politics. Guttoso's words carry great weight: he had done real fighting when he joined the banned Communist Party and fought for the Partisans. He has been damned by the Italian clergy as a '*pictor diabolicus*' for his famous painting of Jesus on the Cross. He is even a friend of Picasso! Laura has fallen into a listening pose, arms and legs crossed, while John and Renato engage in animated discourse. As they talk, they hear the throaty roar of a motorbike approaching. The sound converts to the engine idling and finally silence. These sounds announce the arrival of Robin, the youngest, who bounds in. While Rosemary and the two girls are very still, Robin is incapable of being so, and sets about a great performance of mimicking the musicians. Renato is delighted with him.

The seasons turn; it is deep winter and a fire burns in the narrow fireplace. Peter Peri has arrived, leaving behind his art studio in Camden Town for a couple of days. He is the oldest person in the room, older than Rosemary. He has an air of a man who has been through much – a slim and intense Hungarian émigré, of Jewish ancestry, but now a Quaker. Peter has lived through dangerous times. A Communist in Berlin, he and his wife got into trouble when she was arrested with propaganda in her handbag. 'Like a film!' exclaims Juliet in her beautiful husky voice. John had met him at the Artists' International Association, whose rallying cry was the glorious 'International Unity of Artists against Imperialist War on the Soviet Union, Fascism and Colonial Oppression'! John treats him with great respect, loving him for his gentleness, while his art is definitely not gentle, but conceived on a grand, modernist and provocative scale.

A project is suggested. They will paint some shutters on the theme of Shakespeare's *The Winter's Tale*. Any visiting artist friend will contribute a panel. Peter de Francia comes one day. A large, unshaven figure, a pupil of Renato's, he is half French, an intellectual in the French sense, who created the *New Left Review*. His painting is very human, full of poignant images of human vulnerability. Laura throws her wooden panel onto the kitchen table and starts to paint with a palette strongly biased towards yellows, while Peter sets himself up next to her. They talk about art together: he is interested in who her tutors are, and what assignments they give her. Later he tells John and Rosemary that she has fresh and natural talent.

Every now and then Wilson Plant pays a call. What a relief his visits are! He is so interesting, a former colonial servant who doesn't believe at all in Communism! He is very sceptical about the (revolting) Soviet regime, and believes, like Pasternak, that 'the Revolution wasn't worth a dime'. He is a dear friend.

Winter in the Dark House is like hibernation, but it passes eventually. John has climbed the high stone garden wall; he is kneeling on the top, trying to loosen one of the flat coping stones, while above his head a buzzard coasts effortlessly. Closer to him the blue tits and greenfinches flit about and fill the air with their calls. He stops what he is doing and jumps down with alacrity when he finds one of his favourite visitors has arrived. Victor Anant! When John was working as commentator on art for the *New Statesman*, he received a marvellous essay from a writer on the subject of 'An English Christmas', and on the back of the envelope was the return address: 'Left Luggage Office, Paddington Station'. Berger at once jumped on his motorbike and went to meet a gentleman from Bombay. He fitted the bill as a radical. Distrustful of established power, he had been imprisoned by the Raj before escaping to England. These two never stop talking, so the rest of the household tend to drift off to do their own thing – Juliet to her pony, Laura to her painting and Robin to his mysterious adventures. Mr Anant loves coming so much that eventually he decides to move to the Forest of Dean himself.

Whichever exotic visitor was in residence, Rosemary and her charming, self-deprecating, polite, English children gathered around as an admiring, if sceptical, audience to these strange visitors, creatures from another world – trenchantly intellectual Marxist artists, rather self-regarding, who take the floor and hold forth about their politics, about Communism and the inevitable truth of their Marxist interpretation of history. 'The trouble is,' Rosemary might say in a gap in the conversation, 'the rich will always exploit the poor, the strong oppress the weak and the clever manipulate the stupid.' Whichever Marxist was in the room would look at her aghast – she simply did not understand!

The truth is that Rosemary was rather cast down by all this Communism. One day Robin came home from shooting, a bit fed up from failing to bring home a rabbit. Rosemary was in the kitchen and he could sense her low spirits. 'What's the matter?' he asked.

'It's all right, it's not money.'

'I know,' said Lyon. 'It's something else.'

'Just depression.'

'What about?… Are you depressed about me?'

'Oh, no, no, no, Lyon. Of course not.'

'No,' said Lyon. 'One of your friends?'

Rosemary said nothing.

'Russia?'

She said nothing.

'What has gone wrong?'

Rosemary explained a little about Russia.

Lyon meditated.

'It will be all right in a few months' time,' he said. After a pause he said, 'He will still like you.'

Then he said, 'You musn't talk about politics.'

They went upstairs, and at the top of the stairs Lyon put his arm round his mother.

'Is he a great friend?'

'Yes.'

'He will be just the same. You mustn't worry.'

Rosemary had thought that she wanted to be an intellectual. She had needed this to put her petty social world in its place, hadn't she? But when she actually came across an intellectual system in the form of John's Communism she did not like what she found. She was appalled when the icy fingers of the Cold War stretched themselves all the way to the Forest of Dean and through the cracks in the doors and windows of her stone house. She did not like either side, seeing one side as decadent, bored and degenerate, and the other as hysterical and slightly mad. She was not really that interested in politics, and she was not really an intellectual. She was intuitive, a poet and a dramatist.

Rosemary was a prey to emotion, anguish, self-deprecation and passion, but the fundamental paradox of her character was that she exercised over all her deep feelings a firm, and sometimes icy, self-control. No one ever heard her swear, shout or scream. And so she did not argue with John's politics. Instead 'she emitted an aura of passive and stubborn immutability; John an air of exasperation at her refusal to accept self-evident truths'. I muse on her character and entwine my own with hers. For I recognise things that we have in common – we are both dramatists, we love the most passionate parts of plays, music, books, we love the company of the chosen few but are impatient with the day-to-day trivialities of English social existence, we cast people as either for us or against us, we can be magnetic. But I do not share this icy self-control, and my family have all seen me shout, swear and lose my temper.

After a year and a half at Saligo, Rosemary and John's romance still burned and one day, when the family was in residence and there were no visitors, the following exchange took place.

'We told Lydia we were going to be married. She got up and kissed us both.' (The kiss of a young woman who would in a few short years deny her absolutely.)
'Ah,' she said contemplatively. 'All this marrying…'
'It will have to be you next,' I said.
'Yes,' she said, occupied with her own thoughts, 'Yes.'

Rosemary and John returned to London to be married. The day was 7 May 1955 and the place was Hampstead Registry Office. Is it any surprise? Where else for people trying to escape their background? Despite Rosemary's deliberate break from her past, she couldn't help feeling slightly wounded that her marriage was greeted by absolute silence. She received one letter wishing her well, and that was from Clementine, Winston Churchill's wife.

Rosemary had really made her bed now. After they were married, John settled down to domesticity in Saligo. And there was one important new development in their lives. John decided, with all the opportunity offered by this remote place and the security offered by his marriage, that he wanted to set about writing his first novel. Rosemary already had two novels under her belt, but found herself drawn inexorably into his. Robin's copy is inscribed in Berger's hand: 'For Liz, who worked hard and more patiently than I at it'. The dominance of his enterprise meant that she found it impossible to work on her own ideas, noting in her diary a few self-critical asides about some 'sob stuff' she was trying to write, which all came to nothing. The children came and went. Rosemary noticed the first signs of adolescence in Robin – a slight thickening of the features. She thought the girls were behaving like useless lumps, and observed Alastair's forays into love with scepticism.

Berger's novel, which he called *A Painter of Our Time,* amounted in fact to the exploration of a personal crisis. He had only recently abandoned his own career as a painter. He was struggling with a sense of the futility of applying paint to canvas when Communism was in the midst of upheaval, when everything was distorted by the prism of the Cold War, and when the very real terror of nuclear war hung over all of humanity. 'The greatest violinist in the world cannot be justified in playing his violin on the banks of the river in which a drowning man is shouting for help.'

The political backdrop to the novel was the unfolding situation in Hungary, which had become the People's Republic in 1949, an authoritarian state on Soviet lines, and very much under Russian influence. Developments in Hungary were conveyed urgently to Berger through his friendship with Peter Peri. After Stalin's death in March 1953 there was a moderate liberalisation in Communist Hungary under the reformist Prime Minster Imre Nagy, although the ultra hardline Stalinist Rakosi was still General Secretary of the Party and undermined most of Nagy's reforms. Hungary was being pulled in two directions. The action of the novel begins in 1952 and develops through the middle years of the '50s.

In the novel, the narrator, a lightly disguised version of Berger, also named John, turns up at the London studio of his friend Janos, a Hungarian émigré artist, to find that he has disappeared. It opens like a mystery: the room is eerily still and full of signs of a life suddenly abandoned. The narrator finds amongst the canvases, easels and coffee pots a journal written by his friend. The remainder of the novel takes the form of the missing Janos' diary entries, interspersed with passages of comment from John. John is a sort of alter ego, but you can see the author in both characters.

In the pages of the book that John and Rosemary sweated over, Berger poured out his struggle. Janos cries out over 'the sickening futility of so much contemporary art in the West', yet at the same time rails against complete subservience of art to a political purpose. 'Who wants to live in a Corbusier?' Above all, though, Janos feels that he should be in Hungary, risking his life, joining the struggle, like so many of his friends. Berger reveals his own personal crisis too, through the pages and pages of analysis of the very act of painting, which he had so agonisingly abandoned. Berger found inspiration in the Forest of Dean, which was everywhere around him as he wrote. 'The English landscape is like a garment on a torso that is constantly moving; in fact it is the light that moves, but the effect is like a green shirt worn by a swordsman duelling with an invisible figure in the sky.'

For a satirical view of the English social context of Janos's struggle, the dabblers in art, the collectors and the gallery owners, Berger turned to Rosemary. I think I can see her hand when Janos visits the collection of a certain Gerald Banks:[9]

> A boxer dog ran into the room and then, seeing us, pulled up short and slid on one of the Persian carpets over the parquet. 'Out Tilly. Kitchen! Kitchen! Tilly!' The visit is a disaster; Janos is rude and breaks a priceless vase. Banks is smooth, but then his wife enters. When he saw her, Sir Gerald stopped talking. 'There you are!' she said. It was immediately clear she was angry. It had the metallic ring of polite hostess anger.

It was rather more disturbing for Rosemary, and very much less under her control, to realise that Berger had created for his protagonist Janos an English wife called Diana who was without doubt a version of herself, and even nicknamed Rosie.

---

[9] Modelled on Kenneth Clark, of 'Civilisation' fame – the 1969 BBC television series on the history of Western art, philosophy and culture.

Alastair is keen to point out in the *Memoir* that the fictional Diana is more of a passive handmaiden than the real Rosemary, and cannot be seen as an exact portrait. But Rosemary herself was uncomfortably aware of the parallels, and notes in her diary that every now and then 'a phrase strikes a chill. Too near, I think, too similar'. There are fragments of description, telling little details, which seem to be born of great familiarity: 'Dear Diana. She is loyal, but I can see in her extra upright walk how she unconsciously disapproves.' 'You lie [in bed] like a knight in armour. That is not a woman's way of lying.' 'She betrayed her nervousness only occasionally, and then just by turning over the gloves she carried in her hand.' And Rosemary would have been disturbed to read some of the darker thoughts that Janos expresses about his wife, speaking of 'your cherished cultivation of your own disappointment', and complaining that 'your loyalty weighs me down'.

Towards the end of 1956 matters were coming to a head, both in Hungary and in the snuggery at Saligo where John and Rosemary were struggling over the novel. Earlier in the year, the 20th Congress of the Communist Party of the Soviet Union had completed the dismantling of Stalinism, creating the conditions for the popular uprising that took place in Budapest in October. A new government was installed, under Imre Nagy, who framed the uprising as a legitimate expression of the will of the people, rather than the unforgivable sin of counter revolution. But the new government lasted only eighteen days, after which Soviet tanks rolled in to Budapest and crushed it. Nagy was executed, along with 20,000 others, including large numbers of students and intellectuals.

In Saligo Rosemary had to weather John's personal crisis, which seemed to be reaching breaking point too. In her diary she described him as 'becoming ill' under the stresses. Rosemary's life was shifting from a romantic, arty, lefty scene with a provocative Communist flavour, towards something more real and difficult to cope with. So she took command of the situation, arranging a trip to East Germany to enable her young husband to finish his book and recover his balance. While they were abroad Berger had to decide, in the light of events in Hungary, how to finish his novel. The protagonist, Janos, disappears in the middle of a triumphant exhibition of his work, organised by his long-suffering wife, Diana. It is understood that he has returned to Hungary, finally disgusted by the decadence of life in the West, unable to resist the call to action, and is never heard of again. It is a matter of speculation as to whether he supported the revisionists or the Soviet crackdown. The trip to Germany, with the completion of the novel, was, Rosemary writes in her diary, 'probably the best thing I ever did for [John], or ever shall do'. I think about Mimi and the part she played in William Walton's First Symphony. There are certainly echoes.

It is hard to know what the children thought of all this. It had been Alastair, after all, who had originally discovered John, and was very close to him in age. Now John was married to their mother, closeted for hours in the snuggery working endlessly on a novel about Communism. It must have been strange for them all, as John was so very different from their conventional, shy, charming and well-bred father. But I suspect their feelings were complicated. Robin told me that John was a sort of Daddy figure for him, and he kept in touch with him throughout his life. And Laura, who loved her father Gilbert so dearly, as an aspiring young artist must have enjoyed the lively art scene that her mother created at Saligo. Was it a coincidence that she went to exactly the same art schools that John had?

Through it all, the vast Forest of Dean, ancient and unchanging, absorbed the passions that swirled around the Dark House. The brightness and coolness of the morning, the emptiness of the forest, the fallen leaves underfoot, the restless flocks of birds moving through the trees – the landscape was always there, offering its long perspective. There were no human passions it had not witnessed at some moment in its history.

Chapter 26

J left school in 1982, gradually leaving my painful teenage years behind me. Life in Downshire Hill continued, and my parents' lifestyle did not change much. Their eccentricities became exaggerated. An already austere food regime became even leaner, our diet consisting mainly of chicken wings. A tide of environmentalism swept over Downshire Hill, and we all became fierce exponents of Bill McKibben's book *The End of Nature*. Merlin became so involved that he developed a career out of it. Personally I felt that I had to bear the brunt of the increasing strangeness of our parents' isolated position in the world. Tara, the golden retriever, had died in my arms when I was nineteen. I can remember very clearly stroking her head as she slipped away, and had my first real understanding of that soul-to-soul thing that is your relationship with your dog.

No. 38A Downshire Hill, now dogless, continued to be home. It still had its ancient washing machine, its French windows leading to the back garden that required a hefty boot to the metal panel at the bottom to open, my bedroom door which slammed in the wind; records were still played on the grand hi-fi cabinet and listened to in reverential silence; the yellow carpet was still there in the sitting room, and the Léger print hung on the wall. In the mid-1980s I was away in Oxford, studying a subject that I felt was not for me and coming home for the holidays to find nothing had changed. Laura still kept the household going, with her daily grind at Queen Mary's Hospital. They did not have much money to spare.

One day, when, having left Oxford, I was working at the Victoria and Albert Museum, I found myself at a gathering. One slim man in his sixties was introduced to me as Seth Cardew, a potter, son of Michael Cardew who was better known. He seemed especially interested in me, and suddenly, quite out of the blue, asked me how my mother was.

'My mother?' I answer, surprised. 'She is well.'

'Does she still play the piano?' he asked.

'Sometimes, I suppose. Yes, sometimes we play duets,' I said.

'And how is Alastair?' Of course I had no idea how Alastair was. I had never met him.

I had moved back home for a few weeks when the lease on a flat in Stoke Newington I was sharing with some friends from Oxford came to an end. So that evening I told my mother of the encounter. She was folding some towels or something, but stopped abruptly and pulled me into the bathroom, shutting the door behind us. 'Don't tell Dad,' she said urgently. 'Of course not,' I said. The conversation seemed to have been shut down before I had begun to ease open the door. 'That's good, then,' she said, and went on folding towels and talked about something else.

Seth Cardew, it turned out, had been my mother's first boyfriend.

Juliet has given me some photographs of my mother and in one of them someone has caught her looking natural. Here is the daughter that Rosemary rhapsodises about: she has a centre parting, shoulder-length hair with a kirby grip (it was always long when I was little), a face of lovely lines, a little smile, beautiful smooth skin and a soft, fashionable stripy collar. Yes, I can see why Seth fell in love with her.

A few months after her mother's move to the Forest of Dean, Laura came home from Chelsea Art School with her first serious boyfriend, Seth Cardew. He had a delightful boyish smile and fitted in to the unusual ménage with ease and humour. In fact he already knew John Berger, who was one of his teachers at Chelsea. Seth was from the sort of background that meant he was not to be put off his Love because of the eccentricity of her family. He himself was the son of Oxbridge graduates who had dropped out to search for a simple life. His father, Michael, had apprenticed himself to the famous potter Bernard Leach and then set up his own pottery. Seth and his two brothers were raised in an attic room above the pottery, a life of wet clay, pottery wheels and clay dust, a life where everything happened in one room. When Seth was born, his father wrote to his mentor: 'He is a very nice little boy with good hands and long potters' fingers.'

It did not take long for Seth to become a regular visitor at Saligo. He was undoubtedly a lovely boy, with arcadian good looks, who wandered around the house in bare feet and sported rings on his fingers. With effortless ease he managed to charm Laura's mother, not at all intimidated by her formidable manner, and became a central part of the arty scene. Rosemary herself, with her love of romance, found him to be delightful – he was so modest, kind, unassuming, gentle and thoughtful. She drew him in to her garden of Eden; mother and daughter in love at the same time – what could be more romantic? Rosemary pours out this feeling in her diaries; Seth was given his own fanciful name, a sure sign of acceptance. And what could be more perfect for Seth than an Arthurian knight? She called him Gawain.

'Their early love was bound up with my own.' Rosemary writes that Laura gave up her jeans and took to flowing skirts, with a velvet band in her hair. She describes her, together with Seth: 'From the window I could look down into the paved garden and see them together. Their clothes, their attitudes, their movements, their youth gave them a classical look.' By 1955, Laura and Seth had become a 'constant'. They came to Saligo for weekends and for holidays. Rosemary speaks of summer mornings, Seth brushing Laura's hair in the paved garden, 'Lydia' in green jeans turning Candy loose in the field, 'Gawain' carrying the bridle. 'There was always something poignant in their extreme youth, their rose garden dream of happiness.'

During term times Laura and Seth disappeared into their London lives. Laura shared a flat with some friends. Seth moved on to study sculpture at Camberwell. I imagine cool London, riding around safe streets on a Vespa, classes, earnest discussions about art, parties, old-fashioned chivalry on the part of the men, girls being girls.

The rose garden dream of happiness seemed eternal. But then two years of careless youth, of timeless young love came to an end very suddenly. One weekend at Saligo, Berger called for Laura and Seth. It was strange that they had not set off already to return to London. Where were they? They had not come in to say goodbye. Rosemary went upstairs to Laura's room and found her in floods of tears; her back was turned and she was sobbing, her shoulders shaking. Seth was putting her coat gently around her shoulders, buttoning it up, and setting the collar in place. He had been ordered to the Far East on National Service. Rosemary pinpoints the moment in her diary, she and John exchanging a look as they confronted this sad scene: 'Through my spectacles, I saw [John's] eyes immensely magnified, immensely blue. I could read his thoughts. It was all part of this insensate capitalist idiocy of national service.' Berger was present at this great upheaval in Laura's life, but she never mentioned him once, however many times his book came off our shelves. Laura's Love was leaving her for what seemed like an eternity, and she was heartbroken.

Life at Saligo went on with its strange rituals and seasonal rhythms, a duller place for Laura without Seth. Then finally, nearly two years later, the moment came when Seth returned, more experienced after his time in Singapore, Malaysia and Sri Lanka. Almost the first thing he did was to head for the Forest of Dean, for during all that time he had not forgotten his Laura. He arrived at Saligo laden with presents, eager to see his beloved. But when he got there he found only Rosemary. Laura was nowhere to be seen, and he found that she had, in fact, stood him up. Rosemary wrote in her diary that Laura's behaviour to him was 'farouche, graceless, almost adolescent'. And there was a sense in which Rosemary felt that by ditching

Seth, Laura was also rejecting Rosemary's own personal idyll, which had been so bound up with her daughter's romance.

There must have been a better way to do it, but I know my mother, and I know that she ran from any sort of confrontation. She preferred avoidance, hunkering down, soldiering on, stubborn determination to live for the present. When she thought of what she had to do when Seth came home she must have screwed her eyes tight shut and hoped that it would all go away. That was the Laura way. For by the time he came home, she had met a different sort of man altogether. She had met Tony. And Tony was the opposite of Seth. In her diaries Rosemary describes Seth as sincere, competent, unaggressive, quiet, appreciative. I think we can safely say that Tony was oblique, panicky in the face of practical matters, aggressive, noisy and took no notice of other people. Seth went on to marry Jutta Zemke, one of the life models at Camberwell, and have three children, to work as a model-maker at Shepperton Studios, and then to run his father's pottery in Cornwall. But perhaps he always had a tug of sadness when he thought of Laura, and of what might have been if he had not been called away at such a moment.

And so Seth fell out of Laura's life, until I met him at that party at the V&A in 1989. He must have been overseeing the transference of his father's papers to the museum's archive. In the meantime, however, he had remained friends with Robin, and in 2003, prompted by Robin's news that he had met and was getting to know me, Seth wrote him a letter, a copy of which Robin then sent on to me. Here it is. (Seth uses the family name 'Tiger' when writing to Robin.)

Dear Ti,

Thank you very much for the email, which I got the machine to print out and have it with all your letters from previous dates. This is because it dwells with affectionate regard on your meeting with Fanny.

When I met her in 1989 and was enquiring of her whether Laura still painted, and Fanny replied that although the painting had hardly occupied any time, in fact almost none, during the years of family life, that recently to that date, Laura had taken it up again. I was glad to hear that, because, as an art appreciator, there was in Laura an extremely wide window of awareness of whatever came into view.

One of my major concerns is, Ti, that some of those, if possible all – paintings should be reverently preserved. Now you might feel that it is just my personal devotion to your dear sister, and this cannot be discounted I know; but when I used to look at Laura's paintings, even drawings, each one, or each line conveyed more about the landscape or object or person that her work was describing than you could ever appreciate from looking directly at the view, object or person with you own eyes. Do you understand what I mean?

There was a landscape painted from a place between Newland and Gloucester, and another one that Raffaelle christened 'La Récolte de Mele'. There were also numerous sketchbooks filled with drawings in and around the dower house – Wang the Cat and Suchie and Louisa Titheridge (Nanny) washing up or sewing. What I want to convey to you is that these traces of Laura's awareness were (to my thinking) so penetrating and deep that they amount to statements of things and people as they truly are.

If I can explain – someone is sitting for a head and his name is Tom (say) and a group of people are making models of Tom's head. They all see him differently but they all claim that they want to make Tom as he is. Tom as he is can be measured and copied and there is a reasonable chance that the heads will look alike, however, there is an extension of Tom that lasts from the time he was conceived to the present moment and on through widely divergent choices of action until the day he addresses himself back to the earth. This would be called the unseen part of Tom, and this dear Tiger, is what Laura's awareness was able to convey in her work.

I tell you on my honour, it was a very rare and important gift that we were all privileged to receive on viewing and re-viewing her work.

It nourished us all on a very deep level. So, as an interested person, I wonder if I can ask a favour; that you ask Fanny to try and gather all the work and preserve it somewhere safe – and if it seems right – there could be an exhibition, but only in a gallery that conducts business with a proper respect... (a rare thing!) for these amazing traces of artistic integrity. Got to stop. Bobbi sends love to you both.

Lots of love Seth.

Chapter 27

No. 38A Downshire Hill continued to be home for me during my twenties. After Oxford I moved to a shared house with friends in Stoke Newington, which my mother referred to as 'that place in Hackney'. I became a young twenty-something with a job in London. I moved back into 38A Downshire Hill when the flat-share dissolved and everyone moved on to other things. The world of Downshire Hill was coming to an end. Laura and Tony were trying to work out how to fund their old age, and Laura had a yearning to return to the countryside.

Laura's childhood had begun in London, when her parents set up home in Cornwall Terrace, Regent's Park, and then, as money was tight, 'some pokier place behind Harrods' in Walton Street, in those days not much of an address. It seems astonishing that Rosemary and Gilbert's life should have been 'pinched', considering the stratospheric wealth of her parents, but such was the truth of the matter. Rosemary only had a 'girl's portion' of the money, which was by all accounts comparatively small – her brother Ivor inherited the wealth. Holidays were spent with Mimi at Ashby or at Drumore, a shooting lodge in Perthshire. In Scotland, Rosemary behaved just like a person of her class, and shot partridges and grouse. She also rode very well, side-saddle, top-hatted and veiled. But at some stage, although retaining a London address, family life moved to the countryside – first to Knebworth, and then to Kintbury. I knew instinctively that country life was deeply a part of my mother and it was in the countryside that she was happiest. Here she could wander about, dig in the garden, plan little improvements, sketch and paint, be in her home which was the place she loved to be. And half listen to Tony endlessly talking.

For these reasons, the plan was conceived to sell 38A Downshire Hill and move out of London. My brother tried to come up with a scheme to allow them to stay, but they were very stubborn and insisted that a move was the best way. We three almost couldn't bear it, and certainly with house prices in Downshire Hill reaching into the several millions we have cause to regret it now. I moved out again after a short spell living at home, and moved to South London, and my parents began to prepare the house to sell it.

From that point onwards, the dear old house began to lose its character. First they threw out the aged washing machine, then they replaced the boiler and installed central heating, and finally they re-carpeted *the entire house* with the same beige carpet, including stairs, corridors and all the rooms. The sitting room no longer had its yellow carpet, and the staircase turned from orange to beige. They fixed the door that you had to kick open to get into the garden, replaced the faulty latch that made my bedroom door bang in the wind, and repainted the hallway. They created a sort of fantasy of what an ordinary, suburban person might want their house to look like.

Chapter 28

Although Rosemary's relationship with John had its difficulties, hitherto 'this old bear' had been 'loving and faithful'. But after John had completed his novel, and they headed towards the second anniversary of their marriage in May 1957, there is a sudden change of tone in her diary.

Now suddenly the journal breaks off for an extraordinary poem with an endlessly repeated refrain for nearly four pages, conjuring up all of her familiar spiritual resources. Although she had declared herself an atheist, God was never far away in times of stress.

> *Here is the sun*
> *I must keep faith*
> *Croak of a thrush*
> *I must keep faith*
> *Hoarse blue tit*
> *I must keep faith*
>
> *My shrivelling heart*
> *Keep faith*
> *My knocking blood*
> *Keep faith*
> *My sinews don't despair*
> *Food build me*
> *To keep faith*
> *Sleep, mend me*
> *To keep faith*
> *Death, spare me*
> *To keep faith*

Follow me, fear
I will keep faith
Leap at me, panic
I will keep faith
Threaten me, old God
I will keep faith
Wound me, darling
I will keep faith
I will keep faith
With your broken word
I will keep faith
Keep faith keep faith
For both of us

After the trip Rosemary had organised to the GDR to help John to complete his novel, he did not spend most of his time in the cosy snuggery at Saligo. In fact, he was absent more and more often; Rosemary was fairly sure that he was being unfaithful. This outburst of anguish was prompted by one of his prolonged absences. Alastair in the *Memoir* writes that we feel instinctively that we should not overhear it.

From this point onward, their marriage seemed to enter a period of semi-permanent crisis. John disappeared again to some Communist Party gathering. Then came a telegram. Then silence. Then at last a phone call. The thin thread of his voice over a wire stretched from Central Europe to the Welsh border. She speaks of her body being able to move again, fit into chairs, move with speed and grace. Then came letters, not wholly reassuring.

Berger must have been away for a considerable time. When he returns, everything is different. He goes to the pub twice a day. They no longer sit about together but always have to be doing something. They read, they translate; they never have conversations which could not be listened to by anyone else. Poor Rosemary; her fiction began to crash painfully into reality.

The next section of the diaries reveals Rosemary grappling with every aspect of her marriage. She speaks of the way John filled her life so that there was no room for anything else; she speaks of his dazzling presence, which made everything seem hopeful; when he left the room he left 'a corresponding darkness behind him'. 'Without him I was never confident.' She has a sense of unreality – am I really married to this man? Were we once in love? Did we live an idyll? Rosemary had invested too much of herself in this *one*, as it turned out, unreliable, man. Just like her fictional heroine, Pauline.

She returns to the thoughts she had when she married him – 'Can I take responsibility for this man's enormous passion, his dependence, his absolute love?' But in these sober moments she is thinking that she should have asked herself, 'Am I prepared to accept his infidelities, his neglect, his casualness, his denial of this very moment?' She speaks of his lack of imagination about her, and her lack of acceptance of him. She asks herself whether, if she broadened her understanding, her acceptance, she would not feel so superfluous, so expendable. Through all of this, she still believes that they love. They try in a fog, but are not honest with each other.

Amidst the painful descriptions of this time, there is a defiant flash of aristocratic Rosemary. She and John take a trip to see Renato Guttoso in Italy, along with the actor John Humphrey, a friend of Alastair's and loyal friend to Rosemary. She observes Renato Guttoso and his wife closely, trying to find in them some sort of key to rescue her own marriage. She describes Mrs Guttoso as a peculiar, ugly, not very intelligent woman, who had made herself into the handmaid of her artist husband, 'going forward on her small fat feet in the direction of her husband's life'. She tries to understand what makes this woman stay, whatever the treatment she receives from her husband Renato. Does she not wish that she could have him all to herself and that the charm he spilt over others could every now and then be poured out just for her? Rosemary was given the answer that Renato's wife was patient, and accepting. John Humphrey writes that it was clear that Rosemary was miserable.

Rosemary describes herself and John fumbling back together, revealing in her diary that this was a painful process, and that only in his arms was she free of the pain. 'My love hurt to the point of purity, the thin fine point of purity where it almost reached pleasure. I let go of everything else, he filled every cubic foot of my consciousness. Towards others I felt only half real.' This is almost an exact quote from her description of her fictional heroine Pauline.

But on the next page things have descended into violence. They lash out at each other. Poor Rosemary – her self-control had deserted her, which must have been an extremely painful experience for her. The two magnets, who had attracted each other with such force, had switched polarity. 'My first shot hit him where his eye was still yellow from the blow I gave him last week.' They quarrelled frequently, and she speaks of his eyes being hard with hatred; 'sometimes I thought he would like to kill me. At least once, I would have killed him if I had had a knife and could have got it near his throat.' And then, just as I thought I could take no more of this painful stuff, she says quite simply: 'After five months of *sturm und drang*, I realised, quite suddenly one morning, like any other morning, that Mit had no more romantic love for me.'

During this period, the family, usually so much at the forefront of her thoughts and the diaries, recedes to a shadowy place. Alastair was laying plans to emigrate to Andalucia, and in the winter of 1957 off he went. Her beloved 'Lyon', after years of shared suffering 'on bitter railway platforms, on dreary piers, in tea shops, dentists' waiting rooms, cinemas, streets', became 'arrogantly adolescent, refusing the memory which we tacitly shared'. He no longer needed her. 'Under the chill in my voice…' she writes, 'I was stricken, appalled.'

It had never been like this between us. They all turned and walked way. Lyon was walking out of my life. The spray turned in my gloved hand. Sons are like lovers; they leave you, Lyon of the wood and the water, of the kingfisher, of the caged bird in the shop, would never come back.

I have a memory of my mum standing outside Downshire Hill, her arms folded and tears streaming down her face, when I left home for good.

Meanwhile, a couple of terse references in her diary foreshadow a world of trouble. 'Lydia took a lover' ... 'Gawaine is gone, Lydia loves a stranger'. It would have been reasonable to assume, Laura must have thought, that when she brought her striking new boyfriend, Tony, back home to Saligo, this might have been a recipe for success. Surely this young, intense, Marxist Jewish intellectual would fit right in? For Laura had brought home a man who was inescapably a version of her mother's young husband. I wonder if Rosemary thought this was her influence, or rivalry, or revenge? Was Laura expecting her mother's approval, or trying to demonstrate that two can play at this game?

However, Tony's few visits to the Forest of Dean during the course of 1958 were in fact disastrous. I suspect that he was rather intimidated by the authentic revolutionary scene he found there. Berger and his friends were very high profile in the international Communist world; they were energetic, influential people engaged in a struggle they felt had overwhelming urgency. Perhaps they represented what Tony would have liked to be, but he was not confident enough to embrace, too awkward, too trapped within his own head and beset by insecurities. There is nothing worse than being introduced to a group of people who are supposed to be exactly up your street.

There was another problem. Rosemary was not welcoming to Tony. Her diaries reveal that the admiration of young men, mixing gentle flirtation and homage, was essential to her, and that they in their turn often adored her. Laura's previous boyfriend, Seth, had been all that she had could have wished. But this new rather chippy, unapproachable and ferociously intelligent boyfriend of her daughter's was not going to play her game. Perhaps Laura needed him to stand up to her mother, in a way that Seth had not done, and fully develop her own identity. She felt that her mother had taken over Seth. Rosemary, passionately interested in the young, and isolated from her own peers, was unable to stop herself becoming over-involved in the lives of her children. Tony was absolutely crushing about her literature and her somewhat fey philosophising. He was the true model of an Osborne angry young man, and Rosemary made him angry. In the immortal words of Jimmy Porter, 'I took one look at Mummy and the Age of Chivalry was dead'.

When Laura brought the new boyfriend to Saligo for a visit Rosemary would sulk, Tony would fume, and Laura, caught in the middle, would cry. For all her rebellion, her Marxist husband, her lack of snobbery, Rosemary was still the daughter of a viscount and she could be pretty imperious when you first met her. Once she had taken to someone, of course, this barrier dissolved completely, and she became the engaging, charismatic friend who was loved and admired so fervently. With her deeply beloved eldest daughter's new man this happy development never took place. Tony took deep offence at the way she behaved towards him.

The truth was that Rosemary and my father had more in common than might have appeared on the surface. Both were caught up in their own interior lives, each of them with a strong sense of their own personal narratives; both had a vulnerability about them and were very sensitive to slight. Tony was too immature to discern Rosemary's vulnerability, incapable of seeing that what she needed was in fact kindness and tolerance.

During this painful period from the middle of 1957 to the end of 1958, Rosemary writes in her diary of the uncomfortable sensation of reading the fictional version of herself in *A Painter of Our Time*, as it received its finishing touches and headed towards publication. To me, the language used to describe the feelings of the protagonist Janos towards his wife seems very strong, and strikes a nasty note.

During the last few days I have quarrelled with Diana on every possible occasion. The whole place is heavy with disappointment – like gas from a leaking pipe.

We quarrel about coffee pots or politics. But that is only because we cannot quarrel about what separates us.

You accuse me of my politics. No, the Communist in me is our scapegoat. The enemy is the artist, with his inconclusive one-man struggle. And you are right, you being you: he is the enemy. And in this you are in agreement with the Communist leaders you so ignorantly and maliciously libel… Your jealousies. My suspiciousness. My selfish austerity. My discontent. Our disappointment is never completed… My hell of a Rosie.

We have turned each other's qualities sour. But because we know that originally they were qualities, we do not leave each other.

You unhappy dragging bitch. You Rosie I have made.

Further uncomfortable reading for Rosemary can be found at the end of the novel. In a letter Janos, who has run away from Diana, describes himself seated in a café in Vienna. 'Opposite is a Viennese student – very pretty – round her neck she has tied a silly, gay, piece of green chiffon – as she reads the chiffon bow tickles her chin – as I look at her she re-crosses her legs.'

During 1958, Rosemary and John prolonged the agony. 'Let's go back again, I cried in grief', writes Rosemary. He said: 'We can't go back.' 'It was the only time I ever saw him in tears, and they were the last words we ever exchanged as lovers.' She then writes that she

drifted into the most extraordinary state of mind… I knew no peace, no hope, I could concentrate on nothing… I couldn't read the papers or work for more than a few minutes in the garden… I tried to think of something on which I could concentrate my attention, so that I could build a new life away from him… In a sense I was fighting for my life – fighting for the balance and detachment that would give me life.

10 November 1958, and it was all over. They spent a final week together at Saligo. Rosemary charts it all in her diary:

The condemned man is given biscuits, cigarettes, a companion to play chess with on the eve of the killing.

Then their life together came to an end at Victoria Station.

Somewhere in all of us there exists the strength to enable us to walk unsupported, tearless, to the gallows.

Rosemary says to John: 'Goodbye, be happy.' John is in tears. 'Don't wait. Go now.' Rosemary boards her train and then suddenly her beloved Lyon is there. Young face, boy's face, white and strained. 'Lyon… my darling… how did you know?' 'Jillie… your letter – just come – I made a bolt for it.'

How appropriate that on this very day John's book, *A Painter of Our Time*, came out, dedicated 'To Liz, my wife'. Two weeks later the publisher withdrew the book in the midst of a furore. The offending sentence was one in which the narrator hopes that Janos joined the Soviet crackdown rather than the revisionists, a conclusion which went against the prevailing sentiment in Britain, including the Left. Stephen Spender wrote in *The Observer* that the book 'stank of concentration camps' and 'could only have been written by one other person – Joseph Goebbels'. John defended himself, saying that the book had emerged out of contacts with émigré refugees from Fascism, and was astonished at the reaction.

In the pages and pages of print about John Berger, TV personality and man of his times, Rosemary is passed over again and again, not mentioned, written out of the story. The value of her own artistic life is set at nothing. A ripple of Mrs Jordan disturbs the surface of history here – a vibrant, passionate, brave woman: artist, mother and wife dropped so easily from accounts of their own time, buried and forgotten, while the men of the story are given centre stage.

But Rosemary and John's romance was real, their marriage was real, and Rosemary gave it her best shot. Was everyone embarrassed because she was so much older? Were these radical Marxist circles in fact incredibly socially conventional, the opposite of radical? Was it very embarrassing that a darling of the Left was married to an effete aristocrat? Poor Rosemary. The truth is that he was serially unfaithful to her. Was there no one to tell him that his behaviour towards her was brutish?

During this time Rosemary's diaries are preoccupied with herself. There are signs that she was struggling to reassert the gritty part of herself that could cope with anything. 'Thank God, thank God', she writes, 'my courage has returned and stands against the rails of my heart like some old Clipper captain taking his ship round the Horn. What a softening of the brain is love.'

But this is a temporary reassertion of her courage, and soon her agony returns. In many little asides, moments, she reveals that Laura was very kind to her during her breakup. Rosemary describes Laura leaning on the pump and prompting her mother to acknowledge Robin. 'Look, Lyon is waving.' I expect she sighed, got used to it all, kept her feelings to herself, missed her father, and found Rosemary and John terribly embarrassing. After the breakup, however, Rosemary pens a portrait of her beloved Laura looking after her mother 'like a small child' with some 'instinct for rightness'. What happened, I wonder, to that instinct for rightness?

Chapter 29

*I*n the twenty-first century we pay a visit to my Uncle Robin at his flat in London. We have had lunch on the roof terrace, during which the wine flowed.

'You lived in Nutley Terrace?'

'Yes, in 1964 and 1965.'

I consult the A to Z to remind myself where Nutley Terrace is. It is a Hampstead street which almost joins on to the end of Ornan Road where we lived. There is only Belsize Village between them.

'I used to see your mum in Belsize Village. Yes, Katherine Whitehorn lived on the top floor. I think John Berger's second wife found it for us. Then Juliet moved in.'

I feel I have to apologise over and over again. A quick calculation. We were back from Scotland and living in Ornan Road, while he was in Nutley Terrace. He would have been my twenty-two-year-old Uncle.

Later, in 1978, when Gilbert, their father, collapsed, very ill, his second wife telephoned Robin and said no one knew how to get hold of Laura. Robin, then living in Kilburn, volunteered, and came to Downshire Hill to break the news. That was when Laura called within, saying 'Tony, what should I do?' 'K was in a coma for a couple of weeks,' mused Robin, 'but she didn't go and see him.'[10]

Robin goes on, this time picking up the story of Laura and Seth. 'Rosemary was very upset by the way your mother dumped Seth. He went off on National Service and came back with a ring. Laura found trouble in facing up to him. Rosemary reacted against the arrival of the new boyfriend (Tony) as she hadn't quite worked through the previous one.'

There was one more little detail. Robin was friendly with the Parliamentary Secretary of Tony Greenwood, our neighbour in Downshire Hill. This Secretary would pass on gossip about the activities of Robin's sister and her family living at No. 38A. Not for the first time in this adventure, I feel an uneasy sense of being spied upon.

On the mantelpiece was a sculpture I had not noticed before, or perhaps it had not been there on my last visit. It was a stone sculpture, a figure of a girl; a slightly abstracted nude; simple, beautiful.

'That's your mother.'

'Seth?'

'Yes – good, isn't it?'

'Beautiful.'

'There was another one, that used to be in the garden in Saligo. My mother gave it to someone when she moved out so rapidly. I'm very annoyed – he's still got it.'

Robin paced up and down restlessly, plotting about how he might get it back.

'I think you'd better have this one. I'll leave it to you.'

Chapter 30

*I*n early 1997, my parents moved in with me for a few fraught months. I was relieved when they finally found a house in the Teign Valley, about an hour's drive away from us. It was a perfectly acceptable place with a very pretty view over the rolling hills of South Devon. We were glad that they had their country place, their project, but knew we would never feel the same way as we did about 38A Downshire Hill. It was just a house.

However, it was the beginnings of a grandparental home, and Laura got to work in the garden. There was a tree with a swing, a walnut tree, a little conservatory, a well-equipped kitchen, a narrow little sitting room where they put the telly and a posh dining room they scarcely ever used.

As 1998 wore itself out under the shadow of the impending millennium, Laura started feeling ill. She thought it was a virus. I gave her a hug and said it would be better soon. But after Christmas she collapsed and had to go to bed. The doctor came, performed some tests, and left with furrowed brow.

I have a strong memory of sitting at her bedside in hospitals when she went in for further tests. Tony was advancing some theory about what it might be. I looked at him, at Mum and at the doctor, and I so powerfully wanted him to stop. *Just stop thinking you can control this one.* Because you can't. Just be humble. We left the hospital with the news broken to us that she had an enormous and malignant brain tumour and only a few weeks left to live. Dad strode ahead of me out of the hospital, his feet kicking the floor, muttering 'it's all smashed to pieces', suffocated by his own private agony and unable to share it with me.

After Laura came back from hospital we all gathered at the new Devon house. Tony wouldn't tell her what was wrong with her. He wanted to protect her. She kept saying things like, 'I feel as if my personality is changing', and every time she got up one of us would spring up too, ready to catch her. And yet our talks went on entirely as normal, in so far as they could, with Laura's mind wandering so strangely. Every morning I woke up to a physical sensation. It felt like a huge and heavy weight lying on top of me, like a great big stone. I had to roll it off before I could get out of bed. Every day brought an ordinary chat with my mum, but shot through with the knowledge that this would nearly be the last. The lovelier the conversation, the more pain it carried with it. Amongst the four of us the intensity was almost more than we could bear – we chatted cheerfully around her, watched films, laughed in a way that we hadn't done for twenty years, and then, in intervals away from her, we shared moments of terrible desolation. This was not in the script. She was sixty-four, had lived a good life and seemed built for being ninety. Our little world was designed around her. This was a catastrophe that no one had foreseen.

Strange things happened, like people sending funeral flowers to her while she was still living – lilies – while we were trying to enjoy our last moments with her. We had some walks and talks in the garden; I can remember her saying to me 'you're going to be fine'. She was astonishingly brave in the face of pain, which must have been excruciating. When she died, my Dad's cry came from the bedroom. It was animalistic, like a wounded bull. I went upstairs and there she was stretched out on the bed, stiff and weird and no longer Mum. I had never seen a dead body before. I had never felt grief like this before. And then my Dad launched into a rant, a rant that went on for about three hours, mainly about Laura's family. And I felt destroyed and wanted him to stop.

The funeral was coming up, so the family gathered. I stepped inside the house; straight away I took a deep breath, for the house was filled, gloriously and overpoweringly, with the scent of flowers. Roses, perhaps, with sweet peas, honeysuckle, jasmine. It was joyous and delightful. Merlin's wife shared the experience. But nobody else could smell it. And there were no flowers in the house. I had been brought up in a culture of reductive rationalism, which I had been building a gradual resistance to all my life, but this supernatural experience sent it spinning off into the distance. My experience seemed to say that everything was ok, Mum was with us still, and a heavenly scent filled the air.

Chapter 31

*I*n 1958, Rosemary suffered an almost complete emotional collapse after her split and then divorce from Berger, which makes her diaries painful to read. This was an almost exact replica of the fate of her heroine Pauline. Pauline suffers physically, her body becomes heavy, people seem distant, 'always trying to reach her, coming up to the edge and peering', she can't bear to look at herself in the mirror, she loses all curiosity, alone with her 'amputated passion'. Rosemary's descriptions of her own feelings after Berger left were very similar. She must have been difficult for her children to handle. The author had predicted her own anguish, as if once the story was written it became an imperative and removed her own will.

And so Rosemary found herself alone. Her favourite daughter, Laura, was twenty-four and about a year into her love affair with Tony. Rosemary decided she had to get away and delivered us a section of her diary called Rome, Sicily and Ronda.

> You go to Rome. You take the express; you sit in your wagon-lit and look out of the window. Some shadow of yourself staggers along the rocking corridor to the restaurant. You sit, you eat, you drink, you enter into some mad unreal conversation with others at your table. You reel back along the corridor, you close the door of your wagon-lit, you lean your head against the back of the seat, you cry and cry.

She arrives in Rome and it triggers a memory of a time she came with John.

> You remember sitting in a little trattoria near this magical white station, and the words said then. 'Our love is perfect, it is for ever, and it needs a ring.' You look down at your hands and you see the ring, and you realise that the ring meant no more than the words.

She seems to have made contact with some friends in Rome, before realising that they had busy lives and that she had better move on. She chooses Sicily, and heads for Taormina.

> When you married the man you loved you thought you would never again be in a hotel bedroom alone. When you undressed the night before the wedding in the London hotel bedroom, you thought, for the last time – and you remember going down the stairs in your wedding suit, early, early, in the morning, to be married to the man waiting for you below. You kissed and found a taxi to carry you to Hampstead. And there at eight o'clock in the morning, over a table with a big vase of lilac on it, the man by your side told the registrar that he John Peter took you Rosemary as his wedded wife. And in the taxi to the airport you clung to each other, and you were frightened, and you said 'It is for ever, isn't it?' And the answer of course was 'Yes, for ever'.

Self-dramatising and melodramatic as all this is, more like a teenager than a woman of fifty, I think I am getting to know Rosemary well enough; Rosemary the romantic, to know that she really did suffer. Her marriage to John had taken courage. As well as a romantic partnership she saw it as a symbolic rejection of her past. Its collapse, and especially Berger's multiple infidelities, were deeply wounding, undermining her carefully constructed version of herself on every level. Was there only one inescapable conclusion? That the disapprovers were right? That a safe, conventional marriage was the only option for a liveable life for someone like her?

Rosemary finds a place to stay in a mountain village and lives there for five weeks, and establishes a routine for herself which seems to revolve around a man called Pipo – always a man with Rosemary.

> The rain began. It thundered on the roofs below my balcony windows. Supper time. Out with an umbrella and my duffle coat, and down the steep, cobbled alley outside my house, the water poured in

a torrential rivulet. So up through the torrent, shoes soaking, up the dark steps under the archway, up the steps to Manuli's bar, to Pipo waiting for me, to the espresso machine to dry my gloves, my shoes, on the counter. 'Vino, Pipo,' 'Si, Signora'. Drinking the harsh strong Sicilian wine, standing as close as possible to the machine to get a little warmth, while Pipo cooked my supper in the tiny kitchen. 'Why are you alone, Signora?' And the wine gradually dulling the pain. Others coming in, a few jokes in Italian with me, then noisy and animated conversation between themselves in Sicilian. Pipo coming to my table with a gentle query, 'More wine, Signora?'

In the mornings when I came up for *la collazione* Pipo was there alone, and we had long long conversations about politics. Pipo it was who did everything for me – got my Italian paper every day, told the *spazzino* to call at my house, sent the little boys for cigarettes for me, lent me a pot to boil my morning coffee in. And one morning I sat over my *collazione* in tears, alone in the trattoria, and Pipo came and stood near me – nothing more than that. He did not speak or touch me. He was a rare creature.

There is some of Rosemary's spirit here, some courage in the way she involved herself in the life of Sicily, no doubt drawing around herself a circle of Italian men. I notice that none of the women are mentioned. But at the same time there is no escaping the fact that she was lonely, miserable and defeated.

I stayed on, taking the bus down to Taormina twice a week for small necessities, hoping for a cable which didn't come. I wrote the letter in which I stated my ultimatum. There was no answer, then or ever. I had made my home in a man. One man.

There is an echo of Mrs Jordan – a woman alone, heartbroken, in exile,

---

[10] K was a family name for their father, Gilbert.

waiting for letters. But she couldn't stay forever, and one day she took the decision to return home.

One day I struck camp and left. I took the night train to Rome. I paid the rent to the priest, kissed Pipo and Albina goodbye, went to the station with Eugenio, who sat in a profound silence with me on the platform because I had kissed Pipo, and waited for the Rome express to come in. In the morning Rome loomed and I was alone in that white station again. I had a bath in the Diurno, collected my letters from where I knew they would be. 'I am very much in love' wrote the man I had married at eight o'clock on that May morning.

I went to a bar and had two brandies. I met my friends briefly, I dined with another friend. The London train left at two.

The train de luxe pulled us up through Italy. I was picked up in the restaurant car by one man at lunch and another at dinner. My dinner companion took me out into Paris to eat oysters. He sang operatic snatches walking along the boulevards. 'If you lose something or someone,' he said to me, 'there is always something or someone to take its place.'

She says of the last part of her journey:

Of all the lonely moments in my journey, this was perhaps the loneliest. The green station lights of Victoria glimmered through the windows. I got out, hailed a porter, went to the left luggage depot and deposited my typewriter and suitcase, tipped him, and moved off alone with my grip. I walked through hurrying crowds. I felt that no one could see me, I was so ghostly. It will be like this always. I shall go on journeys and come back like this to find no one waiting for me and nothing to go to. Then I went to Lydia's flat.

So! Laura was still there for her mother, continuing to look after her in her moment of distress, her instinct for rightness still intact.

Rosemary goes back to Saligo, and burns everything to remind herself of her life with John: letters, papers, journals.

> Finally when it was all reduced to ashes, I burned the sweater which he always wore and his torn pyjamas, and then indeed he was gone.

When Rosemary returned home her eldest son, Alastair, invited her to Ronda to live with him for as long as she needed to.

> There was London, cramped in the flat with Lydia's flat mate, out of my element, there was a little shopping for the departure, there was the meeting with the man who had been the friend of both of us, and the hour or so in the pub drinking gin and tonic, unable to talk clearly, the hasty meal at Cromwell Road with this same friend. The arrival of Jillie and Lyon to say goodbye. Then the call for the flight. I saw their three faces, strained and cheerful. I waved and tried to smile. They waved and tried to smile.

This was early 1959, the siblings still together, Tony not mentioned, although he had been with Laura for a couple of years; two years before my brother was born. I need to escape from Rosemary's head and look at her from the outside again.

Chapter 32

*I*n the bleak weeks and after Laura's death, Tony stood in my kitchen – tall, bony frame, fine, soft, white hair, seeming to suck in all the energy of the Universe, and said, 'But there is the darkness, you see.'

He couldn't really bear to live in Christow any more. There didn't seem any point without Laura, so he sold the house and moved to Totnes. The house was smallish, but quite handsome with a racing green coloured front door and a strange sunken garden squashed in between houses, which towered above it. A community of seagulls looked noisily down on Tony's life from above.

Tony began to thrive; he joined a bookbinding class and gave us extraordinary bound and misspelt creations designed for the careful writing down of addresses and recipes. He drew groupies around him; strange females from the hinterland of Dartington Hall with flat shoes, dowdy grey bobs. They adored Tony and became his cult followers. Laura would have seen them off, but she was no longer there to control the flow of Communist frumps. He also developed a very close relationship with his builder. For all his Bohemianism, Tony had touchingly exact habits – his socks always perfectly matched, rolled together and posted into a long, hanging sock organisation system with little pigeonholes. He put triple glazing in the windows; his food regimen was austere to the extreme, with more or less zero carbs and sugar. He taught himself to cook, made industrial quantities of extremely garlicky hummus, and discovered quinoa. His enormously powerful brain, with very little stimulation, was turned towards the minute details of his domestic life; here he could exercise absolute control over his whole environment. The countryside bourgeois scene was kept at bay with his persona of distant and professorial eccentricity, with an edge of ferocity that terrified people. A nasty fight developed with his neighbour about a tree. He stalked about, nursing his grief, and built a shrine to Laura, hanging her pictures on every conceivable space.

Faint feelings of nausea came over me when I visited Tony in Totnes. The shoe shop with flat, round-toed, brightly coloured unisex shoes – in what Universe were these considered fashionable, flattering, stylish? Food shops where people didn't feel it necessary to show any degree of efficiency, deference, politeness and looked pityingly at you. An unspoken assumption that everyone should be a hippy.

Tony was bigger than all this, of course, but he really enjoyed it. It didn't matter whether he was speaking to the man in the hi-fi shop, a former schoolfriend from Dartington Hall, or a new neighbour, he would direct his unedited thoughts about Wittgenstein, the state of politics, the meaning of consciousness in their general direction. And they adored, or they tolerated.

He set his house up with a complete set of amenities – a rowing machine, a precision engineered broom, a glistening set of beautifully arranged tools – and began work on a book which had been taking shape in his mind, *The Self Seeker*. He asked for help with it from my husband, and both my brothers, which they gave kindly and patiently, but not from me. The very name shows a man deeply preoccupied with identity. It was a strange sort of blend of science, poetry and history; a touch of Boethius, perhaps, before the worlds of science and art separated. The book embodied his need to explain *everything*, to tame the chaos, and to impose a pattern on the whole Universe. He set out to explain consciousness, seeing it as existing somewhere in the tension between the Way of Truth (your own perceptions) and the Way of Seeming (the scientific reality of the things you are seeing).

He hypothesised a material particle of consciousness, called an *empsoucon* – a particle of the soul, which exists in the space between the two Ways. Tony had sorted the whole thing out in his head, tamed every part of the Universe to bow down to his system. But the trouble was that his choice to live such an isolated life meant there was a complete lack of the things that give great academic thought its authority. There was no interaction with other thinkers or academics, no real sense of a team, little broad human experience. With the power of his mind, and little reference to anything else, he felt he could remove inconvenient complexities and find the key to everything.

More and more I became convinced that the further the workings of his huge brain quested to understand the Universe, the more he was seeking for something that had got lost in himself. The more he sought, with increasing fervour, to declare religion dead, the more I felt that if you scratched the surface, there lay a deeply religious man. He finished the book and self-published it. My sister-in-law, a scientist, frowned and declared it 'more poetry', my friend a philosophy professor declared that it 'didn't quite work as philosophy'. Maybe one day it will turn out to be the truth.

One day I went round to Dad's flat. I was shocked to see him pulling himself around on his hands; he couldn't walk. He had ignored a medical complaint until it floored him. I wanted so much to have a tender moment with him, but he just issued instructions, his voice as clear and dictatorial as ever, and he wouldn't let me help him.

'Yup Fan. Just get that bottle for me could you? Pass it over.'

I was stricken, appalled, close to tears, as he pulled his big, tall frame along the floor with astonishingly strong, sinewy arms, and I mutely did as he asked. He pulled himself into the lavatory and peed into the bottle.

'Good lord, my back,' he said. 'This is really… something… terrible,' he said, dragging himself out and finally settling into a chair. He still wouldn't let me help him.

'Why didn't you tell us about this before?' demanded the doctors. He thought he knew better than the doctors. His mind encompassed the whole Universe, from infinite space to the tiniest nanoparticles – how could mere mortal doctors tell him anything? I was overwhelmed by the poignancy of his illness; everything about him tended to the immortal, his brainpower so awesome that it should be able to *solve* this death thing.

Then he was in and out of hospital, lying on his hospital bed, a performer to the core, while dozens of horribly sick people around him cowered and felt iller. He commanded the staff, nurses, ancillary staff and doctors like they were there to serve him, so he did well in hospital. 'Shit's just shit.' He made friends, he talked, entertained, and said it was a race against time, when we all knew there was nothing that could save him. 'Fan's here,' he said into his phone. 'She's looking absolutely *stunning*!' Oh Dad, sometimes

I remember how I felt when I was a small girl, your warmth, your charm, your certainty – you were just my dad.

And he came back to his house, with a panic button rigged up and a battery of rails and wheelchairs and ramps. He had everything covered off. I rang anxiously to see how he was, only to be told in his most Cambridge drawl, 'I'm fine. Very relaxed. Janice is massaging my feet.' That's all right then, I thought.

He bought a new armchair, very fancy and uncomfortable. His and Laura's taste had gone more *nouveau riche* in their old age. He sat in it, rather enjoying the homage that was at last paid to him, with unquestioning devotion, from far and wide.

'People treat you differently when you're dying,' he said calmly and ruminatively. He didn't show one ounce of fear, and all of his charm came to the fore.

At last, he and I began to talk.

'Fan,' he said, 'You know I've made so many mistakes I feel almost embarrassed about it.' I murmured something reassuring about everyone making mistakes, but all his words were stripped of anything but truth.

As our talks progressed, the surface radicalism began to peel away, and traces of wistfulness about his Jewish roots began to emerge.

'Darling, to think I am the grandson of Rabbi Hyman. Surely I deserve a visit.' Did he mean from any old rabbi? He wanted someone to confess to.

'I should have been more forgiving in my life,' he said, looking closely at me to see my reaction.

'Yes, Dad, we all should.' I thought about that ecstatic praying that ultra Orthodox do, swaying and muttering, joyous connection with the eternal; he would have enjoyed it. What was the Self Seeker but an attempt to connect with the eternal?

I think I reminded him of Laura, and he was pleased to see me. I pushed the wheelchair around Totnes and we visited the cake shop quite a lot; he always had memories of Mitzi, the pastry chef that his parents had brought out of Nazi Germany and who became their cook. He had strange dreams under the influence of medication, including one where he was the captain in charge of a North Korean submarine. 'Trust your Dad!' exclaimed my father-in-law, who actually was a captain in charge of a submarine. But not a North Korean one.

Another day there was a great to do as he wheeled his wheelchair around the room with a fistful of euros, trying to find a place to hide them. 'Ah, Fan, look, I'll put them in here, shall I? You'll remember?' He put them in a copy of one of his books on sculpture – and we all promptly forgot about them.

I spent a whole day with him every week, and my brother flew over from Germany most weeks to spend a couple of days with him. His mind was absolutely sharp, his intellect not one tiny atom diminished throughout his illness. I wheeled him into the Totnes bookshop and he picked books off the shelf, devouring their contents.

I invited everyone to Christmas, including Francis, and Dad stage-managed his departure. It was a piece of theatre. Dad so thin and frail sat in his wheelchair at the end of the table and made a speech. He spoke of his meeting with our mother all those years ago. All this is the result of that one chance encounter, he said wonderingly. He opened his presents feverishly and hugged them to himself, as if to take them with him.

And then just after Christmas 2012 he was rushed to hospital. He removed his breathing mask and started to give me some financial advice (as if! He never had any money). 'Darling. Never let money matters go outside the family.'

'Please Dad, can we not talk about this.'

Then the phone went and it was Big Brother. His face lit up. 'Ant!' he cried and moved to a discussion: 'Never give up – keep going with your work.' I got up, desolate, squeezed his hand, and said goodbye. It was the last time I ever saw him.

I thought it was just a brief hospital visit, but a couple of days later the phone went in Scotland where I was visiting friends to celebrate Hogmanay. It was Merlin. His news was that Dad had really died. I let the phone drop and stood, stricken. I simply could not imagine a Universe without him in it. Later, at the New Year's Eve party, I was very savage to a well-meaning lady who kept coming up to me and rubbing my arm, saying 'You're doing really well'. How did she know if I was doing really well? She didn't know me.

The will was read. Dad had classically over-engineered everything, and left his little legacy in trust for the education of all his grandchildren. None of his own children got a penny, nor had he ever given us any, not even pocket money. My little brother had to give me the news that, as if we lived in a previous era when women had no control over their lives, I was not allowed to access my third of the legacy without it being signed off by both my brothers. The moment was excruciating, and I shook with anger. At the same time a huge and mighty weight of guilt, which I had carried about with me ever since I could remember, seemed to lift. I had had no alternative but to fight him.

∿

There is no escaping this question.

The question of the blueprint.

I happened to catch on television one of the episodes of a four-part documentary made in honour of and concerning the somewhat cultish figure of John Berger in old age. There, sitting in his pleasant conservatory and talking, talking, softly, intently, was the great man. He does a little sketch of a snail, and it is effortless and beautiful.

I had only just learned of my grandmother's marriage to him in the '50s, so what might have been a casual interest took on a keen and fascinating edge.

The really startling thing, as I sit glued to the documentary is that HERE WAS DAD, or something very like.

John Berger is SO like Tony it is almost funny, and not a little disturbing. The family trope that Laura's relations were reactionary, right-wing and anti-Semitic is completely undermined by this truth: here was my grandmother married to a Jewish intellectual terrifyingly like Tony, right down to the shape of his head, the way he sits, and the way he expresses himself.

In the documentary Berger, as an old man, draws a portrait of Tilda Swinton. She sits very still, while he crouches over his paper and does a quick portrait of the actress. While he paints he talks, in a soft, deliberate voice, with long pauses between his words.

'We… who… draw… do so… not only to make something observed… visible to others, but also… to accompany… something invisible… to its incalculable destination…'

He comments on the fact that he and Tilda share a birthday.

'That is something that we share… quite deeply… I think it's as though… in another life… we met, or did something…'

He defines the edge of her face with a sepia wash.

'Not in the sense of reincarnation… we are aware of it in some department that isn't memory… maybe in another life… we have landed together.'

Alastair in the *Memoir* talks of his mother's 'surrender' to Berger's 'personal magnetism'. He goes on to speak of 'a passport to membership of the avant garde, far outvaulting decadent Bloomsbury and all that elitism, introverted, snobbish apology for intellectual life which her parents had toyed with in a languid sort of way'.

'Surrender to his personal magnetism' is of course exactly what Laura did when she met Tony. Here were two charismatic Jewish patriarchs, 'reading from the Book', enjoying the sound of their own voices, veering towards the conceited. Two men with restless minds which ranged across disciplines, who wanted to delve deep under the surface of things. Tony, like Berger, could be immensely charming; he too wanted to take on the established order and promote a controversial line on any question, partly just to provoke debate and fend off boredom; he loved to command an audience, to communicate, to argue.

The documentary follows Berger's move in 1962 to a French village to live amongst peasants. Tony, too, was attracted by the simple life: he had a philosopher's nostalgia for manual tasks, perhaps as a relaxation from all that tortuous thinking. In one YouTube clip John Berger speaks of his interest in Spinoza; and when I hear him talking of dualism, the material and spiritual world, this is so like Tony, who was a dualist to the core. He took to drawing, painting and sculpture, and so often the things he produced were bright, bold abstract pieces, with the same pattern produced on both sides of the page, but with the colours inverted.

The arguments we used to have with him about art! His portentous way of saying certain artists were 'very bad' – as if there was an absolute good and an absolute bad in art, and that it was 'all incredibly simple!' This 'reduce' tendency was probably a product of his undoubtedly extraordinary mathematical brain; he would observe the world from the heights of his exceptional intellect and be amazed by its sluggish movements, its emotional complications. As the rest of us grappled with the moral complexities of life, the small ups and downs, I sometimes think we seemed to him like tiny stick figures who had wandered into a gluey area on the table and were writhing around trying to find their way out. He tried to understand us all, but couldn't really. He was a sort of Doctor Who figure – a Master of the Universe.

I turn back to YouTube and watch a 1983 programme called 'Voices' where Berger sits opposite Susan Sontag for an earnest discussion about 'Storytelling'. Here Berger reminds me of my father with his 'its all incredibly simple' approach pitted against Sontag's deep subject knowledge.

Berger crouches forward, trying so hard to articulate his thoughts about storytelling, narrowing his eyes, looking to one side, frowning, raising his eyebrows, speaking with his hands. It seems to me that it is a little painful watching John Berger. With Susan Sontag you are in authoritative hands: she knows what she is talking about, she illustrates her points with references to the Brontes, to Edgar Allan Poe, to Flaubert, she speaks of her delight in language. With John Berger, he has defined himself as a storyteller, but he is an autodidact, with the slight sense of insecurity that brings. 'A story,' he says, is always a rescuing operation – a shelter 'against that endless terrifying space in which we live.' Oh dear, poor John! Did my grandmother help with or contribute to this fear?

Berger's techniques to counter the sophistication seem kinder and more empathetic than my father's. There is that characteristic narrowing of the eyes and searching so earnestly, as if his life depended on it, for the right word, which is rather endearing in a way. Tony was inclined to stoop to '*ad hominem*'.

Why, I muse, after saturating myself in all the material I could find about Berger, were these duffle-coated Marxists irresistibly attracted by aristocratic women? These two men, John Berger and Tony Hyman, tortured intellectuals, or pseudo-intellectuals, were drawn to the social confidence, resilience, inner resources, charm and easy manner of the upper classes. So, in another generation, was Karl Marx to Jenny von Westphalen, herself a descendant of Scottish nobility. And so, in another way, was working-class boy and composer William Walton to Mimi.[11]

'If I'd known,' Tony said portentously, 'that your mother was connected to *that lot* I wouldn't have touched the whole scene with a bargepole.' Is that really so, Dad? Why then did you edit so carefully the proofs sent for correction by Debretts? Made sure that Laura's chequebooks were signed 'the Hon.'? I'm not convinced.

---

[11] Walton is a slightly different case, for the other three were all Jewish, whereas Walton seems to have been a pronounced anti-Semite. In 1939 Dora Foss wrote: '[Walton] is very anti-Jew au fond. Thinks that they do want war and that they create the "jitters" that the ultra-Left intelligentsia get. He says they have got a German 1924 outlook – completely démodé. He says he can't afford to be rude to the Jews as they are so powerful musically. He says he thinks it's a menace all the German Jewish musicians that are coming in the country and taking work from Christians.'

This question of anti-Semitism in the circles I have been writing about is very hard to unpick. Here is a profoundly shocking statement from Mimi's lover (himself working-class of course), and there is, or was, without doubt a measure of casual anti-Semitism in English haut-bourgeois and upper-class circles, a subtle 'othering', an inflexion of the voice, perhaps, very difficult to distinguish from reactions to class, rather than race or religion. If my dad was on the hunt for anti-Semitism in Laura's family and circle he certainly would have found it, but he wouldn't have found it in Rosemary, as I do feel that she was free from prejudice. Perhaps Mimi, had she met a Jewish artist instead of Walton, would have behaved just the same way, and my mother, had she found a genius who wasn't Jewish, or even had hints of anti-Semitism, would have adopted his views with perfect equanimity.

Chapter 33

*J*n 1959, after her return from Sicily, and with the sale of Saligo, Rosemary knew that she had to pick up the pieces and make a new start. The children rallied round their mother in distress: Laura welcomed her into her flat in London, and Alastair stepped forward with an invitation to his mother to come and live in Ronda for however long she needed to. Laura waved her mother off as she set off for Spain, with that anxious look on her face that I know so well.

Alastair busied himself with preparing for his mother's arrival and found her a place that would suit very well, with a refined lady called Doña Isabel Riquelme, who lived right next to the great bridge in Ronda. It was beautiful, with a fine wall-tiled room, and a private bathroom (which was almost unheard-of in Ronda in those days), and a terrace with views across the spectacular gorge. The family sighed with relief that their mother was settled and the crisis had passed.

Rosemary moved in and gradually began to recover some of her spirit. She exercised her intellect by starting to learn Spanish. As part of her sense of putting a marker in the sand to demonstrate the beginning of her new life, it somehow does not surprise me to learn that she decided on a slight change of name. From now on she would be known as Rose. Alastair, Juliet and Robin all learnt to 'think and speak' of their mother as Rose. 'I found myself will-nilly in the Rose camp', writes Alastair, although he thought that 'Rosemary' suited her better. I am touched by this. It seems to reveal the humanity of all three of them, as it isn't an easy thing suddenly to call your mother by a different name. The extended Guest family refused, and continued to call her Rosemary.

The arrangement with Doña Isabel was only a temporary fix and before long Alastair came up with a more permanent solution. In 1960, he took a 'magical old farmhouse' in the countryside near Ronda, El Duende, rent-free, but with the undertaking to refurbish the long-abandoned owners' quarters. Rose was installed there with a maid and a cook and Alastair kept two horses. When Robin came to visit he was sent off to buy a car, returning in triumph with an MG two-seater sports car in which Rose drove herself and her maid Salvadora, who soon became devoted to her, up the precarious track to Ronda to do the shopping. A satisfactory life was established, thanks to the kindness of her eldest son. Rose's move to El Duende more or less coincided with Ali and Di's move to Mondragon, and the establishment of their language school. Rose became an institution.

Her arrival at the bar was distinctive, and had a degree of ritual in it; first the uneven sounds of her footsteps coming down from the upper floor, then the walk across the patio, always in black trousers, then the Gauloise being lit with a flick lighter, and her adjusting to a comfortable position on the bar stool. Then conversation would start.

Seated on her bar stool, Gauloise in hand, Rose became a Socrates-like figure among the young students at Mondragon. They gathered around her, vying for her attention, as she made them discuss every subject under the sun. Love (*'Hombre*, I have known many men'), Politics, Happiness, Sex, Inhibitions, History, Religion (she shocked her acolytes by declaring herself a committed atheist). The young students who gathered around her found that intellectual and moral doors were opened that they did not know existed. They discovered that there was a great warmth and exhilaration in friendship with her. Conversely her disapproval could be icy: her dissent was expressed through a long, wheezy drawing in of breath through half-closed lips with a hint of a shudder.

During the daytime Rose worked on her Spanish, went riding, visited the magical white villages that clung to the craggy landscape – Zahara, Villaluenga, Montejaque – and bashed away on her typewriter. She was irresistibly attracted to the drama of the bullfight, and loved the excitement as the Goyesca drew nearer. Robin can remember Ernest Hemingway being present at one of them. There was much to help her forget the bitterness that trailed in the wake of the collapse of her marriage to John.

Then in 1960 an event took place that changed everything again. Rosemary took a trip to Seville, which lay about an hour's drive from

Ronda, and made plans to meet Robin there. Laura, also on holiday, with her boyfriend, Tony, arranged to come and stay in Seville for a few days and meet up with her mother and brother. It didn't take Rosemary long to find her way to the dramatic heart of the city. She headed for the Calle Sierpes (the Street of Snakes). This narrow street twists and turns its way through the centre of Seville, lined on both sides with shops where you might buy delicious *yemas*, meringues and candied fruits, or browse in shops selling flamenco dresses, embroidery or fine leatherwork. Here in this crowded street, difficult to negotiate, but so bursting with life, Rose stepped out in front of a motorbike and was knocked down. Because of her deafness she always found it hard to hear things that were coming from behind.

When Robin, Laura and Tony came to join her, finding pandemonium and a jabber of Spanish voices, they reacted with all the concerned dutifulness of young people in the presence of a stricken parent, vying to give the best and soundest advice. Both Robin and Laura's boyfriend immediately voiced their opinion that she *must* go back to England to have her leg seen to. In Franco's Spain in 1960 healthcare was pretty-hit-and miss, and Andalucia was a neglected area of the country. Despite all of their pleading, Rosemary point blank refused their advice. She had nowhere to go *back home to* she said bitterly, and would much rather stay in Spain and take her chances. Before long she was in an operating theatre in Seville; the surgeons smoked as they worked, and they made a shoddy job of her leg. The charming weekend in Seville had been comprehensively ruined. Every time Laura tried to bring Tony together with her family something went wrong. Everyone went their separate ways, feeling cross and resentful.

For Rose, the most hurtful thing about the whole affair was that it led to a terrible rift with Alastair. With typical courage and stubbornness she saw the leg incident as a minor inconvenience. While still in the clinic in Seville she formed a plan, when reasonably mobile again, to come back first to Doña Isabel's and then finally to El Duende, with the devoted Salvadora to look after her. Gradually she had begun to recover her old self there. She did not want to return to England with all its bitter memories. Alastair opposed her plan, believing, with the others, that she should indeed go back for therapy on her leg, and that the Duende plan was madness, given the hazardous and precipitous access in winter, the dodginess of the car, and the lack of a phone. Alastair's view, when expressed, was dynamite. Rosemary accused him of the deadliest sin in her book – betrayal – leading to a huge row. She wrote him a letter from the clinic saying

> I am very sorry indeed that the happy relations of years should have come to grief as they did on Sunday. The bitterness of the hurt you dealt me was responsible for my harshness. I still don't know whether your sudden anxiety to get me back to England is due to your concern for my future, or a desire to be rid of me in Ronda.

Alastair muses, with hindsight, that she was in a state of extreme vulnerability, and reacted in accordance with some bedrock aspects of her character – her sensitivity to slight, her obstinacy and the great importance she attached to loyalty, which in fact meant accepting her viewpoint unreservedly.

As Alastair tells us in the *Memoir*, a compromise was found. A grand friend of Mimi's called Pomposa Escandon de Salamanca had built a few villas in the grounds of her house in Marbella which she called Santa Petronilla, and it was arranged that Rose would have one of these, and Salvadora would go with her. It wasn't the magical El Duende, but it did mean that she could stay in Spain, and continue to hold court as she always had done amongst the students at Mondragon. Her leg never did recover properly, and from then on she had a pronounced limp.

Chapter 34

$\mathcal{I}$ have been getting to know Francis's sister, Micky. She is a curly-haired, loquacious, confident French woman, tough, with a senior position in local government in France. But her English is certainly good enough to communicate, and she has been filling in her side of the story. She has a family of her own and lives in Grenoble, her hometown since childhood. She and Francis don't seem to get on very well, but they are not estranged, and perhaps on some level are fond of each other. Her cheerful chat, combined with a visit to Francis in May 2018, allowed me to build up a closer idea of the family as it headed towards more dangerous waters of recent history.

Francis meets me at Plaza Catalunya and we take the metro, just a couple of stops, to his flat. A slightly awkward cramped lift ride takes us to a pretty top floor apartment, painted a warm ochre yellow, and hung with just a few treasures, opening onto a pretty balcony filled with jasmine and bougainvillea; part of a Moroccan-tiled tabletop leans against the railings. I take a deep breath of warm, scented, Mediterranean air.

He gets into his stride again; he is tall and thin, effortlessly talkative, his voice husky with an educated British accent, the tiniest trace of difficulty pronouncing his 'ths', his hair soft and grey, his large eyes analysing; he speaks with his hands. You can't help but watch, mesmerised, and your job is to listen.

I mean absolutely *gorgeous*… Jeremy Corbyn – the guy is just so wacky… The British are all pirates and whores… It's European, it's Arab, it's whatever you want. It's betwixt and between. Freedom is recent. Let's stop being hypocrites. People think they know – what do they know? The French Ambassador got out of the pool in Jerba and said, 'I'm pleased you're looking after yourself!' I mean it's a non-stop show – jumping out of windows, fucking everyone. The British love to *nanny* everyone. I mean what do I care, if people want to tie each other up, as long as nobody gets hurt – who cares? Dubai? Everyone knows it's the biggest knocking shop in the world.

He shows me a picture of an Italian artist friend, pictured in a long red Berber cloak. 'I mean, speak of personality, the women swooning everywhere; my mother said, "Ah Vito, if only I were ten years younger".'

And, as usual, from the moment he said to me when he first messaged me 'you bear the name of the woman I admired most in the world', Francis' deep admiration for and influence by these two extraordinary women thread through his discourse – our shared grandmother, Fanny, and his mother, my Aunt Margaret.

He kicks off with one of his favourite anecdotes, which I have heard before. Fanny and Alexander would always book into the finest restaurant in France. She would order *fraises des bois* with three different types of cream, whipped, Chantilly and one other. She surveyed this display of creams and said, 'Mix the lot!' My grandfather *adored* her but he didn't

Francis with his beloved grandmother

know how to take it. An American leant over and said, 'Gee is that how you eat strawberries in France?'

Soon we were on to her clothes. He leans forward.

> There was that thing your father had, a shoulder thing, some kind of fox thing you put over your shoulders. There was a Chinese chest (I don't know what your father did to it, it was horribly chipped and knocked about once he got hold of it) containing a huge blanket of silver fox tails all sewed together. She had twenty-eight pairs of Ferragamo shoes, a metallic handbag (*absolutely gorgeous*), a set of cultured pearls for every day and natural pearls for the evening, and a black Persian lamb fur coat.

Then we were on to the tensions. 'Alexander absolutely *adored* his wife, I mean he *adored* her.' But as the children grew up, things got worse. Anthony in particular clashed with his father; the atmosphere was always close to nastiness.

Francis opens his family album and turns the pages. He has been exploring the roots of his father Marcel, in a quest to understand the Berber side. He had paid a visit to the prison where his father was held for six months by the Vichy Government – a narrow damp corridor with little doors leading to prison cells running down its length. 'You know your father was quite something,' a friend of Francis' had said, and added, to someone else: 'You know Francis is very handsome. The older he gets, the more he looks like his father. You're looking more and more like him!'

'I'm *well* aware that I'm like my father!' says Francis forcefully.

Seated on the sofa in Francis' open-plan living space, we pore over his album. Here is a photograph of Marcel's brother, he who during the war, in Tunisia, had thrown the bread pellet onto Margot's table. He wears a flat-topped, straw hat, zoot-suit-style loose trousers and long jacket, with his arms thrown out theatrically; he has the huge and charismatic eyes, such a feature of the family. He was an impresario, says Francis – he launched the career of Claudia Cardinale. '*Speak of characters!*' But he was a disaster in the end.

Francis expands a little on the family history. Marcel's father was a Muslim Tunisian Berber who converted to Catholicism, and then, aged thirty-five, married a sixteen-year-old Sicilian girl who could neither read nor write. Marcel was always ashamed of his mother's illiteracy, and ashamed of his Berber origins, claiming that his father was a Spanish diplomat. Francis is very preoccupied with the Berber blood that runs through his veins:

Berber culture is the bedrock of North African society. Berbers fight with knives, to cut the balls off the Christians. They say if you meet a Berber you don't know whether he's going to make love to you or slit your throat, and he probably doesn't know either. They're temperamental. My father was very temperamental, but my mother said it made him a wonderful lover. My parents were madly in love, and my mother swept all before her.

Francis brings dinner out onto the balcony. We have risotto, followed by delicious little puddings in glass containers, a good bottle of wine, and round off the meal with a little glass of limoncello. I retire to bed but can't sleep for a while. Eventually I get up and walk to the window, pulling back the blind. The window gives out onto the backs of flats, some unpainted brickwork, some concrete, some of those thin, metal shutters you get on the front of shops. Washing hangs from lines strung in awkward vertiginous places, making me wonder how their owners reach them. I look down; it is a long drop.

The next morning I get up late, but am pleased that in the end I did sleep. While Francis makes coffee I wander over to a picture on the wall. I study it closely – a beautiful group of little sketches of theatrical costumes, some pencil drawings of the Seven Deadly Sins, and then some coloured ones – a green flowing dress, simple and long, medieval style. They are by a friend of Francis' – Abd'Elkader Farrah, theatrical costume designer who worked with the Royal Shakespeare Company. The lady in the green dress is Margaret of Anjou in a play directed by Terry Hands in 1977. Other sketches are of Henry VI and Richard III. Francis lifts a framed document from the wall and shows me a poem on the back by W. B. Yeats. Then he flips it over and there is the same poem translated into Italian. It was Pierre de Ronsard's 'Sonnet pour Hélène', a famous poem about unrequited love which Yeats rewrote more than three centuries later. 'That was the third man who loved my mother,' says Francis. Her devoted admirer Gino de Sanctis translated the poem one evening over a glass of wine on the terrace of the palazzo where Margaret was billeted.

*Gino de Sanctis, Italian journalist and
friend of Margaret's in Rome*

Francis runs over the now increasingly familiar story of the postwar period. Margaret and Marcel were in Tunisia and then Grenoble, bringing up their family of three – Francis, Micky and Thierry. Fanny and Alexander were in Richmond, Alec clashing terribly with his son Anthony, and not sharing a bedroom with his wife. Fanny was involved as far as she could be with Margaret's children, and visiting her in Grenoble. I splice in some details Micky has recently told me. She remembers Fanny – Nanou – coming to stay in 1959 when Francis' little brother, Thierry, was born.

We lived in a very small flat and she was staying in a fancy hotel. Nanou and I went to the mountains for a day trip. We took a bus and then a cable car. Nanou was dressed as usual with a beautiful dress and large sun hat. At the top of the mountain was a very chic restaurant where we had lunch. I simply remember I spent a happy day with a kind and caring lady. I was impressed by her beauty and elegance. It was the first time I saw such an impressive woman. Every Christmas Pop and Nanou sent us large parcels full of books, clothes, chocolates and toys because they knew we were broke. I remember the beautiful kilts from the Scotch House, the frilly panties, and the fancy and elegant summer dresses Nanou chose for me.

∿

Fanny's visit to Grenoble to see Margot and her family was only a year before catastrophe. For the first time I learn that she experienced her third major breakdown, but this time she did not recover. She was treated, Francis tells me, with electric shock therapy. In the summer of 1960 Fanny tried to commit suicide, and in 1961 she succeeded. She threw herself in front of a train, and a few months later she died.

How easy it is to type those words 'threw herself under a train'! But this is not an easy thing to learn about my beautiful grandmother, whose portrait had always hung on the wall in Downshire Hill, and of whom I always felt so proud.

I am not sure why, at this particular moment in her life, her mental health went awry so badly again. Perhaps those inescapable things – ageing and hormonal changes – contributed; her lifelong capacity for self-dramatisation; and of course the poorly understood mental health struggles she had had on and off during the course of her life. I cover the distance in my mind between her house and the train station, and try to imagine the moment of decision. A romantic conception of herself as a tragic heroine was perhaps playing out in her mind. Now my cousin Micky tells me, and this knowledge settles sickeningly in my mind, that she was very closely attached to Tolstoy's novel *Anna Karenina*. This must surely have shaped her choice of method. The novel was part of the inner landscape of her mind, and perhaps she almost felt she was playing a part, like an actress, so much so that she just followed it through as though working through a script, her imagination taken over so fully that her life, her children, her grandchildren receded to a distant, half forgotten place. I hover around this knowledge carefully.

I open the book towards the end of the novel. Anna Karenina, like my grandmother, analyses and dissects her fellow passengers, just as Fanny shredded everyone so acidly.

> They talked nonsense, insincerely, only in order that she should hear them. Anna saw distinctly how weary they were of each other. Directing her searchlight upon them, Anna thought she saw their story and all the hidden recesses of their souls. But there was nothing of interest here, and she continued her reflections.

I think of all that I have learnt of my grandmother – an absolute prima donna, with a magnetic presence, strong intellect and a natural but charming superiority to everyone around her. And yes, I can see why she identified with Anna Karenina.

But the aftermath? Alec and his children, Margaret and Anthony, were left reeling, devastated; guilt, terrible recriminations and blame erupted uncontrollably in all three. Whose fault is this horrible thing? Alec's for bullying her? Margaret's for abandoning and worrying her? Anthony for being a 'little Hitler'? Or was it the recent death of her psychiatrist, who had been her rock for years? I do not know what passed through the minds of Alexander or Margaret and Anthony; how many bitter words they replayed to themselves. But I have a strong sense of novelistic determinism, of the ultimate control over her own narrative represented by this final, desperate act.

Chapter 35

*I*n the opening years of the 1960s, a perfect storm had erupted, a storm which changed everything, which left a trail of havoc in its wake. Laura's mother had been following a self-destructive path for some years, but it had all come to a head in 1958 with the collapse of her marriage and her breakdown. Laura was already feeling burdened by the angst of it all. And, moreover, Tony was feeling pretty rejected by Laura's family – initially when he visited Saligo, and then in Seville when Rose rejected his advice, cold-shouldered him, made him feel he was not part of the club. Relations were tempestuous. But the Rose stuff turned out to be just the first squalls. The heavy weather was soon to intensify almost beyond anything that could be borne. Tony's mother's suicide in 1961 inflicted the ultimate rejection – an unimaginably terrible blow. Tony was an emotional man, deeply sensitive, who loved and revered his mother. He stared into an abyss of darkness. Where could he look for something to hold on to? A spar from the wrecked ship to cling to for dear life?

The spar was Laura. His calm, kind, optimistic girlfriend was his future. Tony was reeling, lost and damaged – dark and chaotic emotions threatened from within. But when he was with Laura, a future seemed possible. He set about casting her in the role not just of wife but of mother, too. Yes. Together they could claim a new life. Tony's mind gave birth to an idea – an idea that took an increasingly firm hold. They would make a pact to reject everything that had gone before. They would be free from all the encumbrances from their past that had held them back. This was the 1960s after all – the era of rejection. If both of their mothers were prepared to melt everything down so violently, their own reaction would be equal and opposite. Tony was developing a frame of mind that would give no accommodation.

I am conscious, at this juncture in my narrative, it would be easy to fall into my father's habit of *irritable reaching after fact and reason*. Keats would not approve. Tony himself would search for a complete solution – *we must really get to the bottom of things here*. I must not go down that straight and easy path. I will review again those decisions taken in the aftermath of his mother's suicide, in the hope that the truth will offer itself somewhere in the spaces in between.

Tony took swift action. First, only just waiting for everything connected with his mother's death to be dealt with, not long after the brand shiny new year of 1962 had begun, they got married. Next, Tony arranged for a year's internship at the Technical Institute in Haifa, Israel – a new land full of hope and promise.

Tony and Laura moved to Israel. In a physical embodiment of their resolute turn towards the future and rejection of the past, Laura was already five months pregnant. On the surface, the move looks like a pure escape, but underneath lay something more complicated. My father always said it was quite by chance that he ended up there. But Tony never did *anything* by chance. In truth, Israel hummed with poetic significance for the Zionist Hymans of Slutsk. Rabbi Aaron Hyman had settled in England, but his final destination was Israel. Here he came in the 1930s, and here he was buried, on the steep, sunbaked slopes of the Mount of Olives, overlooking the holy city of Jerusalem. His descendants search restlessly for his grave amongst the many even now. Some of his children trod in his footsteps to Jerusalem – pioneers of the early state of Israel – like Cecil, who rose to be an ambassador. When I myself visited Israel in 2015, I met a marvellous, earthy, liberal, secular woman with a dirty laugh who had been in love with one of Cecil's sons – Johnny – who had fought and died in the war of 1948, killed by Palestinians. He was a hero of that ferocious early struggle for the right of Israel to exist as a refuge for Jewish people from all over the world.

All these years later, Johnny's lover, now married to someone else, became wistful when she began to speak of the way Israel was going – the move to the right, the settlements, the mass immigration of the ultra-Orthodox from Eastern Europe. She emanated something of the spirit of early Israel – the courage, the hope, the sense of being part of a tightly knit band of settlers. Her house in a leafy Jerusalem street felt *so* familiar to me.

It breathed Hampstead, with its shelves of books, its important modern works of art on the wall, its sense of order, and with its highly sophisticated academic (her husband) who gloried in describing the Dead Sea as the Cunt of Israel, glancing across at us to see if we were shocked.

Tony and Laura rented a fresh, white, sunny flat in Haifa. Their baby boy was born in May, under the care of the excellent Israeli health service. Tony, as he sat shirtless on the balcony, while Laura held her new baby in her arms, closed his eyes and turned his face up to the sun. This really was blissful. Somewhere in his soul, when he moved to Israel, he was searching for a sense of belonging. He gave their baby a Jewish middle name – Arie, and planned for this to be his given name.

My father wanted to belong, and yet when it came to it he set about sabotaging his own quest. He and Laura treated their time as if it was a honeymoon that lasted for a whole year – they took holidays in the paradise on earth that was Eilat. Neither of my parents ever gave me a sense that they had visited or marvelled at the wonders of Jerusalem, placed their hands on the Wailing Wall, or walked the shores of the Sea of Galilee, followed in the footsteps of Jesus of Nazareth, or described the wider context of Israel in 1962. Above all, they did not make contact with a single member of my father's family in Jerusalem. Israel was a small country where everyone knew each other – a club where everyone participated in a shared enterprise, so if you were searching for a sense of belonging this would be the place to find it. But something... something was getting in the way. When faced with the actuality of a club of people, and perhaps a hearty pioneering culture that he found philistine and coarse, Tony reacted strongly against it, and withdrew.

Tony's posting, and with it the idyll, came to an end. All of the turmoil seemed poised to return to their lives. But their pact to reject everything that had gone before had survived their year in Israel and was more firmly cemented than ever. Their return journey amounted to a sort of ritual renunciation. A farewell tour. First stop: from Haifa they took a boat to Naples, where they stayed in the Cappuccini Convento in Amalfi, the glorious hotel in a thirteenth-century monastery on the coast. Here, in this idyllic place, with its lemon gardens, its cloisters and its panoramic view, Tony had spent a blissful holiday with his mother a few years earlier. A symbolic replacement of his mother by his wife. Next they made their way up through Italy and into France. Second significant stop: Grenoble. Here Tony left Laura with the baby in the hotel, and paid a visit to his sister and her family. Micky was eight years old when this visit took place, and she remembers it clearly. Even at this tender age she had a strong sense that her uncle did not want them to meet his wife and son.

Tony sunning himself at the Convento Cappucini in Amalfi

When they arrived back on the shores of Britain, after their farewell lap of honour in Europe, they pored over a map and put their fingers on the wilds of the West Coast of Scotland. They headed for the Mull of Kintyre. Another escape? Not quite. Of all the places they could have chosen in the vast, wild landscape of Scotland they chose to settle in the stables of Carradale House, the dwelling of a certain Naomi Mitchison. She was at the heart of a network of aristocrats, scientists and Labour politicians that should have been a perfect and congenial set for Tony to be a part of. She was also, incidentally, a great friend of Richard Crossman, Margaret's wartime boss at the Political Warfare Executive. Once again my father seems to have been in search of a place where he could feel he belonged. But Tony did not embrace this opportunity. Something weird was preventing him from being a part of it all. In spite of his charm, his intelligence and the respect in which he was held, he could not convert this into a happy band of brothers and a support network. Instead, he continued the withdrawn life he and Laura had begun in Haifa. Laura loved Tony and was content with motherhood, happy sketching and looking after her little boy. And here I was born.

Carradale

∿∿

Rose continued her life in Spain for two years after her accident. But things were not quite the same as before. After a while, she started to think about an eventual return to England. In 1962, she took a practical step to bring this about when she bought a flat in Swiss Cottage, right by the station at the top of Avenue Road. And so she came home. She moved into her new place, which was close to Robin and Juliet.

Another new life began for Rose. Another reinvention. She called her new flat 'Panorama', and decided that she would spend the summers at Mondragon, so that she didn't have to abandon the charms of her Spanish life altogether. Everything had been patched up with her essentially kind and easy-going eldest son. Rose began once again to rebuild her life, this time from her base in Swiss Cottage. It was unfortunate that her beloved Laura had gone and married this man whom she found so uncongenial, but there was no escaping the new reality. Laura was now in Israel, soon to have her first baby, and Rose must surely have been looking forward to becoming a grandmother.

Poor Rose, all of her hopes of love had foundered, her pride and sense of herself had been severely shaken. But she gathered herself together and began to embrace the role of friend and mentor to the young. All of those whose lives she touched during this time write nostalgically of their friendship with her. The actor John Humphrey, friend of Alastair, reports being overwhelmed by her and of loving her. Her nephew, Julian Guest, remembers great parties at her flat where she listened to the inane statements of her young guests with amusement and understanding. Her niece, Meriel Boyd, remembers her as fascinating company and young in spirit, and another niece, Mary Talbot, remembers going to the opera with her every two weeks for four or five years and seeing absolutely everything. Rosemary used to croon bits of the opera *Otello* – 'O salce! salce!' – on the way home. Alastair perceived something heroic about her performance during this time. She gave more than she took, and she had moments of terrible loneliness. Everyone was moving on. 'This winter is more solitary than the last, the last winter was more solitary than the one before. It seems only yesterday that there was a life, a life which everyone but me, I suppose, has forgotten. They have gone on to other lives, I alone am left with the ghosts of that time.' But her habitual self-control meant that not a trace of this bitterness was in evidence when she was with others. Only her diary listened.

Rose's loneliness was exacerbated when it gradually became clear to her, after Laura's return to Britain, that she had been renounced by the daughter she felt such a passionate attachment to, and that she would never see her again, or be allowed to meet her grandchildren.

A friend of Juliet's called Caroline Clegg remembers meeting Rose during this period: 'I found the flat very peaceful. It was full of pictures, books and ornaments, and had a curious smell of furniture polish and garlic. Rosemary always made her salads by rubbing crushed garlic round the bowl before she started. She was a very good cook.' Caroline Clegg met her husband Silas at Rosemary's flat, and Silas remembers it too:

> 95 Avenue Road was an oasis of peace. The ceiling was decorated with wallpaper depicting huge butterflies all flying in the same direction. I thought of bombers as I fell asleep. In the sitting room there were pictures and a sculpture. One picture was of a beautiful white cockerel set against a midnight blue background. Am I dreaming when I remember that she told me it was a gift from Chagall himself?

'The sculpture', Silas goes on to say, 'was of a girl playing a guitar. It stood in the window and plainly meant a great deal to Rosemary. She said it was of her eldest daughter, Laura. I remember looking at the sculpture as the afternoon sun set and the gramophone played.' As Rose derived what comfort she could from Seth Cardew's clay sculpture of Laura, with rounded shoulders and bare feet, playing the guitar, we were a mere twenty minutes' walk away, living our lively family life, all of us children quite unaware of the close proximity of our grandmother.

Rose wrote a poem at this time, ruminating on her lost love affair with Berger.

> *You knew him in the darkness*
> *You told him in the darkness*
> *You held him in the darkness*
> *He left you in the darkness.*
> *(You have not forgiven him*
> *For leaving you.)*
> *Oh Lady, walking in Hampstead High Street*
> *Just a little faded*
> *A little used*
> *But respectable*
> *And gallantly mincing, gallantly wearing blue.*

The same friend of Juliet's left her two-year-old daughter with Rose for an hour or so. 'When I came back, they were chatting by the fire and looking at books. They obviously got on extremely well. It is such a shame Rosemary never knew her grandchildren, as she would have been a wonderful grandmother.' Yes, I think, such a terrible shame. My granny.

In 1969, Rose was diagnosed with cancer. Alastair writes that she faced her disease with great courage. The fatal nature of her last illness seems to have wrought a final transformation in her; a new light was shed on everything around her. 'The admirable way she handled her endgame is best summed up for me in the series of half a dozen or so letters she wrote to me in her last year, full of interest in and concern for my affairs.' She was reconciled with her adoring sister, Cynthia, and went on a last holiday to the French Alps with her. Robin describes the last time he saw her.

I realised that the effort of making lunch and talking to me had tired her out and she needed to rest. Feeling guilty I got up to leave. She did not try to delay my departure. She limped up to the front door of the flat and opened it to let me out. I kissed her on both cheeks. 'Goodbye, darling,' she said. 'Take care and don't work too hard.' 'Goodbye, Ma,' I replied. 'See you soon.' I pressed the button to summon the lift and turned to face her. She forced a smile, waved and shut the door. I never saw her again. The noise of the lift momentarily distracted me, but as I descended by myself towards the main entrance of the block I thought – no self-pity; no emotion revealed; great stoicism and extraordinary courage and self-control.

Juliet and Alan saw her through the last stage of all. Where was Laura through all of this? Nowhere to be seen.

I have in front of me two photographs. One is of Laura in Ornan Road holding the flower of a clematis and looking at the camera; she seems a little awkward, as if she has been told to pose in this way, but is kindly going along with it. Next to it I place a photograph of Rosemary – a black-and-white photograph of her in a dark jacket with a white scarf around her neck, her hair parted at the side and slightly longer on one side than the other, just as Alastair describes in the *Memoir*, and with the same expression that she wears as a small girl on the front cover of his book. I put the two of them together again, just as they should be, a mother and daughter who were like sisters.

Laura

Rosemary

Chapter 36

J am still in Barcelona with Francis. With our minds on our shared grandmother, we take a few hours walking around the city. He has some shopping to do – a beautiful enamel necklace and earrings for a friend's wedding, and some coffee from the best coffee house in the city. He treats me to delicious tapas – artichoke hearts, tomato and olive oil bread, sardines. The day is rather humid and my lack of sleep drags my footsteps. Francis, although twenty years older than me, seems never to flag.

He continues to talk, and the story unfolds. Francis was personally devastated by his grandmother's death. He possesses a poem he wrote at the time containing the words 'Something in me has died', and every year on 7 November, the date of her death, Francis would closet himself away.

Alec too was shattered by his wife's suicide. Now retired from Shell, he went on cruises and sought comfort with 'women who were clearly tarts'. He developed diabetes, which he did not look after, and some time in the mid-to-late 1960s he lost a leg. I am starting to understand Tony's obsession with drying between his toes with a hair dryer. Alec converted most of his substantial wealth into an annuity for himself, and did not financially help his son-in-law, Marcel, who had lost his job and pension during the war.

Meanwhile, Margaret's life with Marcel was not always an easy one. They remained passionately in love all their lives, but at the same time Margaret had to tiptoe around his sensibilities. He would often lose his temper and shout, causing her to cry. His shame about his illiterate mother dogged him and one day, when a letter arrived written in capitals, which his mother had commissioned someone to write for her, he threw a terrible shouting fit. Micky felt that her mother chose her husband over the children, and that she, Micky, wasn't allowed a proper childhood. When one of the children had a cough they were told not to cough near Marcel, as he had terrible health anxiety after suffering from TB during the war. Margaret managed her husband by ignoring his overblown posturing and getting on with things in her own way. I get a sense of a marriage that has a distant flavour of my parents' marriage: the way Laura carefully skirted around Tony's problems, and the total devotion to one another (sometimes to the exclusion of the children), feels familiar. Marcel and Margaret's *ménage* was more tempestuous, more Gallic than ours, but still two households, uncannily close in values but completely divided, developed on either side of the Channel.

Margaret included her father Alec in her life, and he used to go and visit Grenoble every June. She had a strong sense of duty and never criticised him in front of the children. She always had a sense of proportion and determination to do what was right. Micky remembers the visits clearly, describing them as 'very surrealistic'. Her grandfather, 'Pop', would stay in an impossibly expensive hotel and invite them to a fancy restaurant. It seems that for them, just like our family across the Channel, money was tight and that their grandparents' wealth was a contrast and a source of bad feeling. She revels in her memory of 'fancy drapes', and of being treated like a princess by her grandfather, trying to impress her. The visits must have been full of tension, as Alec still couldn't accept his son-in-law. 'I understood he was snobbish, greedy, selfish,' Micky had said, 'but I could also understand he felt my father had stolen his daughter. He used to send me presents, little girls' fancy handbags, books, ivory elephants.'

As time went on in the 1960s, Margaret's family spent every summer in Corsica. Pop came to join them one year, in 1967. He offered money to buy the teenage Micky a bathing suit. 'But that's not even the price of one of your cigars,' Micky shot back at him. Gradually, though, tensions between her father and her grandfather were reduced now that Alec was handicapped by the loss of his leg. 'We were the only grandchildren Pop had, and in his own way he was probably thankful to his daughter to allow him to be a grandfather.'

But he was only allowed to be a grandfather to his daughter's children. Alec found that he was barred from seeing his son, and not allowed to meet or get to know his other grandchildren. Tony assigned to him the role of monster, blamed him for his mother's suicide, and hated him.

In the light of all of this, the extraordinary thing is that Tony was surprised, when his father died in 1968, that Alexander's will was biased in favour of Margaret.

As soon as the news of Alec's death reached her Margaret flew to England and went straight to the smaller flat Alec had moved to nearer Chiswick. His nurse had drunk all of the wine and whisky that he had stashed away. Tony joined her there and opened the conversation with the words: 'Margaret, we're going to have to change the will.' Margaret got £20,000 plus £50,000 to buy a house in Grenoble. My father got about a quarter of the amount of money, plus all the furniture and the carpets. Margaret refused her brother's request to change the will, as she felt that it would be wrong to disrespect her father's wishes.

Tony did not put a notice in *The Times*, and there were only twenty people at the funeral on that July day in 1968 at Chiswick Cemetery. Francis remembers choosing a couple of things from his grandfather's possessions – an ivory-handled paperknife, and a gold cigarette holder inscribed to Alexander Hyman from the City of Lviv in honour of the status of his father, Aaron. Francis likes to find something not of value but of significance.

Tony had already 'renounced' Margaret, as we have seen, back in 1963. But the will was the final nail in the coffin, and afterwards brother and sister never spoke again. Tony wrote Margaret completely out of the narrative of his life; he hardly mentioned her to us, and behaved as if she did not exist.

That evening I decide to drink a lot, and Francis and I sit out on the terrace amongst the bougainvillea. Francis folds his arms and half closes his eyes.

Some people just have a stronger sex drive. People have their lives. People get so censorious about this or that. Take my father – women would swoon, and my friend Farid – he needed a woman every second or third day. He couldn't survive without it. Women are much freer, what with the pill, and one man is out to get someone else's wife, but you pay a price for freedom. I mean yes, people get married – but some people are more sexually adventurous than others. Then there are different social mores. The French, the Arabs and the Turks accept much more, sexually. It's part of the cultural code. It's like eating kidneys or offal. The English get so *censorious*. They love to nanny people. It's about what gives you pleasure. That's it. Full stop. You look at some of these old English horses[12] – have they ever had a real lover? All this endless talk about sex is a form of pornography. People go on about women's rights in Tunisia – I mean do they know how Arab women behave? Stop saying that all the past was ghastly! That all of the world was one great misery. People project backwards.

Francis moves on to kidneys, which we bought on the way back to his flat from the fresh and well-presented food market. 'You just cook them with plenty of oil. Absolutely *gorgeous*. We know beer gives you a belly, wine doesn't. I had a medical checkup. "You're in such good form, it's amazing!" my doctor said.' (I think of Tony and his determined preservation of his health; he kept himself lean and fit to the end of his life.)

In Tunis everyone knows who's screwing who. You just learn. Now you walk down the road, and one pats the bum of the other. *La mano morta.* If you invite it, you mustn't complain. What do we have now? Faltering democracies. Globalisation has handed power to big companies. The Brexit vote corresponds to the influx of Poles and Romanians. There are more Romanians than Irish now in England. People abuse their powers and privileges. Look at the Blairs' holidays in Tuscany, Tony Blair with his 450 euro swimming trunks.

'Let's have a drink for my mother, Margaret,' he says. 'Tomorrow is the 28th of May – her birthday.' We raise a glass to toast the aunt that I

---

[12] Some of Francis's vivid narratives don't sound entirely British.

never knew. I look across the table at my extraordinary cousin. Despite the difficulty of getting any words in, I have grown very fond of him. He has kindness and generosity, he is courageous in challenging humbug and stupidity, he doesn't bear grudges, he never allows life to get boring, and he reinvents himself when life throws obstacles in his path. He is a force of nature and he has gone his own way.

Chapter 37

So far, we can understand that Tony and Laura had an extreme reaction to the emotional distress they weathered in the crisis years from 1960 to 1963. Then in 1964 came the strangest move of all. Realising, after six months of life in the wilds of Scotland, that it was not really going to be possible to earn a living out there, they were on the move again. They could have gone *anywhere*. Anywhere in the world.

How about Cheshire, where Tony's patron Basil de Ferranti lived? Or indeed America?

But no, in 1964 they chose to move with their toddler and six-month-old baby to *Hampstead*, slap bang in the middle of every player of significance in the complex drama of both of their families. It was a landscape that was utterly familiar, full of people that they would know and bump into at every turn; bristling with connections. All of the people Tony had so

formally, in his own mind, renounced, were *right on their doorstep*. Rosemary lived in Swiss Cottage, just ten minutes' walk away from the house they chose to buy. Robin and Juliet lived in Nutley Terrace – even closer, just a few minutes' walk. Tony's childhood home in Hollydale Road was fifteen minutes' walk away, the flat where Margaret had brought up Francis after the war was just down the road in Belsize Park Gardens. Margaret had many friends in Hampstead and came there often. Further complications ensued when Francis moved to London from France in 1976, buying a flat in Glenmore Road, just ten minutes' walk from us. He and his mother had picnics on the finger of the Heath that stretched down into South End Green every summer for twenty years. If my parents had searched for a way of torturing themselves, they couldn't have devised a better one. What on earth were they *thinking*?

After the move, Tony's position in relation to their families had if anything hardened still further. It was quite clear in his mind that their decision to cut off all contact with both sides of the family must remain firmly in place. That would *really sort everything out*. With his usual inability to understand the crooked timber of humanity, everyone was to be inserted into a sort of mathematical equation. You feed into the equation 'the complexities of family life', and receive the answer 'Zero Contact'.

But once they were installed in Ornan Road, that was tortuously difficult to achieve. And with their second move, to Downshire Hill, my father chose to place our little family on the main arterial route from the High Street to the Heath, the very street that everyone inevitably walked up and down all the time. How utterly baffling and upsetting for the Boyds that Laura had returned with her babies, settled amongst them, but then let them know in her embarrassed way that she would not see them. But how could she avoid seeing them? Mutual friends found themselves 'cut', including an old Communist friend called George who saw Tony regularly at the Working Men's College and was baffled when Tony pretended he did not know him. Francis, too, found himself 'cut' on the streets of Hampstead, and used to try and avoid Downshire Hill. How anxious must everyday life have been for Laura, keeping her eyes on the ground, changing direction, lurking in porches and letting herself back into the sanctuary of No. 38A with a sigh of relief?

Tony and Laura created a daft, mad farce on the stage of Hampstead. They were on constant alert. Walking up the High Street – isn't that Juliet? Panic… panic… panic… Quick, into this shop until she has gone past. Has she really gone now? Phew, crisis over. On the main stage of Downshire Hill, Robin – a young medical student, fair-haired and primed for laughter – finds himself thirsty and in need of a drink. He thinks to himself Why not? He pushes open the wrought-iron gate, walks down the little red brick path, and lifts the knocker. The door opens and his big sister stands before him. She is contorted with embarrassment, turns round and calls out, 'Tony what shall I do?' Robin looks anxiously and humorously at her. 'Whatever the spirit moves you?' She mutters something under her breath, looks at the floor, and closes the door. Robin turns and walks away down the red brick path with a sigh, his thirst unquenched. Just by South End Green, not far from the first pond on the Heath, a smartly dressed, striking-looking, tall, thin young man with curly hair and bright eyes sits with his mother to partake in a picnic they have just purchased on Hampstead High Street, talking incessantly. Enter Laura and Tony from Keats Grove – a sighting – Margaret with Francis – a quick swerve with eyes down – onto the 24 bus

Laura and Tony were on constant alert, ready to swerve if they spotted someone unpalatable coming towards them

and out of danger. If you go to Swiss Cottage, be careful – for you might happen upon the elegantly trousered figure of Rosemary, with her slightly asymmetric haircut, limping along, on her way to go shopping, or getting on the tube to meet someone at the opera. But now farce has tipped over into tragedy, for at this time Rose had moments of terrible loneliness and missed her eldest daughter. Just out of sight, but so nearby, were three grandchildren whom she was prevented from knowing, and who never knew her. It wouldn't have taken much to change all that, to welcome her into No. 38A Downshire Hill, and for us to know what it was to say the word Granny.

What on *earth* was going on in my father's head? In truth the move to Hampstead was part of the same pattern: a desperate search for a sense of belonging, followed by an instinct to sabotage his own quest. He had had a parade of opportunities to be at the heart of lively groups of people throughout his life. From Dartington through to Cambridge, the Communists, Israel, the Mitchisons, the Boyds, St Anthony's College, Hampstead – and yet he was too shy, awkward and prone to feeling slighted, to be able to make anything of them. Instead he felt that all these networks had in some way rejected him. Instead of deploying ordinary explanations – like friends, colleagues and family members being a bit annoying, or chaotic, imperfect and making mistakes – my father's determinist mind, which craved patterns, systems and explanations, created a malign conspiracy against himself. And although he felt the networks had rejected him, he still needed to feel he was a part of them. So in his mind the only possible truth was that he was an *enfant terrible* whose genius they could not cope with, and they were plotting against him. He needed to be right in amongst them for his paranoia to be stoked on a daily basis, and for it to bloom to its fullest extent. He became addicted to it in a way that seems redolent of self-harm. In some ways it reminds me of those parts of Jerusalem where the Jews traverse the Palestinian areas of the city across the rooftops to avoid any unwelcome encounters.

First in Ornan Road, and then in Downshire Hill, Tony built an invisible wall around us. From his safe haven within it he would create a perfect family, and beyond he saw betrayal and conspiracy everywhere. He became addicted to the literature of conspiracies – the Albigensian heresy, the works of Dan Brown, stories of spies and the British Establishment – Burgess, Philby and Maclean. He strode around the streets of Hampstead, seeing spies everywhere: behind the most innocent people he passed in the street he was sure he could discern the deep state at work. He had an obsession, which ran through all his life and work, that Britain was being run by an anti-scientific conspiracy. 'Even paranoids have their enemies,' he used to say to me, half joking. He overthought everything to a heroic level. And of course he assumed that everyone else thought in exactly the same way as he did.

Ripe matter for his mighty brain, as it constructed these conspiracies, could be found in Laura's family. They were all around him! Whispering in corners, hatching their plots, turning people against himself and Laura. They were aristocrats – part of the Establishment! And they were out to get him. But of course not a single member of Laura's family was remotely capable of acting in this way. The truth was much more prosaic. Laura's mother behaved badly, that is without doubt, but it would not have been the first time in human history that a man found his mother-in-law a bit of a handful. All of her own children found her difficult. Robin tells me he rather liked Tony, and certainly found him entertaining. Juliet was a thoroughly nice and capable young woman who married a very intelligent working-class 'bloke'. No doubt she was robust with Tony, but would have been horrified to think she could have contributed to such a reaction. No, the Boyd siblings were chaotic, took life as it comes, made lots of mistakes, were tolerant of human imperfections, both their own and those of others, with problems of their own and lives to live. They expected to be teased themselves, and certainly would have teased Tony. Unfortunately, Tony, raised by his mother to have an excessively high opinion of himself, took terrible offence when anyone challenged his self-assessment. He could not see that the Boyds meant him no harm, and he felt rejected by them. He would rant that they 'never lifted a finger to help us', but why should they? Laura and Tony had definitely been helped by the family to buy their houses; the other Boyd siblings weren't rich and had to earn their own livings the same as everyone else.

As for his own family, Tony's enmity with his father became worse after his mother's death. He cast Margaret in the role of Alexander's accomplice, and mentally banished her, along with her husband and children. The truth was again less extreme. In fact Margaret simply took a more balanced view of the family tragedy, and a more pragmatic and practical view of the future. Micky remembers one final visit, before the banishment took force. In 1964, when she spent a summer in England, Margaret, Francis and Micky came to see us in Ornan Road. Micky remembers me in 'diapers and white lace tights'. We only had educational toys, and Laura did not utter a single word. '*Had she been told not to speak?*' Micky demanded robustly.

Tony was a man with an exceptional mind, of great warmth and depth, with a rich interior life, who loved his wife and cared desperately about his children. He was a thinker of great complexity and sensitivity, but also highly emotional and, possessing little self-knowledge, he was incapable of adjusting himself to others, or doing any work of self-improvement. He was plagued by fears, responding to the worry and unpredictability of the world by exercising iron control over everything and everyone in his power. He reacted very badly to slight himself, but was capable of inflicting terrible hurt on others. With his height, his imposing presence and his enormous intellect and ferocious temper he could be quite terrifying. All of the peripheral characters in this drama who tentatively wished to reach out to us were absolutely intimidated by him, and Tony used this. People mustn't be allowed to meet each other, for who knows what version of events might emerge? Only then could the dark places be expunged, and his life could be constructed in the light.

Years later, when I moved to the West Country, Laura and Tony sold No. 38A Downshire Hill and came to stay with us for a while. In no time at all Tony had begun striding the leafy lanes of Devon, muttering to himself. He came to the conclusion that a modest, retired Establishment couple who lived nearby were *undoubtedly* spooks. A harmless piece of gardening equipment protruding over the top of their hedge was of course a listening device – it would be *dangerously* naïve to assume otherwise, and best to keep quiet as you went past. He said all this with a humorous glint in his eye – knowing that he was teetering on the brink of absurdity. Perhaps some self-knowledge after all. During the course of a walk in the woods he ran into the mistress of the largest house in the village and came back muttering loudly to himself: 'I said to her – don't pigeonhole me!'

Having cased the joint of our new neighbourhood and warned us of all the dangers, he and my mother finally found themselves a house of their own, about an hour's drive away. Here his conspiracy-finding radar homed in on the local churchgoers – '*Hypocrites*!' he designated them in disgust. He built up the same narrative around Charles' churchgoing. 'But Dad,' I protested, 'There is no organisation more benign, harmless and inclusive than the Church of England.'

'If you say so, dear,' he murmured, clearly unconvinced.

As the years rolled by my father's narrative grew more intense and more entrenched. He fed, nurtured and encouraged the fiction as tenderly as a child until it grew out of all proportion to everything else, like a wicked fairy imposter. Over four decades later, when Laura died, strong and powerful after all those years of care, the narrative overwhelmed him. It was the first thing he reached for on the very evening of her death. His extraordinary rant against Laura's family, many decades on from the events in question, through which I sat mutely listening and feeling increasingly miserable, went on for three hours.

After Laura's death, Tony's absolute control of his fiction started to slip; the moment I went to him with Robin's letter was a seminal moment of its dismantling. He reacted by drawing Robin inside the invisible wall – 'I actually rather liked him,' he began to say. By the time of our long conversations during his last months, I think he was starting his own process of dismantling. Some truths were starting to creep up on him. 'I should have been more forgiving in my life,' he said to me. 'I've made so many mistakes in my life I feel almost embarrassed about it.' 'I am the grandson of Rabbi Hyman, surely I deserve a visit.'

I feel myself drawn towards the straight and easy path of explanation that

I warned myself against. My father was too great, deep and extraordinary a person to be stuffed into some category and given a pill to sort him out. But knowing what I do now of the remarkable qualities possessed by his mother, Fanny, qualities that shine through the admiring talk of my cousin, Francis, and knowing what a close relationship, what a meeting of minds she and Tony had, I cannot be in any doubt that her suicide in 1961 caused him terrible suffering. His state of mind must have set him up for the extremity of the construction he built inside his head. He really despised psychotherapy and psychoanalysis. Any discussion of the subject would set off a rant of some sort. He hated the idea of some 'mediocre do-gooder' telling him what he should think – and indeed it would have taken a remarkable one to take him on.

In those days there was still a lot of shame attached to mental health struggles, and he would not have admitted to having a need for help, accustomed as he was to relying on his mighty intellect to solve every problem. But these days, after the trauma he went through, nobody would blame him or think any less of him for seeking it. I think of all those years I watched him chewing away at the side of his hand and loudly talking to himself. Some professional therapeutic assistance would surely have been beneficial to help him understand that peace was not to be found by rooting out people from his past life, by blaming and demonising others, but rather should have been sought within himself. I wish this could have happened so that he could have been spared the torture he meted out to himself and others, and particularly in his last years that he could have achieved the real greatness that he was capable of, so that we could have better enjoyed all that was brilliant, life enhancing, fun, kind and utterly extraordinary about him. I am glad that he found such peace as he was able to, with Laura.

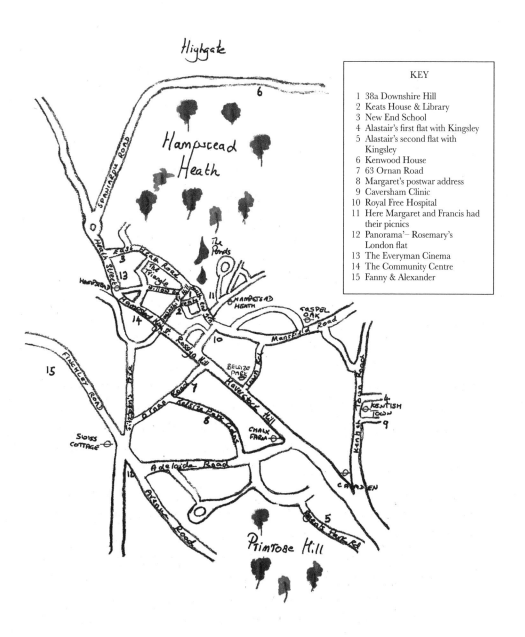

Highgate

Hampstead Heath

The Ponds

Spaniards Road

Heath Street

East Heath Road

The Triangle

Hampstead

Hampstead Heath

Gospel Oak

Mansfield Road

Belsize Park

Haverstock Hill

Finchley Road

Swiss Cottage

Ornan Road

Chalk Farm

Adelaide Road

Primrose Hill

Heath Park Rd

Camden

Kentish Town

Kentish

Avenue Road

Chapter 38

The curious reader who has come so far with me might well ask, 'But what about Laura? Why did she allow it? Couldn't she have found a way of soothing Tony's ruffled feathers?' But Laura was, in fact, a full participant in the project. Tony used to say to me, 'You see it really was Laura and Me, *contra mundum.*' Of course he never explained *why* they had to be *contra mundum*, and I used to feel that I was trying to be a part of the *mundum*, meaning that their stance of being *contra* it was not at all helpful.

One clue to Laura's behaviour can be found in the long line of strong women from whom she was descended. Her ancestry was not a history of settled families but one of dramatic rifts and exclusions, of blood feuds that lasted, in the case of the Boyds against the Darnleys, for centuries. Antisocial behaviour and standoffishness were entirely normal, the main thing being to get what you wanted, regardless of any collateral damage. Laura was a quieter character than Mimi or Rosemary, but she had her own methods. Out of the limelight, without drama, cloaked behind an artlessly chatty exterior, disclosing very little of her private mind, but just as prepared to disregard the norms of compromise and conciliation. The tradition was the same in all three women – you care nothing for the reinforcement or validation of a social life, you are utterly stoical, never let your self-control slip, pursue your desires, and live with the consequences. Because Laura was on the surface of things so prepared to go along with other people's forceful action, it was easy to miss the ancestral core of ruthlessness deep within her.

Almost as deep in Laura lay her character as an artist. Under her kind and charming exterior she possessed an artistic detachment which could border on brutality. Robin recalls her quality of 'passive acceptance of events', and others have used this word 'passive' as well as 'shy' to describe her. I think we must look further into her character to see that her passivity was all part of the same artistic detachment: she let others rage, storm and grab the headlines, while she watched, absorbed, synthesised everything she saw into her own vision. In this private space she created for herself, she developed the 'amazing traces of artistic integrity' that Seth wrote so admiringly of in his one-time love. She was, as an adolescent, undoubtedly affected when her family life became so turbulent, but her response was to switch off and disappear into a world of art. She learned how to screen out distasteful things, to keep her thoughts private. When she and Rosemary sat opposite each other in silence in the snuggery at Saligo, Rosemary had no real idea what her daughter was thinking. Her bohemian boarding school, Langford Grove, was the kind of place that indulged this slightly spaced-out sense of not caring about anything but art. After practising the piano, she would go to the headmistress, 'Curty', and ask what she should do next. 'Practice some more,' Curty would say, with otherworldly vagueness.

Laura developed, without anyone really noticing, a deep inner life and great determination. Rosemary writes in her diary of her daughter: 'I called her to join us but she went on in haughty silence with her drawing book and pencil. Sometimes she was like that, proud and virginal.' Laura watched and shielded herself as her mother behaved dreadfully, her father was treated badly, and eventually they separated and divorced. She was certainly affected by the mess of it all, and during her teenage years she was quietly on the lookout for a way of making the emotional turmoil go away. To begin with there was Seth, accomplice in her world of art, but then he became too immersed in the toxic angst of Saligo, too close to her mother, with Rosemary's habit of taking everyone over. Then she found Tony. Here was a man who would erect a wall within which she could live the life of an artist, undisturbed in her beautiful garden. Here was a man who was prepared to guard the wall of her paradise like a rottweiler, and could make all of the unpleasant things go away.

Juliet remembers visiting her sister, Laura, soon after she moved into Abbey Gardens with the new boyfriend. Laura was doing the ironing. She had just made a mark on Tony's shirt.

'She was very upset about it,' Juliet tells me. Juliet said, 'Why don't you just laugh it off?'

'The trouble is it keeps happening,' Laura said, looking anxious.

This vignette made me think for the first time that Laura too was intimidated by Tony. That he was exercising his controlling behaviour right from the start on her too. It casts a darker hue over their partnership. But there was something about it that Laura found attractive. His absolute certainty and intellectual power seemed to dispel the mess that she found so difficult. She took a deep breath and put all her chips on Tony.

Laura must have imagined that even though Tony didn't get on very well with her family, she could probably keep it all going in an intermittent sort of a way. Then, when Tony said in his forceful way, 'It's either me or them,' she must have wondered at the finality of that, but then thought she must just get on with it. Having made her decision, Laura was absolutely determined to stick with it, her eyes focused firmly on the future and the family that she wanted so badly to create. She would have said to herself, 'So be it. My family is the past. This is the future.' Tony's cruel decision to place them in Hampstead, right in the middle of it all, seems to have been an extreme test of her resolve and her loyalty to him.

Laura accepted the reality of her position. As her marriage progressed, she gradually, with quiet focus on the everyday business of life, reversed the early dominance of Tony and became the stronger of the two. She was the important parent, the one who kept everything going, the centre of the family. She set about her grand project of creating a typical English bourgeois family. Years later she said with satisfaction of her children that we were 'middle-class, with a certain *je ne sais quoi*'.

The only tiny snag was that she and Tony between them hadn't the faintest clue how to go about it. They went hell-for-leather for the education side of things – intellectually you couldn't fault us. But bourgeois life in England is a complex, interdependent structure based on good manners, considerateness, connectedness and reciprocity. With their decision to ban almost all humans from their lives, our parents ensured that they remained perpetual, slightly bolshy students, and they sent us out into the world without any of the proper equipment needed for full participation in the middle-class life they dreamed of.

During my teen years my dear mother passed on no tips about make-up, boys, washing of hands, a basically normal wardrobe. (I turned up for my Oxford interview in a donkey jacket, a tartan kilt and DM boots – perhaps they gave me a place out of pity.) Later, visits to the homes of various friends, and the experience of living in the English countryside, introduced me to all sorts of new social rituals of the *haute bourgeoisie*. I had no idea at all that after a visit you were supposed to say to your hostess something along the lines of 'I've made the bed, but would you prefer I stripped the sheets?' The reply might be something like, 'I'm sure it is very pure'. Then you were supposed to spend much of your time folding chairs in parish halls, offering to make cakes and biscuits for things, doing flower arrangements, enquiring after everyone's health, convening endless gatherings of distant relations, inviting people to things, and being invited back, spending time with people you found dull. At the dinner table you were supposed to have excellent manners, ask for the salt to be passed, converse in an interesting but not too confrontational manner, offer to help at every opportunity. And so on. Like Eliza Doolittle, I had much to learn.

You might also ask why my brothers and I did not pull down the house of cards more quickly. I can only say that before the internet it really was possible to turn your house into a fortress. Ant used to blurt out at the supper table, 'So how about this Uncle Al then?' and the three of us did have a joke about it, featuring Uncle Al in our conversations; but somehow the reaction was so weird and tortured that we usually just left it alone. Our parents were, on the whole, good together, so the atmosphere in the house, at least in the days before teenage angst crept in, was relaxed and happy. Like most children we thought mainly about our own concerns, and since we never saw any of the actors in the drama, and seldom heard their names mentioned, they just didn't feature in our lives. It was exactly as Tony planned all along. Only as time passed did certain vexed questions of personal identity start to trouble us; the need to know began to develop and grow stronger.

Chapter 39

The other day, I went back to Hampstead for the first time in years. I met my old school friend, Sarah, for lunch in Belsize Park and then walked on. I came first to Belsize Village, the little triangle so familiar, just at the end of Ornan Road. The bakery where we bought iced buns was now a delicatessen. It is very 'lifestyles'. I have seen countless delicatessens just the same throughout the country: the shop sign has 'naive' pictures of bottles of wine and country loaves, the exterior is painted cream, and there are tables spilling out onto the pavement. There would *definitely* not have been tables when we lived in Ornan Road. Where was the bakery with the fat lady proprietress called Candy, wearing an apron and white hat, and the shop counter full of buns of differing types and colours – little cupcakes, macaroons, various fingers, some dipped in icing, and loaves of all sorts?

I walk on through Belsize Lane and on into Ornan Road. The two road signs are immediately next to each other, without the slightest change in road directions. Here we are. I imagine if my heart rate, pulse, temperature and all that sort of thing were being measured there would be a change now. My young and old selves morph into each other, the screen pixelates and screeches as the two interchange. The red brick Victorian terraces fall away and on the right hand side of the road is a row of glass and brick terraced houses. A '50s dream of modern living. A bright, shiny new modern couple with their two very young children and a dream of a perfect future move in here in 1964.

These houses are not uniform. They differ subtly from one another, but all have large areas of window, sometimes as much as half the façade. I pause, glance, move on a bit so that it doesn't look too weird. I cannot see through into the inner life of any of them; I can only see the reflection of plane trees. All of them have unpainted brickwork as an important design element, interspersed with the glass. Here is one differently styled, with grey wood panelling. I cannot remember the number. Is it 43? This one has a garage next to and slightly in front of it, fenced off with a bright green mesh barrier with a 'Danger of Death' sign with a poor stick man falling backwards with a spiky shape bearing down on him. There is a lime tree in the garden. It has a wood-panelled fence with a bamboo hedge. I continue my dance, walking on, snatching a stare through the windows, I see only dark geometric shapes revealing nothing. No. 51 is more pretentious. It has more purplish coloured brickwork and a central archway. Everywhere is very smart, narrow wood panelling, and the door has a huge brass knocker. Was it No. 63? This one does seem more familiar – it is plainer, with white windows and yellow brick. The garage is set back and would have been easily reachable by us; such a perfect hideout when we carried a forbidden cargo of illicit sweets. I'm sure this must be the one, and it is nearly at the end of the road. Not far to go before the multi-storey car park which has been a Premier Inn for years. I remember it as the place with garages with green doors where I rode my bike. Strange, and yet I don't remember the number being 63. I must check with my brother.

My contemporary self pauses and turns around to check out the other side of the road. Here are much taller, three-storey, triangular-gabled, red brick Victorian buildings. Did they bulldoze a load of these to build our modernist dream house?

I shake off my four- to seven-year-old self and turn left into Haverstock Hill. I stroll up the main road in the direction of Hampstead Station. I pass the Royal Free Hospital on my right and have memories of Laura when she worked there. A conversation about the racetrack theory of hospitals comes to mind. Here is Hampstead Green, a little triangular patch of green surrounded by railings and now full of forget-me-nots, cow parsley, bluebells and daisies. Some building work is in progress at the Royal Free. A pile of rubble is imperfectly covered in sheeting. On the other side of the road are large, red brick terraces. Now we are in Rosslyn Hill and I pass St Stephen's church. The noticeboard advertises a concert by the Linden Baroque Orchestra called 'The Madness of Love', which seems rather appropriate.

I am seized by an incredibly powerful memory of intellectual snobbery.

You had to be so careful what you said in Hampstead. It could never be foolish or ill-informed, and any gathering was always full of people of a similar cast of mind, ready to judge your every tentative adolescent remark. 'Oh dear... no... the Linden Baroque Orchestra? There's really no point when you could go and see the Academy of Ancient Music... Nicholas? Yes, he's in New York doing a PhD in particle physics... and what are you doing?'

I pause at the top of Pond Street; an Australian woman is crossing the road with her small child and a scooter. The child randomly sits down and the Australian woman says, 'What are you doing? Git up!'

I walk on past Hampstead Hill Gardens, whose elegant houses curve away out of sight, their front gardens full of lilacs and laburnums just come into flower. A plane tree shakes its seeds into the warm May air. This is more like it. I pass a couple of white-haired old boys in tweed jackets, baggy trousers and sandals, earnestly in conversation. A Hampstead type does persist in pockets. Like a disappearing species of plant you happen upon unexpectedly, and you tug the sleeve of your companion excitedly to point it out.

I have somehow arrived at the top of Downshire Hill. Here is the Police Station. A handsome building in pale red brick, all triangles, the door flanked by two handsome police lanterns, which actually say POLICE on them, and a black bench divided into individual seats. I have a memory of being taken up to the Police Station to visit the horses. They were enormous and all of them jet black.

I proceed slowly down the hill. Past the Magistrates Court. Here I once met my history teacher, a precise lady with a toupee, which shifted about during lessons. She gave me an innocent greeting and I was so shocked to see her on Downshire Hill, so far out of her proper territory, that I jumped out of my skin and ran past without even saying hello. I pass a woman with a Spanish accent saying into her mobile phone, 'I don't know what to do!' No. 50 is a handsome cream house with a black balustrade; it used to be inhabited by a primary school friend whom we called 'the genius up the road' in our household. Then there is Hampstead Hill Mansions in red brick. On the other side is a run of exquisitely pretty Georgian houses set back from the road with quite extensive front gardens. When we lived here this one belonged to a strange man, a mysterious figure who wore a long mac, rode a motorbike, and I have since learned was eventually murdered. The garden was always unkempt and a thick weeping tree shrouded the house. Not any more. The whole row of houses is immaculate. I walk past the low-level house which is really just a glass box with blinds. Opposite, a white house with a crenellated finish stands out amongst the simple brickwork and flat roofs. A car goes past and hoots, someone shouts out of the window.

Downshire Hill

I pass the turning to Keats Grove, marked by St John's, handsome as ever. The houses are smaller now and set nearer the road, all of them terraced. We are getting closer. Then suddenly there are some three-storey houses again; this one has a blue plaque to mark the residence of Lee Miller and Roland Penrose. And there is a blue plaque to Peter Medawar, whom we knew, sort of. Well, my parents sucked up to them anyway. My mouth has gone a little dry and I know it is coming, and yet it comes upon me suddenly and with a shock.

It is No. 38A, the number in strange unfamiliar chrome rounded Ariel font. The red brick path is gone. The pretty ironwork 'Moel Lys' is gone.

The pretty small panes in the bow windows have gone, replaced by long, uniform panes of glass. My mother's little front garden with paths she laid twisting here and there, and the hydrangea and the Dicentra spectabilis, miraculous little flowers in the shape of hearts which she nurtured with such love, all gone. The waist-level gate which I pushed open as I swung home after a day at school, my army surplus bag on my back, gone and replaced by a tall 'sod off' gate and a burglar alarm. There is a general air of disregard for what has gone before, of money being conspicuously spent. I can't linger for too long.

When I was very young I had a favourite book called *The Little House*. It was the story of a little house in the countryside that was living happily ever after, until one terrible day bulldozers started arriving. They cleared patches of countryside, and built tall, dirty, ugly buildings and gradually all these buildings came closer and closer to the little house and started to tower over it, and slowly its coat of white paint turned grey and all the flowers died. Then one day a truck arrived, picked up the little house and transported it away from all the horrible new houses and placed it back in the countryside where it was happy, and where it felt it belonged. I had a similar sense of a dear old familiar house turned into something unrecognisable.

I move on. No. 38 looks more or less the same. I have a memory of running my hand along the wall as I returned home, and being yelled at by someone from the other side of the street. How mean! I was only little. There is a bright blue cotoneaster in the garden; always there, I think. Pru Hannay's house, two down from us, is much the same except for a neat garden full of spiky plants – she would never have tolerated them.

I walk on to the Freemasons Arms. It is a sickly colour of purple grey and bustling with life; the day is warm but slightly fresh. The collapsed parasols blow in the breeze. The railings are still there where I used to set up my guy to ask for 'a penny for the guy', and once got into a long conversation about abortion with somebody or other.

Since I have tortured myself with intense memories this far, I decide I may as well continue. So I approach the Heath via the 'Triangle'. It is quite steep, with rough grass and a bench inscribed with the words: 'And when the Earth shall claim your limbs, then shall you truly dance. For Brian Chapman 1913 to 1938'. I take the main route and follow the path between the 'near ponds'. The bathing pond is pretty, lined with copper beech, silver birch, oak and plane trees; the water olive green, shimmering with their reflection; a line of white buoys and smaller orange ones skim across the surface. I strike off up to the left and find the path has been tarted up with wooden edges. Everything seems more *managed*, and I can't find the shiny tree we used to stretch ourselves out on like pumas.

A poplar, just like the venerable one which local government arbitrarily destroyed on my own village green, its bark a series of deep black ridges, like crocodile skin. Its leaves rustle gently, just like they used to do on our Devon village green. I have been told about the parrots, and there is one now screeching in the trees. I strain to see it, but it remains invisible. I walk amongst my teenage footsteps across an area which is more prairie-like, all the way across to the 'far ponds', passing that familiar little copse of trees on a little mound. We used to talk about it quite a lot, but I have filtered out any of the information that was bandied about. I've come quite a long way now and am starting to feel a little footsore, as I have newish ankle boots that are giving me blisters, so I decide not to press on to Kenwood, but turn in my tracks amongst the buttercups. Straight ahead of me is the Shard. The Heath is artificial, like a dream, or a romantic painting of a classical landscape. I am used to rough working countryside these days.

I come back a different way. Here is a path that spills over to a slope where there was a tree you could walk inside. Here is the football field with its pavilion. I see Tara digging a hole right in the middle of the smooth grass. Lime Avenue is now a mixture of the old trees with a lot of new slender trees. I can remember these coming down in the hurricane of 1987. I was living in Stoke Newington and working in London at the time. I can remember the vast old trees coming down everywhere, ripping up pavements and smashing windows.

I finish my visit in South End Green, approaching from the 'finger of the Heath', and passing a happy figure of a father on a bike, two cool speakers strapped to the front with a stream of mellow jazz emanating; his little girl sits back in a comfy seat attached to the back. What is there now in South End Green? An astonishingly fashionable and elegant charity clothes shop, Daunt Books, Paradise India Cuisine, Topps Tiles, a vet, a cheap food shop and, then, at the bottom of Keats Grove, Keats Hair. 'Keats would probably have loved it,' says Charles. 'He had pretty great hair.' A poster in the window offered 'shimmer silver, colour addict'. And further on, painted onto the window, it said: 'Thy hair soft-lifted by the winnowing wind'. Someone has made some very creative use of 'Brand Hampstead'.

Before I go, I must just check the bakery where I used to work – still a bakery but now 'Euphorium Bakery' and a little more styled; is this a mixture between Euphoria and Emporium? The garage – now a posh gated mews; the number 24 buses – still there but a different shape, more rounded. The Hampstead Classic Cinema is now a food hall, and Hampstead Heath British Rail Station has an orange sign. What the…? Orange? I finish my visit in a very gloomy café, served by a dolled-up woman with long grey hair who has seen better days, and warns me to be careful because my teapot 'might splash'. A hipster says, 'My other half loves carrot cake, so… nice little treat.' With that overheard sentence, I decide it is time to bring my wanderings to a close.

Throughout the late 1970s, my secondary school years, the blanks that stood in the place of my extended family remained in place. I imagined them far, far away, in some distant land, or living in a castle, with a gateway and deep moat, steeped in wickedly right-wing views. I had no idea that their footsteps might have been threading amongst our own on Hampstead Heath, or up and down the High Street, or even coming right up to the steps of No. 38A itself.

I reflect again on Robin's visits – on the two occasions he walked up the red brick path, stood under the Moel Lys sign and knocked on the door. There was the famous glass of water incident, and then he came once again in 1978 to tell Laura that her father had died. Where was I? Perhaps I was at school. But I wish it had been me who had opened the door.

Chapter 40

*I*t was my job to organise Tony's memorial service. First of all there was the crematorium. I went with Merlin, just the two of us. We agreed that there was much that Tony would have found hilarious about the undertakers and the way they behaved. I chose a Schubert piano trio, which I can't listen to now. Merlin and I sat next to each other in the empty room. Eventually Merlin broke the silence.

'So, are you going to read this poem then?'

'Oh yeah, ok.'

Ant didn't come over from Germany, deciding to keep himself for the big memorial service. I thought perhaps he should have, as this was the moment his father was consigned to the flames.

I invited everyone I could think of to the religious service we held in Dartington Church for Tony's memorial, and there was quite a crowd in the end. The guest list of course included Francis (whom we had only known a year) and his sister Micky (whom at that point we were about to meet for the first time).

I held it together, just about, and the service and party afterwards were a joyous celebration. I divided the tribute between the three of us. Francis read from the Bible, and Micky read the Kadish – the Jewish prayer for the dead. She spoke of Fanny, our grandmother, and her love for her son. She spoke of her one memory of meeting her uncle: he had been wearing the famous fawn duffle coat, and her description brought him vividly into the room. To please Ant, we had a pair of earnest ladies singing Couperin – he is very close to music. The vicar said that he had never met Tony, but wished he had.

The party afterwards was lively and full of fun. He would have enjoyed it.

There was confusion over a casserole. A friend who lives just up the road from me had kindly prepared a dish for us, but the delicious, comforting stew had unfortunately been left behind; my husband and Francis drove all the way back to collect it and bring it south to Tony's house in Totnes. My friend opened her front door and nearly had a heart attack. (She had met Tony quite a few times – and he was an unforgettable figure.) What? A ghost? Isn't this supposed to be Tony's funeral? Why is he here? All this passed through her mind at lightning-fast speed before she dragged herself back to the present world and noted the obvious differences.

'This is Francis,' Charles said. 'Tony's nephew.'

'Ah, hello, yes. Good to meet you. I'll just go and get the casserole.'

After the party, close family all gather at Tony's house. Francis singled out a stoneware mug from Tony's stuff – once again picking over the remains.

Micky sat on one of my father's uncomfortable chairs, just by the rowing machine. Things seemed un-relaxed between her and Francis. They sniped at each other constantly, while my brothers and I, well brought up by our mother, tried to spread a nice atmosphere. Micky's husband had not long ago had an accident and his leg was trussed up in a strange device.

'The Hyman men were all *hard*.' Micky said the word with great emphasis. 'Hard and *mean*.' Yes, I think, I can see traces of that in Tony, although he would not have liked to think that of himself. I remember him speaking of 'the hard rabbinical tradition'.

'I wish,' I said politely, 'that I had had an opportunity to meet your mother.'

'Why?' she asked robustly, with a gallic shrug. 'She did not wish to meet you!'[13]

'Oh.'

My brother Ant emerged, with his eager look, from somewhere deep in the house, waving a dusty old photograph album – a small leather-bound book with a plaited double string with tassels. It contained small black-and-white photographs of Fanny and Alexander's exotic cruises. Inside the front cover was written in white ink 'TRAVEL SNAPS 1936 AND 1937', in crude capitals. The pages were grey brown and contained tiny prints with

---

[13] Francis is convinced that this is not true, and that Margaret was saddened that she wasn't allowed to meet her niece, and her two nephews.

white borders and rough edges, the corners of each one slipped inside little arrowhead-shaped photo-fixers.

We peered closer, and read the descriptions – white ink to show up on the thick brown pages.

We learned of voyages from New York to Havana on 24 October 1936; then on 31 October they were in Cuba; on 3 November in Vera Cruz; on 5 November in Mexico; then Antigua, Costa Rica, Columbia, Panama, Trinidad, Rio de Janeiro, Buenos Aires, and so on, all the way to 15 January 1937 and beyond.

Fanny and Alexander travelled for three months of the winter. The pictures are of things they saw, of bustling markets, cathedrals, jungles, but above all they are of Fanny. Elegant, poised and beautiful in every setting, here her head and shoulders are framed in a porthole, here she is 'with Mr Poliakov' at the Havana Yacht Club in a sun hat and white sleeveless dress blowing in the breeze, here crouching down as part of a group of Cubans just outside Havana, here in silhouette leaning on the balcony in Vera Cruz, her '30's bob silhouetted against the light, here leaning on the window of the hotel at Buenos Aires.

At the end of 1937, Fanny and Alexander set off on another long winter trip, cruising to Cape Town. Here she is in a white blouse and dark trousers sitting back in a relaxed pose in a basketwork chair on deck. The white ink letters say 'GETTING WARM'. Here she is in Cape Town in a dark dress with puffed sleeves, a belt with a large buckle, and a string of pearls, looking a little more severe and a touch mannish. Here she is in the same outfit in a strange photo marked in the familiar white ink, 'IN DARKEST AFRICA', with a group of local boys carrying sticks and guns; she looks as if she is engaged in banter with them. Fan loved being photographed. Another page is marked 'NATIVES IN THE RAND AMUSING THEMSELVES ON SUNDAY WITH DANCING'. Then they are in Zanzibar and there are snaps of locals – bare-breasted women staring bemusedly at the camera. Then they are in Mombasa; a shop with pots and pans and baskets of produce; two dogs lie hot and exhausted, asleep on the dusty road.

Everything peters out then. And we realised the significant fact about these old, old collections of family photographs – that Tony had methodically removed every single photograph of his own father, Alexander. As this fact sinks in, we all look apologetically at one another.

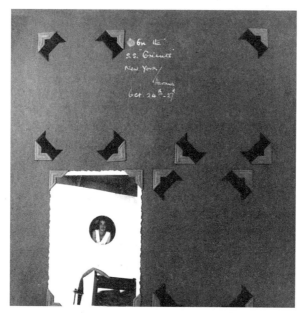

*Fanny and Alexander's photograph album with all
the pictures of Alexander removed*

∿

A few months later my brothers and I and our families piled into two cars and drove to Dartmoor, to Hound Tor, for a final farewell to Tony. We walked along the closely sheep-cropped ground, my brother clutching to his chest the sealed container with Dad's ashes. He stood on the edge of the rocky outcrop and vigorously shook the container, releasing the fine ash into the Dartmoor air. It was a breezy day, and I watched the fine particles twist and turn, carried away on the wind.

'A fine figure of a man,' he said cheerfully.

I wondered where in that dust were all the fights, the fury, the rage, the bitten hands and furious conversations with self. As with anything connected with my dad I did not feel release, peace, contentment, straightforward grief, but a sort of tortured anguish and misery. Time would heal, though. Time would heal. Charles put an arm round me and said, 'You know you and your brothers are really quite sane, considering…'

∿

I have been putting off the moment to listen to Dad's tapes. On my computer is a list of short sound clips. I press the play button and his voice comes through from beyond the grave.

I am touched by my brother's reassuring, tolerant voice in the background. 'It's fine, go ahead. No, don't worry about that light.'

'ANT!! It's not playing back at me. You'd better come and explain.'

I make my way slowly through the sound clips, a Brechtian commentary on the process running in parallel with Dad's reminiscences. 'The machine seems to have gone into a misfunction, so I'll have to redo something.' 'I have a new method of writing things. I have a black book and am noting down subjects when I am in bed at night.'

Dad's voice is soft and posh, but with some twanging vowels that give him away. I realise that somewhere in my mind I am attempting to recreate my grandmother from fragments, and something in the spectral voice of my dad as it breaks off to laugh, with warmth, but a laugh that is entirely within himself, is the voice of Fanny, my namesake.

And I realise something else. Dad's tapes are all about the extraordinary place that transformed everything for him – Dartington Hall. He spent five formative years, from 1935 to 1940, at the school set up by Leonard and Dorothy Elmhirst to be a truly avant-garde social and educational experiment. It was like nowhere else.

In truth Dartington was something that turned me off whenever Dad mentioned it, just like Babbage. But here, sound clip after sound clip on Dropbox, letting out Dad's over-articulated and eccentric ways of speaking, are all about the place. My grandmother opened up a door for him to a sort of paradise – only *that* was good enough for her son.

I imagine at the age of seven he must have been pretty insufferable. 'Dartington was just fabulous,' he said, 'after being in a home where nobody ever *did* anything.' I notice how he dwells in the world of his own personal narrative. 'I was accompanied to Dartington on my first day as I was considered very nervous. It turned out on the first night I was perfectly happy and a whole lot of the other children were in a mess. So much for maternal views.' It sounds as if he is talking about someone else. Very remote from his emotions. He describes a vivid little scene: he must have been refined, educated, superior and highbrow almost beyond comprehension for a seven-year-old. 'One of the first things that happened,' the soft and articulate voice of my dead father says from my computer, 'was that a child by the name, I believe, of Timothy Brown attempted to scratch my face. I was completely astonished as nothing like that had ever happened in my life before. I must have replied adequately because he ran away howling and never... again... gave... me... any... grief.' Those last words separated and emphasised.

'Everyone felt,' Dad's voice continues, 'that the arts belonged to us.' He remembers an extraordinary French teacher who wrote a play and set up a casino for them. There was a complete set of pottery kilns, and Dartington paid for Bernard Leach to go to Japan. The head of metalwork had been the head of metalwork at the Bauhaus. Everyone painted and drew. Drama was central to the curriculum too. He remembers Dorothy and some of her acolytes walking down Totnes High Street wearing long cloaks, much to the astonishment of the locals. I discern a slight tendency towards delinquent behaviour in my father – he and four friends used to raid the cider mills (part of the Elmhirst experiment was to have 'industry' on the school campus), and he remembers going on strike.

We went on strike for higher pocket money. You must understand the significance of this. A water ice cost a penny, a cream ice cost tuppence, and luxury of luxuries, thruppence bought a choc ice. We went on strike. Aller Park was blockaded, pavement stones were torn up, some of the staff were for us, some were against us. The headmaster must have found all this highly amusing. After a week, he came down and read the riot act, explaining our parents couldn't afford another ha'penny a week, and we were defeated. A… useful… lesson… in… state… power…

These last words delivered with a flourish. I start to understand something fundamental. Dad's early years were in this paradise, and in the rest of his life he sought to recreate this. Fanny gave her son an idyll and he never really recovered from it. For the world is not like that.

Dad's voice comes through again.

I have now put new batteries in the recorder and all seems to be going well, and I hope it continues to last. I hope that the hiccups that I have been going through will be over. Ah… it seems that I cannot get all of these various connections correctly. I hope that it will settle down and tomorrow afternoon I will have to go for a retinal scan. To play, press button… yup.

The next tape goes right back to the beginning of his arrival at Dartington Hall, for the third time now. 'On the train was a boy called Michael Havinden and some boys were rather charmingly kicking him. My mother and I took him under our wing, and he became a friend for life.'

And I feel sad because I realise he was lonely, living on his own and struggling with the machine, and Ant is no longer with him. And I feel sad that I had to keep away from him by then, for my own sense of wellbeing. Everyone misses Mum.

POSTSCRIPT

$\mathcal{A}$nd now I still find that I search for someone I can natter away within the same untrammelled freedom as I did with my mother, and I still set up unsuspecting people to fight with, as if they were Tony. My brothers and I are all aware of the parts of ourselves that are like our dad, and warn each other when we see the signs; we know that he gave us a lot too. And we are also scions of our mother's family – who fought alongside Robert the Bruce – and we all make strenuous efforts to bring our inner Hay/Boyd to the fore.

Before the pandemic, when we could all still meet in one another's houses, Robin convened a lunch party in his flat in London in honour of his eldest son who was visiting from South America with his wife and two children. He is a successful artist whose works reflect the place where he lives. Their colour is absolutely vibrant, and the imagery suffused with magic realism. I sat next to him and found him to be delightful. Also present are Juliet and Alan, Robin's other children, and two of my children. Robin is a marvellous host, the wine flows, and there is a noisy din of chatter. Robin entertains his two grandchildren with all the same gifts for comedy and creating a comfortable atmosphere that his mother wrote about back in the Forest of Dean days. Robin's other son is incredibly good-looking – he reminds me of Leonardo DiCaprio. His daughter looks so like my mother that it is hard not to stare at her – long straight hair, the same face shape and strong limbs. The occasion is jolly and full of humour – everyone seems content and easy going. As I look around the table, I think that it is all… what is it? Just ordinary.

ACKNOWLEDGEMENTS

$\mathcal{M}$y first thanks go to my brother Prof Anthony Hyman – without his support there would be no book. His open, optimistic, problem-solving generosity is really exceptional. And to my brother Merlin who shared the wonderful weirdness of it all with humour, kindness and complete equanimity – for not minding me telling the story as I saw it.

My special thanks go to my uncle Dr Robin Boyd, whose decision to pick up his pen and write me a letter changed everything. And for his steady support, emotional intelligence and avuncular interest ever since. I am so very happy to have had the chance to know you. And to Juliet for allowing me to experience what it is to have an auntie, for her sane and balanced view and kind hospitality. For all the hours looking through binoculars and for lovely swims, meals, walks and talks. And to Francis, for his hours and hours of family reminiscences, for his support of my children, and for his friendship. To Micky for long chats during lockdown.

To my children Sam, Silvia and Victor for their love and support, for reading my manuscript, and for being so wonderful.

Above all to my husband Charles, who has supported me with love, faith, and endless patience (well perhaps not quite endless), and continuous gentle criticism. Also without him there would be no book.

Grateful thanks to John and Tina Micklewright for being amongst the first to read my manuscript and for all their improvements, to Beth McHattie for her unflagging support and brilliant networking skills, to Monica Bohm Duchene for giving me a platform on Insiders/Outsiders, to Sarah Tucker for her friendship and lovely feedback on my manuscript, to Nicky Barrie and her daughter for reading my manuscript and for all of their wonderful support and suggestions, to Cecilia Hemmings and Charlotte Grant for reading my manuscript, and to Tabitha Pelly for her incredible energy, skill, knowledge and support. To Patrick Mills and Pip Carson for their photography. To Robin Boyd, Juliet Bloss, James Boyd, Francis Ghilès and Henry Guest for their generosity in allowing me to use their lovely photographs. To Robin Boyd for his generosity in allowing me to read and quote my grandmother's diaries.

To everyone at Unicorn, especially Simon Perks for suggesting it might have legs, to Ian for taking me on, and to Ryan for answering all my many questions, to Lauren, Emily and Viv.

To all the people I missed out on knowing – my Aunt Margaret, my grandmothers, and especially to Alastair Boyd, my uncle, for his balanced, thoughtful, clear sighted Memoir of Rosemary without which I would never have got to know my grandmother.

To Mum and Dad for being at the heart of my story – if you were here, I hope you wouldn't mind too much.

REFERENCES AND QUOTES

pp. 24–28
Claire Tomalin published her brilliant biography, *Mrs Jordan's Profession*
https://www.penguin.co.uk/books/15327/mrs-jordans-profession-by-claire-
tomalin/9780241963296

pp. 42 –44
JewishGen and the Yizkor Book project have gathered together the memories of the
Jewish diaspora from Slutsk

'the nest of our good and warm childhood'
https://www.jewishgen.org/yizkor/slutsk/slu008.html
Heavenly Slutsk by Y. D. B. (Translated by Sara Mages) in Slutsk and

Vicinity Memorial Book: (Belarus) 53°01' / 27°33'
Translation of Pinkas Slutsk u-benoteha
Edited by: N. Chinitz, Sh. Nachmani, Yizkor Book Committee
Published in Tel-Aviv, 1962

'each like a limb of the city itself, from it, and in it. Slutsk was the hearth, the fire of
the Torah blazed there, and each House of Sparks, from near and far, was lit by its
fire'
https://www.jewishgen.org/yizkor/slutsk/slu008.html#Page11
The City and Its Fullness by Y. D. Abramsky (Translated by Sara Mages)

'it was possible only with difficulty to squeeze between the wagons, whose shafts were
very high'
https://www.jewishgen.org/yizkor/slutsk/slu041.html
Professions and Vocations by Nachum Chinitz (Translated by Jerrold Landau)

pp. 52–53
The Red Earl: The Extraordinary Life of the 16th Earl of Huntingdon
by Selina Hastings
Bloomsbury (Publisher): https://www.bloomsbury.com/uk/red-
earl-9781408187371/

p. 57
Dora Foss description of party at Wimborne House

Taken from: *Music in Their Time: The Memoirs and Letters of Dora and Hubert Foss*
Boydell Press : https://boydellandbrewer.com/9781783274130/imusic-in-their-timei-the-memoirs-and-letters-of-dora-and-hubert-foss/
Permissions: https://boydellandbrewer.com/rights-permissions/

pp. 84–86
James Fox, in his book *White Mischief*, paints a vivid portrait of the scene in Kenya

'gave out the atmosphere of Thames Valley gentility and Betjemania'

'terrible grievances took root in the libidinous, drunken atmosphere'

'another married heiress and beauty, also older than himself, a petite, slender, animated woman with auburn hair'

'The Scottish lord must have felt at home here, beside this beautiful lake, that had the look of a wild highland loch, encircled as it was by mountains and plains, its wide grassy shore bordering the water which, seen from the veranda of the Djin Palace on a fine day, was a clear, cool blue pool. For decoration there were flamingos, herons, black duck, chalk white egrets, and hippos rose and sank in the water among the floating islands of papyrus. The bedroom doors of the house faced an inner courtyard with a tiled pool and a fountain in the centre. There was a sunken marble bath lined with black and gold tiles – to facilitate, so the story goes, the vomiting of over-indulgent guests. The rooms and terraces were furnished with deep sofas and armchairs loose-covered in flowered chintz. And Erroll's full-length portrait, in unpaid-for Coronation robes, hung at the top of the stairs.'

'boredom and an acute sense of his own abilities'

'Give the woman as much as she wants to drink. If she wants to die, let her have it. If she wants a drink, let her have one.'

Penguin: https://www.penguin.co.uk/books/356593/white-mischief-by-fox-james/9780099766711

pp. 91–92
Ways of Seeing by John Berger
Penguin: https://www.penguin.co.uk/books/56465/ways-of-seeing-by-berger-john/9780141035796

p. 92
Berger's Booker Prize-winning novel *G*
Bloomsbury: https://www.bloomsbury.com/uk/g-9781408834343/

pp. 175–176
A World to Build by David Kynaston
https://www.bloomsbury.com/uk/author/david-kynaston/

pp. 189–191
The Szum and the Ching by John Berger,
The Szum and the Ching is a short story, one that makes up the 'Here is Where We Meet' collection.
Bloomsbury: https://www.bloomsbury.com/uk/here-is-where-we-meet-9780747573180/

pp. 204–206 and 222–223 *A Painter of Our Time* by John Berger
https://www.versobooks.com/en-gb/products/2148-a-painter-of-our-time

pp. 240–242 'The Seasons in Quincy: Four Portraits of John Berger', TV programme, one of the episodes of a four-part documentary made in honour of and concerning the somewhat cultish figure of John Berger in old age

pp. 242–245
'Voices', TV programme with Berger and Susan Sontag, 1983 description
Episodes can be found at: https://www.channel4.com/programmes/voices/on-demand/811-007

PICTURE CREDITS

COLOUR PLATES

INDEX